TERENCE WONG-Lr.

S0-AIU-220

Of Comets and Queens

Oscar Nemon's bust of The Queen commissioned by Cunard for the *Queen Elizabeth 2*.

(R W Loosemore)

OF COMETS
AND QUEENS

Sir Basil Smallpeice

Airlife
England

©

**Sir Basil Smallpeice
1980**

First Published in 1981
by Airlife Publishing Ltd.

ISBN 0 906393 10 8

All rights reserved. No part of this publication may be reproduced,
stored in a retrieval system or transmitted, in any form or by any means,
electronic, mechanical, photocopying, recording or otherwise, without
the prior permission of Airlife Publishing Ltd.

Airlife Publishing Ltd.,

7 St. John's Hill, Shrewsbury, England.

Printed by Livesey Limited, Shrewsbury, England.

For Rita

without whose constant encouragement, and patient typing and retyping of my long-hand manuscript, this book would never have seen the light of day.

Contents

List of illustrations

1 The beginning of it all

Shortly after the takeover of Cunard by Trafalgar House in 1971, I went to Australia to see the Government and the board of the Australian National Line. I wanted to assure them that the change would not adversely affect their shipping partnership with our London containership consortium – a partnership of which I had been one of the principal architects.

On my way home I stopped off in New York for a couple of days. I wanted to see our containership management and our Port Elizabeth terminal across the Hudson river in New Jersey.

Now I was in a BOAC jumbo jet climbing out of New York's Kennedy airport on the 6½ hour overnight flight to London. It was about half an hour before my sleeping pill had its full effect. I had put on my airline eyeshades to keep out the light of the cabin and tomorrow's dawn. As I dozed in my private darkness I reflected that my mission in Australia had gone rather well. It had been a bit exhausting, of course. I had been out and back in only eight days. But any uneasiness there might have been in Government circles or in the shipping line had been entirely removed.

I asked the stewardess to awaken me in good time for the London landing. 'Certainly, sir,' she said, 'top of descent?'

I kept repeating in my mind the words 'top of descent' and started thinking about the parallel between airline flights and the various jobs one takes on in life. Top of descent is a point on a pilot's navigation chart at which he has completed his present sector, be it hundreds or thousands of miles, except for the final complex task of the approach and landing. After that, he takes off again on another sector. So, too, the jobs that one takes on in life are all part of a larger whole. They are never all complete in themselves, but are always followed by yet another challenge.

★   ★   ★   ★   ★

The Smallpeice family came from Surrey, and were originally centred round Guildford. There are branches in other parts of the country, but there has been a Smallpeice as Mayor of Guildford fourteen times in the four hundred and more years since the reign of Henry VII. The spelling of the name changed down the years. It is first seen in its present form in 1836 when my great-great-grandfather, John Smallpeice, was Mayor. Black Jack, as he was called, no doubt due to the colour of his hair and long side-burns before he went white, was Treasurer of the County of Surrey for 36 years.

I myself never set foot in Surrey until I was 20. I was born in Brazil in September 1906. My father, Herbert Charles Smallpeice, was at that time a senior clerk in the London & River Plate Bank's branch in Rio de Janeiro. He and my mother lived in a pleasant suburb facing the Atlantic called Coppa Cabana – as the clerk in the British Consulate spelt it when he wrote out my birth certificate. In those days there was no road tunnel from the city's waterfront to the golden beaches south of Sugar Loaf mountain. Copacabana was then still undeveloped, and the journey into Rio had to be made on foot or by horse-drawn vehicle over the hills. Or so I am told. I had to be brought home to England by my mother before I was one to recover from a near-fatal bout of malaria.

The reason my father went to Rio would be almost unbelievable these days. He was born in May 1872 when his father was Vicar of Nutley in Sussex. My grandfather lived to be only 30. According to a press cutting of the time, he was playing cricket in mid-June that year and 'whilst at the wicket, he had a sunstroke'. Sunstroke in England! Be that as it may, he died a couple of weeks later and my grandmother was left to bring up my infant father. Two years later she remarried. My step-grandfather was Algernon Langston Oldham, then curate in Nutley. Oldham later moved on to Shrewsbury where he became an Archdeacon.

The class-consciousness of English society was as its zenith in the latter part of the nineteenth century. And it was to alter the course of my father's life when he wanted to marry. My mother was born Georgina Ruth Rust. For many years Rusts had been shopkeepers along the North Norfolk coast from Mundesley to Wells, having founded the principal shop at Cromer in 1780. But when my father sought his stepfather's permission to marry Miss Rust, the Archdeacon would have none of it. He did not think it right for his stepson to 'marry into trade'. My father was told to go and work abroad for several years to get his mind straight.

This was at the turn of the century, the end of the Victorian era. My father was 28 and his chosen bride 24. Though neither liked it, both accepted the decision as inescapable. My father joined the

London & River Plate Bank, and was sent to Rio, with five years to wait before he could come home on leave. When the Royal Mail ship brought him back to England in 1905, Georgina Rust was waiting for him. They were now allowed to marry, and took ship back to Rio.

I was too young to have any memories of Rio in those days. When I went down the South American route for BOAC in the 1950's and saw it again I could recall nothing – though I found the small house where I was born just before a 10-storey apartment block was built on the site. Nor have I any recollection of Bahia (now Salvador) where my father got his first managership and we lived until his next leave came round in 1910.

At the end of that year we returned to Brazil, this time to Pernambuco (now Recife). This was the heart of the coffee country and only eight degrees south of the equator. The house and garden at Parnamarin, a suburb of Recife, is the first home I can remember. It was a squarish house with a garden large enough to have banana trees and a coconut palm, with a hard tennis court and plenty of room to ride a bicycle. There were horse-drawn trams in the road outside the garden wall. I remember my father being brought home after suffering from yellow fever from which he all but died. I had a large black nanny and was taught by my mother the beginnings of how to read and write.

*   *   *   *   *

My father's next leave came round in four years not five. So we left Pernam early in 1914 and came home in the Royal Mail ship Andes. That September, soon after World War I had broken out, I was sent to my first boarding school – the junior section of Hurstpierpoint College in Sussex. It was my 8th birthday. My parents handed me over into the care of a master on the school train at Charing Cross. After we had waved good-bye I felt horribly lonely.

In those days before there was any air travel, there were few options open to parents working abroad. They had the hard choice of staying together and cutting themselves off from their children for five years at a time, or of separating from each other so that the mother could be with or near the children. And in this case my brother and sister, four and five years younger than me, would be going back with them to Brazil. On arrival at school I knew that I shouldn't be seeing my father and mother again for another five years, when their next leave came round.

So I was pretty miserable and didn't like Hurstpierpoint very much. Whether my mother sensed this or not, I don't know. But she didn't in fact go back to Pernam with my father that autumn and in December she met me off the school train in London. I was delighted to be told that in April I would be going to a normal preparatory school with only about 40 young boys.

For that rescue from distress I have ever been grateful. My mother must have left soon afterwards to go back by ship to Brazil, for that was the last I saw of her, too, until after the War. There was no sense in pining about it; one just had to accept the inevitable, and learn how to cope.

My new school was Hydneye House, at Willingdon, just north of Eastbourne. The headmaster was a Mr Norman, whom I never got to know or like very much. He and his wife were somewhat severe and reserved, and Mrs Norman had a black Pomeranian which smelt and all of us loathed. However, there were two assistant masters there of a very different order, neither of whom were fit for war service – E G Maltby and J R W Tanner. Unlike Norman, both were dedicated to the traditional school sports of cricket, soccer and hockey. In 1917 Norman retired and the school moved to Baldslow, outside Hastings. Maltby and Tanner became the joint headmasters. They ran a good school – ably aided by their wives. I didn't excel at work; I was too interested in sports.

My father and mother came home to England again in 1920. He came down to see me at Hydneye soon after he arrived, and I had the misfortune to be in the sick-room with chickenpox. But time had changed things. We seemed strangers. The weekly letters we all had to write home while at school, and in my case had to continue between terms, were no substitute for the intercourse between minds and personalities that would have taken place naturally during the three holiday periods each year.

Being cut off from my parents for the past five years must have had quite an effect on me, which I was not conscious of at the time. It had begun the process of forcing me to become much more self-reliant and self-contained, going my own way. I had to work out my own bearings, as it were, and to a great extent develop my own rules of life.

In September 1920 I was taken to Shrewsbury School. My father left the school site soon after we got there to catch the train back to London, and I did not see him or my mother again for another five years.

Shrewsbury had been chosen because my uncle and godfather, Basil Oldham, was a housemaster there and had generously offered to take me into his house without my father having to pay any house fees.

Soon after arrival as a new boy, the public school process began of taking one down a peg or two. Some people tend to regard this as a somewhat cruel and almost sadistic exercise. But I think it is a useful one, if reasonably applied. When a boy leaves his prep school as one of the head boys in it and captain of its first XI in three sports, as I was, he considers himself no end of a swell. And, for his own good, it is not a bad thing to be made to start again at the bottom and make his own way up in his new environment.

I enjoyed my years at Shrewsbury, though I would never claim that they were the best years of my life. Having rather a flair for games, I became a double school first fairly early on, getting my first XI colours for cricket and football. Scholastically I wasn't much good. Once again, my mind was too much on the playing fields.

One thing I learnt about myself then was that I only performed well when under pressure. When things came easily I slacked off. I needed the continued challenge of new achievement to keep me giving of my best.

While at Shrewsbury, I had no particular ideas about the sort of work I wanted to do in later life. The idea was that, after leaving school, I would go up to The House at Oxford – Christ Church had been Basil Oldham's college. But in 1923 there was a revolution in Brazil, and word came that my father had lost all his money – how or why I never knew. So the Oxford plan collapsed like a child's house of cards.

So, what to do? I was due to leave school in just over a year and hadn't a clue. My housemaster uncle talked things over with me. One day he said: 'Well, you are good at maths; what about going into accountancy?' His suggestion seemed logical enough, and arrangements began to be made accordingly. Later I was to find out that, although basic arithmetic was obviously a necessary attribute in an accountant, there was actually less scope for advanced mathematics in accountancy than in many other fields; and I have long since forgotten, through disuse, all that I ever learnt of that subject at school. But I have never regretted the decision to embark on accountancy as a career, even if it was made for no good reason.

★   ★   ★   ★   ★

I left Shrewsbury at the end of the summer term of 1925, two months before my 19th birthday. My father and mother had returned to England in the summer of that year. He had worked for twenty-five years in the tropics and sub-tropics in an age when there was no refrigeration, no air-conditioning, and little if any preventive tropical medicine; and this had earned him the chance of early retirement from the Bank. While in Brazil he had picked up a couple of unpleasant tropical diseases as well as yellow fever; also, both he and my mother had missed having their children around; so he decided to retire, although only 53. My parents bought a house at Cromer, and looked for a firm of Chartered Accountants in Norwich to which I could be articled. As soon as I got home from school at the end of July I was taken to meet the senior partner of one of them, Granville Bullimore, who gave the firm its name. I must have been considered acceptable, because everything was fixed up almost before I knew what was happening. Without more ado I started my apprenticeship early that August.

Nowadays a raw articled clerk with absolutely no experience can expect to earn a reasonable salary from the start and be paid about £3,500 a year – admittedly in sadly depreciated currency. But in those far-off days of over 50 years ago, no articled clerk could expect to be paid a single penny throughout the five years of his articles. The opportunity of learning a profession wasn't something you got paid for! Indeed, my father had to buy my articles for me and it must have involved a considerable self-sacrifice. He also provided me with pocket money for all those years. Actually, the firm I worked for did relent a bit in my last year, when they graciously made me an allowance of thirty bob a month (£1.50 in these days of decimal currency).

Although rising 19 I was therefore not earning anything, nor expecting to for the next five years. Not surprisingly, my father found it necessary to supplement his pension and found himself work that he enjoyed with some foreign exchange brokers in the City of London. And by one of those fortunate coincidences that sometimes turn up in life, Bullimore's decided at the same time to open a branch office in London in 1926. By chance, too, it was their junior partner, Arnold Kent, to whom I was articled, who went to London to start it up. I went with him.

My parents bought a house in Surbiton. Although I had seen my father during the summer holidays at five-yearly intervals, this was the first time for twelve years that we had the opportunity to get to know each other. But then one Friday in March 1927 he was taken ill in the afternoon and went to bed with a high fever. Our doctor diagnosed pneumonia. On the Saturday morning a letter arrived from the Bank to say that their medical officer had found him two days previously to be in good health; his pension could accordingly take care also of my mother – at a reduced rate of course – as soon as he completed the application form and returned it to the Bank. By then pleurisy had added itself to the pneumonia and he was too ill to cope with the Bank's form. The crisis came on the third day, as it always did before antibiotics. On the Monday he died, aged 54.

My mother was then just 50, and lived on to 94. I have always thought it sad that my parents had only 21 years of married life together. But she enjoyed her life, all of it; and she was never really ill until the end.

I had to see the Bank, which through mergers had become the Bank of London and South America, at their head office in Tokenhouse Yard in the City. To their eternal credit they stood by their decision to look after my mother. The business of signing the application form was regarded as no more than a formality. They promptly started paying her the reduced rate of pension. This decision was to cost them dear – in the sense that she drew it for another 44 years – though actuaries assure me that these things average out. But what the Bank did made all the difference to our lives. For this, my mother and I always felt very grateful. Had they not acted as they did we should as a family have had no income – my father left no capital other than the house in which we lived.

I worked out my five years' articles with Bullimore, but not before we had given serious thought to whether it was fair for me to go on for another 3½ years without earning. I was very doubtful. But my godmother had recently died and left £1,000 to help with my education. That could finance my unpaid work under articles. My mother insisted that, as I was already 1½ years through the five, it would be folly to give it all up – unless, of course, I were to fail my exams.

I got through both intermediate and final at my first attempt – as I also did my examinations for a Bachelor of Commerce degree, which I took externally at London University while still under articles. To have undertaken the two concurrently, as I did, was really rather mad. But it was what I set out to achieve; and, to my relief, I pulled it off.

Getting down to learning about accounting proved to be tedious and unsatisfactory at first. At the end of my time at Shrewsbury I had been a school prefect (or praeposter, as it was called there), head of my house, and a double school first. But school accomplishments counted for nothing in an accountant's office. I had to start right at the bottom. I spent endless hours adding up the postage book, which I remember had masses of penny-ha'pennies in it because Britain had finally had to abandon the penny post for letters. But this kind of drudgery brought me quickly down to size.

I soon began to go out on audit as a raw junior attached to a senior. The senior put me on to checking the accuracy of all the additions in the daybooks and ledgers of the firms to which we were sent, while he got on with more interesting work. I soon wanted to consign adding-up to the devil. But after a bit it became almost automatic. I gave up cigarette smoking at this time; smoke got in my eyes while casting, and ash fell on the figures so that they didn't add up correctly.

However, when Arnold Kent and I went up to London in September 1926, life became more interesting. Although I was still less than halfway through my articles, I had to be in everything, because it was only a small office and there was no one else to do the work. And the great thing about being a member of a small team was that, even as an unqualified articled clerk, I talked to the heads of the businesses we worked in and tried to understand the management problems of different enterprises. And with this my training in accountancy began to be worthwhile.

★　　★　　★　　★　　★

By early 1930 I had virtually completed my five years' training. I began to think out what I would do when I had completed my articles at the end of July, assuming that I passed my final. I could stay on with Bullimore's for more experience as a qualified (and now paid) accountant. But I found auditing to be boring. I had had enough of that sort of experience. The checking of other people's books was to me unproductive and unsatisfying. I wanted to produce things or services.

Money entered into it. But it was not my main motive. In those days a good newly qualified English chartered accountant could earn £156 a year, or £3 a week. But he didn't always get it, not by any means. For around that time, 1930, a lot of newly qualified Scottish chartered accountants came south to gain London experience and were taking jobs at only £110 a year, ruining the market.

Going into industry was more difficult; but a successful applicant could get £300 a year from the start. But for qualified accountants to 'leave the profession', as the phrase went in those days, was new at that time. Among the pioneers were men like Frederic de Paula, who gave up his accountancy practice to go into Dunlop, and Percy Rees, who gave up his practice too to join Lever Brothers as chief accountant. As industry came to appreciate the value of employing professional accountants, opportunities opened up for the newly qualified. What began as a trickle soon became a regular stream. Those who went into industry at the start, as I did, were lucky enough to acquire valuable experience of management at an early age.

Looking at the commercial world of the late 1920s, I was attracted to the new, growing and exciting world of aviation. When I had taken my final in May 1930 and felt reasonably sure of having passed, I wrote to Imperial Airways and to de Havilland to ask if they had any vacancies for a budding accountant. As I half expected, I received courteous but regretful replies from both – from S A Dismore of Imperial Airways at Croydon and from de Havilland's W E Nixon at Stag Lane. By one of those ironies of history, 20 years later in BOAC, Imperial Airways' successor, I found myself negotiating with Nixon over our de Havilland Comet 1s and their problems.

Having found no possibility in 1930 of entering the challenging field of aviation, I went to employment agents. I was given particulars of a job with Hoover, distributors of the top-ranking American vacuum cleaners. Their offices were in Hanover Street, London W1. At that time they were still importing all their vacuum cleaners from the United States but they expected to build a factory in England within 18 months. I was offered the job and took it, to start in August 1930.

I had now reached top of descent. I only had to complete the last few weeks of my five years' articles. And then I would be ready to climb away on the next sector.

2 Situations Vacant

A few months later our managing director, Charles Colston, came back from a visit to the States with the news that the decision to manufacture Hoovers in England had been confirmed. We were to buy about 9 acres of land and build a new factory outside London.

I wondered where. I was to be the accountant of the plant and would have to work there, not in the West End any more. And I was about to get married.

I had first met Kay some four years earlier, the sister of a school friend of my own sister. We were part of a set who went to dances together, belonged to the same tennis club, and now and then on Sundays in summer drove to the Sussex coast to bathe. I didn't have much spare time because I had to work hard at the two sets of exams I had set out to pass. But I spent my summer holidays each year at Mullion in Cornwall with Kay and her family, and we came to know each other very well.

We couldn't think of marrying while I was still under articles and not earning a penny. But when I was almost 24 and had got the job with Hoover at £300 a year we made plans for our wedding in August 1931. But we wanted to know where to live.

I had read some economics in the course of taking my BComm, and had learnt that the location of a factory should be decided entirely on economic grounds. The factory should be near the source of its main raw materials, close to a supply of suitable labour, and conveniently placed in relation to its principal markets. What really decided our location was the fact that the three executive directors of Hoover lived at Gerrards Cross, Beaconsfield and High Wycombe. A factory alongside Western Avenue at Perivale meant that all three could get there easily in the same car every day instead of having to commute by rail into London. So much for economic theory!

Kay and I found a house to live in some 6 miles away, near Pinner. But only a few weeks after we got married we had a financial shock. In the autumn of 1931 the country was in the grip of a severe economic crisis and the Government decided that everyone's pay should be reduced by 10 per cent. So, we suddenly found our income cut from £300 to £270. Like everyone else, we managed. Unlike most others in our walk of life we had no maid or 'daily woman'. We did the housework ourselves, and our little Austin 7 took me to the factory at Perivale each day.

But all our friends lived south of the Thames. So, after three short years near Pinner, we sold the house at the end of 1934 and went to live with Kay's parents while we built a new house at Esher in Surrey.

We had to live on a very tight budget. I persuaded Kay to keep a set of household accounts, which she could never make balance.

'I seem to have lost seven and sixpence this week,' she said once. 'At least, I can't balance the account. What ought I to do about it?'

'Don't worry,' I replied. 'Just put it down as sundries, and then the account will balance.'

'Well, you're a fine accountant,' she said. 'That's cheating. If you get rid of differences like that at the office your accounts can't be much good.'

'Why not?' I said. 'There's no sense in pursuing accuracy beyond the point where it is useful. Balancing the books is not the purpose of accounts; it only provides an arithmetical check, which it is not worth wasting time on if it is not significant. The purpose of accounts in a business is to enable you to decide whether you are spending too much or too little on this or that and whether you ought to be doing something different in order to improve your position.'

Neither of us enjoyed our household book-keeping and we soon gave it up when we found that we could manage to live within our limited income. I have spent so much time looking after other people's money in the companies I have served that I have never been able to worry about my own finances.

In those days there was an amusing and perfectly legal way of raising money. Hire-purchase facilities for buying new cars were all too easy. The only deposit required was about ten pounds, with the balance payable over the next two years. When you traded in your old car against a new one, you got paid for the old one in cash (less the deposit on the new one) and suddenly you were in funds again. It may seem ridiculous nowadays. But in the 1930s that's the way we raised the wind.

*   *   *   *   *

Devising a system to control all the costs of running a new factory was a thrilling challenge and a great opportunity for a young man of

25. In those days very little was known about the use of accountancy in the control of costs and efficiency in every part of a factory's operations. It was an entirely new field.

That was in the early 1930s – the years of the Great Depression, when millions of people up and down the country were without work and often without hope of work for long years. So for me to be cultivating new ground was a wonderful piece of good fortune. And I was not only developing new professional techniques. The Hoover cleaners I would be helping to make were especially well suited to the times; like it or not, more and more housewives were having to learn to manage without maids; and more and more homes in Britain were being supplied with electricity. There would be no lack of demand for our product. Thus I never experienced the fear of unemployment.

I had no practical experience to draw on. But the Hoover factory at North Canton sent over their accounting manual; and I was able to borrow a book on works accounting in America from the Management Library. But best of all I was able, through Management Research Groups, to visit the Morris Engines' factory at Coventry and to study the control system in operation there. I learnt a lot from that – not least that qualified accountants have no monopoly of accounting expertise. The Morris Engines' accounting system of those days had been developed from scratch by an unqualified man, who walked the floors with an authority born of achievement. I have long since forgotten his name; but I owe him a great debt, because of all that he triggered off in my mind.

As the Hoover factory got going, I felt the need to bring in a few additional people to help develop and operate the new accounting system. Almost the first to join me was Harold G Meads – known to all as George although his middle name was Godfrey – who had qualified the same year as I had, 1930. Like me, he had gone into industry after qualifying and had had a couple of years' accounting experience with Crosse & Blackwell, makers of jam. Together we developed the process of continuous accounting control throughout the factory at Perivale.

I ought to explain a bit about this phrase 'accounting control'. We accountants didn't seek to control anything, except the costs of our own departments. But we provided management at all levels of the business with information which enabled them to control the cost of the operations for which they were responsible. It was financial control with a loose rein. I came to see that the best use of accountancy in industry was not to restrict but to encourage. Our role was akin to the relationship between the jockey and his horse.

For this reason accounting control does not only have a value in the factory. By supplying the right sort of financial information to district sales managers, for example, we increased the productivity of the sales force. I was taken by surprise at the end of one Hoover sales conference on being presented with a silver cigarette box inscribed 'for staunch assistance to the sales force'.

My years with Hoover gave me a fascinating insight into the running of a thrustful and progressive business. It was an efficient business, too, in spite of the costly method of door-to-door selling. I personally disliked this intensely but, my word, it was effective. In the five years following 1931 – against the trend of the depression – the factory was enlarged twice and its productive capacity doubled.

Hoover's business economics at that time were fascinating. The standard cleaner complete with accessory dusting tools cost us about £7 to import from the United States, and there was no duty. We sold it for £21, a mark-up of 200 per cent. The cost of selling was £11, of which £8 covered door-to-door selling, distribution and administration. The other £3 went to the retailer, who took the risk of the buyer defaulting. This left us with £3 profit, which was nearly half what the cleaner had cost us – though it was only a modest 14 per cent on turnover.

I often wondered what the thing actually cost to make. I was soon to find out, when we received copies of the American company's cost sheets; less than £4. Their profit was also £3 per cleaner. When our factory at Perivale got into regular production and we began to match American costs, this profit accrued to us in England on top of our own. No wonder our American parents had been somewhat reluctant to let us build a factory over here. In due time they cleared a handsome capital profit when they floated their English company on the stock market. But in essence the economics of the business at that time were clear; it cost £11 to market what had cost £4 to make, and the company netted a £6 profit – a return of 150 per cent on cost.

Yet I never met anyone with a Hoover who did not think it was value for money. Remember that the low production cost I have quoted could have been achieved only with a substantial volume of output. The great gamble was then to sell enough to ensure that Hoover costs per unit were low.

One lesson from this I have remembered all my life. Almost the greatest mistake in manufacturing industry is to underprice the product. If you price your product too low, you can never make much of a sustained profit, and the business stagnates at best. If you price it high, and it is a good product, you can generally overcome price-resistance with harder or more effective selling.

We employed about 1,500 at Perivale to make the cleaners and about the same number to sell them. The sales force turnover was fantastic – as high as 500 per cent a year. The average door-to-door salesman stayed with us for little more than two months, and we had to recruit 7,500 new salesmen each year.

It was a time of great unemployment. A Hoover salesman in those days drew £2 a week in advance of a £3 commission when he sold a cleaner. If he ran up a deficit of £8 his employment was terminated. The average chap who joined us was no salesman really; to him it was work, when jobs of any kind were hard to come by. He managed to sell half-a-dozen Hoovers to people he knew and then called it a day. But there were some real salesmen who stayed with us a long time and earned good money.

About this time in the mid 1930s, I got more and more interested in studying how other businesses worked. I was working flat out at Hoovers so I had little time for visiting them, but I did succeed through Management Research Groups in visiting the Steel Peech & Tozer plant outside Sheffield, where H A Simpson, one of the leading cost and works accountants of those days, had his base. From his experience I learnt that, however good an accountant is technically, he can achieve nothing constructive without good human relations. The people he is helping to manage must understand what he is trying to do, and want him to do it.

I learned, too, from books borrowed from the Management Library in Bloomsbury Square and from talking to and coming to know the man who ran it, Esmond Milward. He was an individualist and never an organisation man. But he understood the problems of those of us who were organisation types, and he was a man who inspired others.

Esmond contributed much to my mangement education by encouraging me to read the works of two Americans I was never able to meet. A P Sloan of General Motors and E A Filene of Boston. General Motors then led the world in big business organisation, motivating people at all levels. Filene was in the forefront of marketing and selling methods.

He had developed an attitude to pricing a product which caught my imagination. It certainly expanded his business enormously. He judged that there were three best prices at which any particular product could be sold most profitably. A more varied price structure could be wasteful through having to carry unnecessary stocks. The reason for three was simply the very human one that there are three types of customer; those who always pay the top price because if they pay less they feel they are not getting the best; those who always buy the cheapest; and those in the middle.

I was amused to learn from George Meads that the jam industry seemed to have the same philosophy. Exactly the same strawberry jam, for instance, was packed in three different jars with three different labels and sold at three different prices – and all three types of customer seemed satisfied. The manufacturer didn't mind either, because the small profit on the lowest price was offset by the big profit on the highest price – and overall he increased his business.

By 1936 Hoover had become a very different kind and size of business from the one I had joined in 1930. We had grown fast in five years. I persuaded our directors – Charles and Eric Colston and Jimmy Wykes – that we needed to review the organisation and management structure of the business. The rising consultancy firm of Urwick Orr and Partners was called in and Lyn Urwick himself supervised the assignment. His proposals were never implemented because they were unwelcome to the three directors.

I myself had developed a great respect for Lyn Urwick and we became good friends. I learnt much from him about management and administration. He contributed more than anyone in the 1930s and 1940s to improving the standard of business management in Britain. And yet, perhaps because he could not suffer fools gladly, he has never received due recognition in his own country. Now retired, he lives in Australia, near Sydney.

The decision not to accept Urwick Orr's recommendations made me feel it was time for a change. I had achieved what I wanted in financial control. There was not much more to do there other than to keep it running – and I had some good lieutenants who could do that perfectly well. I wanted a new challenge. So early in 1937 I started to look for another job.

★   ★   ★   ★   ★

After seven years in a go-ahead American firm I decided I would try a typically British business with, preferably, several factories in different parts of the country to widen my experience. I stipulated in my own mind that I wanted to remain in or around London, where there was the greatest stimulus for new thought and experience in management-accounting – as I had come to call the work in which I had become immersed.

I first came into touch with Doulton's as a result of answering an anonymous advertisement in the Situations Vacant column of *The Times*. I went to see the managing director, Lt Cmdr E Basil Green. I took to him immediately and thought he would be good to work with. He had come out of the Royal Navy in 1923 and set about getting business experience by working in the accountancy practice of Price Waterhouse & Co as an unqualified senior.

Doulton's, too, seemed to be the sort of business I was looking for. It was very English. It was a household name. Its head office was in London but there were eight factories in different parts of the country, covering the whole range of pottery from fine china through industrial porcelain to stoneware drainpipes. It was still very much of a family business. It was unashamedly old-fashioned – so much so that there was still a speaking tube connecting the chairman's office with that of the company secretary, who acted as chief executive.

Basil Green had been brought in a couple of years earlier on the advice of the firm's auditor, Sir Nicholas Waterhouse, who had recommended the appointment of a strong managing director at the centre to take over the reins from the company secretary who was about to retire. The head office was to be moved out of the dingy terra cotta building in Lambeth High Street into a new building to be erected on the Albert Embankment, looking across the Thames to the Houses of Parliament. And the last pottery in central London, where uneconomic salt-glazed stoneware was still being made, was shortly to be closed down. Change was on the way. Green paraded me before the chairman, L J E Hooper, who must have liked the shape of my face because after about 20 minutes I was offered the post of chief accountant. And I moved from Hoover to Doulton on 1 May 1937.

A reluctant chairman can bring disaster to a business. Eric Hooper was a lawyer, married to a Doulton, and had never wanted to go into the family firm. But when his wife's father died, he had to. Fortunately, he had the wisdom to bring in Basil Green at a critical period in the firm's history. Even so, he all but frustrated every effort to put new life into it. He didn't want it to grow. He wanted it to remain as it always had been. His patriarchal visits to the works were rather like visits to tenant farmers on a large estate. I never understood why he could not see that you cannot stand still in industry; a business must either grow or decay.

But there was a lot I could do below the surface of company policy, particularly in the field of financial control. The company was far from prosperous – partly because the ceramics industry as a whole was underpricing its products, and partly because works-accounting was almost non-existent, beyond what was needed to calculate the wages, pay the bills, and collect the debts.

Doulton's largest works was at Burslem, in Staffordshire. Here we made fine china and earthenware, and employed over a thousand people. There was no systematic control of the multitudinous work in progress through the factory. The traditional method of stocktaking in the Five Towns at that time was purely visual – look at a section and guess how many basketfuls of pottery were scattered around in it.

Apart from works making drainpipes and sanitary ware in different parts of the country, from St Helens in Lancashire to Erith in Kent, there were others specialising in industrial ceramics – chemical stoneware, crucibles and high voltage insulators – all requiring control systems. But because we had to start management-accounting from virtually bare rock, we had not achieved much by the time war broke out in September 1939.

Basil Green was in the RNR and was promptly called up and posted to Great Yarmouth. I had not reached my teens when the first war had ended and, when World War II broke out, I found I was in a reserved occupation, in a business covered by the Essential Work Order. But Green wasn't away for long and returned to us early in 1940 towards the end of the 'phoney war' period.

Soon afterwards, I was approached by Lyn Urwick who had been recruited by the Treasury to set up an Organisation and Methods Division to eliminate unnecessary work in the Civil Service. Would I join him on secondment? Now that Green was back in Doulton's I said I would. And there I chanced to meet R H Wilson, a brilliant chartered accountant in private practice, who had also been pulled in from outside – a meeting which was to have a significant effect on my life eight years later.

Shortly afterwards, Basil Green was appointed Deputy Regional Commissioner for south-east England, which meant he had to leave Doulton's for the duration. I was needed back in the business to exercise control at the centre. So I could not stay on the Treasury staff for more than about 10 weeks, all of them in the Ministry of War Transport. I wasn't sorry to go back, because it seemed difficult if not impossible to make even the smallest dent in the armour of Civil Service procedure. Perhaps, in all fairness, I hadn't tried for long enough.

With the coming of war, the balance of production in Doulton's changed considerably. We concentrated on industrial ceramics and other products required in the war effort, whether for the manufacture of explosives, for warships, or for airfields and army bases. We cut back on all else. We also stopped development of our management-accounting because in war what had to be made had to be made, regardless of financial consequences. I found myself ceasing to be an accountant and becoming instead a deputy for my absent managing director.

But the job at Doulton's was not a satisfying thing to do in war. I suppose most of us in reserved occupations felt the same. When the Local Defence Volunteers were formed in 1940, I transferred to them from Air Raid Warden. The LDV soon became the Home Guard. Night duty twice a week, and field practice at week-ends, provided a bit (but not much) of an outlet for one's frustration at not being able to do more.

So I, for one, started using my mental energies to re-examine the basis of my thinking.

★   ★   ★   ★   ★

At the start I concentrated on my own profession. I gathered together about five or six chartered accountants working in industry around London. They too were concerned about the way accountancy was – or rather was not – developing. We used to meet of an evening at my office in Doulton House. We considered how to turn sterile and unimaginative auditing in directions that would make accounting of greater value to industry and commerce after the war. I wrote a paper on behalf of the group, challenging many prevailing ideas about auditing. The paper was published in *The Accountant* in 1941 as a series of four articles under the title of 'The Future of Auditing'. It attracted a good deal of attention and triggered off a minor revolution in the profession.

But being excluded at that stage from playing a direct part in the Institute's affairs, I joined the council of the Office Management Association, as it was then called. In that capacity I came in contact with Paul (later Sir Paul) Chambers in urging a change in the method of collecting income tax, then almost wholly in arrear. Chambers had been taxation adviser to the Indian Government and was now at Somerset House on the Board of Inland Revenue. It would surely be better for employers to be made responsible for deducting tax from earnings at source and for passing it to the Inland Revenue. The Revenue would thereby receive the tax a year earlier; and the employee would be spared the embarrassment of having to find the money to pay the tax a year after he had probably spent it. To Paul Chambers I argued my thesis as persuasively as I could. E H Carr, then assistant editor of *The Times*, invited me to write articles advocating the new procedure. In due course it was introduced by the Government as PAYE (pay as you earn).

Until then, the Institute of Chartered Accountants regarded those of us in industry and commerce as being beyond the pale and having left the profession. Rubbish, we thought; we were using our professional skills in far more productive ways.

After the war, I organised a monthly lunch group of London industrial chartered accountants. We used to meet in a private room on the first floor of Antoine's Restaurant in Charlotte Street. It was a small group at first, but of high standing. Two other founders were Eric Hay Davidson of Courtaulds and Jim Sandford-Smith of Metal Box. Other early members were Harry Norris of Vickers (and later Geo Wimpey), George Myers of Harrods, Jack Clayton of John Mowlem (and later Rediffusion), Joe Latham of the National Coal Board (and later AEI and Thorn) and Patrick Ravenhill of United Africa and Unilever.

Our influence soon made itself felt. The President of the Institute came and heard what we had to say. It was agreed quite early on that a few members working in industry should be brought on to the 45-man Council, the governing body of the Institute. But then we ran into a procedural difficulty. Under the Institute's Charter, the Council could be drawn only from Fellows of the Institute, and no one could become a Fellow unless he had been in public practice for five years. The rising generation of industrial chartered accountants, however high they climbed in their various businesses, could rank only as Associates.

In due course, however, the Council revised our Charter. In 1948 it became possible for an Associate to stand for election. Various members of the Council put my name forward and I was elected – the first industrial chartered accountant who had never been in public practice to serve on the Council of the Institute.

★   ★   ★   ★   ★

I had become a member of the Reform Club shortly before the war, and often went there at lunch time to read. At one stage I got fascinated by Arnold Toynbee's *Outline of History* and his analysis of the ebb and flow of nations – how the course of history is determined by the challenges people meet and how they respond.

Challenge and response – that is what fashions the future. And if that is true of nations and peoples, it is also true of institutions, businesses and individuals. Every different situation presents a new challenge, and our success or failure depends on our responses. Where there is no challenge there can be no response, only stagnation. Repeated challenge seems to me to be a necessary stimulus to human progress, individually or collectively.

There are challenges in plenty in the course of married life, for instance. If it weren't for that, the achievement of a happy and long-lasting marriage wouldn't be half so rewarding. The greatest challenge I had to face was our early realisation that we weren't going to have children. I fretted and wondered what on earth to do.

Getting my mind straight on this took some time, because I was then going through a period of spiritual uncertainty. In my third year at Shrewsbury I had been duly confirmed and became a regular weekly communant. But after my marriage I let it lapse, and for some years I never went to church.

However, in the course of confronting the fact that we could not beget children I turned to the Bible for guidance and found it.[1] There could be no question of divorce and a fresh start. From then on I resumed churchgoing. I brought myself to realise that begetting children isn't the only object of marriage. I also came to see that disappointment in one field provides time, energy and money for creative activities elsewhere. Certainly, I was able to find compensation in group activities of various kinds which, had I been a father, I doubt if I would have had time for.

Basil Oldham, my uncle-godfather, sent George Bell, then Bishop of Chichester, a copy of *The Future of Auditing*. Why I never knew, but it started something. The Bishop sent it on to Dr J H Oldham (no relation of Basil) who was the secretary of the Christian Frontier Council, on which Bell suggested I might be useful.

By this strange chain of chance began some of the most educative experiences of my life, experiences that helped me to gain some understanding, however imperfect, of what trying to be a Christian means in the world of the 20th century.

The Christian Frontier Council was a new development in the Church of England. Its purpose was to provide a centre where lay men and women could meet to help bring about effective Christian action in modern society. We met not to discuss the abstract principles of Christian ethics but to consider together, as Christians engaged in the affairs of society, the concrete decisions we had to make in our daily occupations.

The Council comprised an interesting group of people, to whom I felt it a privilege to be admitted. It included writers such as T S Eliot, author *(inter alia)* of *The Idea of a Christian Society*, and Barbara Ward, then working for *The Economist*; the industrialist Samuel Courtauld; Arthur fforde, the solicitor who subsequently became headmaster of Rugby; and public servants such as John Maud (now Lord Redcliffe-Maud), Henry Willink (Minister of Health in the 1940s) and Henry Brooke (Home Secretary in the early 1960s and now Lord Brooke of Cumnor).

I learnt a lot from being one of such a group and from the personal

---

[1]Mark 10: 11 and Luke 16: 18.

contacts and friendships which developed. But I learnt most from Joe Oldham himself. He was one of the wisest men I have had the good fortune to meet and his religion was very practical. He had studied theology at New College, Edinburgh, but had never been ordained. Instead, he devoted the greater part of his working life to being the secretary of the International Missionary Council until he became the secretary of the new Christian Frontier Council in the 1940s.

He led me to see that, if Christianity is to have a meaning for the ordinary man like myself, it must prove itself as a faith in which men can find re-inforcement and sustenance in the acute conflicts of social life. It must make a difference to the way people think and to what they do as they go about their daily tasks in factory, shop, administration or politics. Otherwise, it would have little relevance to our present life; and that cannot be true.

But it is a mistake to think that there is a specifically Christian solution to business or political problems. Economics and science have technical laws of their own which must be obeyed. But this is no reason for the Christian to shrug his shoulders and take the line that his beliefs have no part to play in business or public affairs. Christians play a part, like it or not. In the end almost every situation comes to a point where someone has to make a decision. And, hopefully, someone who is a Christian will make a decision that has more rather than less Christian content in it.

I came to believe that one of the ways in which God works in the world is found in the relations of men to one another – in the meeting of man with man and the interplay between their minds and characters. Out of this belief, the Christian in public life will develop a disposition to treat other people as persons in his dealings with them. This, I came to appreciate later, is fundamental to the role of leadership in industrial management.

*   *   *   *   *

Of the interplay between Kay's character and mine, it is not easy to write because it is difficult to see oneself as others do. But two people cannot share life together for over 41 years without gaining a lot from each other in the process. I know that I owe Kay more than I can possibly acknowledge. All through a man's life he is making decisions – not just in business, but in all of living. They can be made for the worse just as much as for the better; and Kay's influence certainly worked for the better.

Kay was, I suppose, a noble example of the good pagan. The only time she ever went to church was for an occasional Red Cross parade during the war, which she regarded as duty. She eschewed anything at all churchy. Yet she prayed on her knees night and morning – to what god I never knew; I found it impossible to talk with her about religion. She loved visiting old churches, but because of their architectural interest and not because they were shrines of worship. And with all this, she was one of the most considerate and straight-living people I have known. Perhaps her intelligence was too practical to feel drawn to religion. She had all the virtues that one associates with a good Christian. Yet it seemed that she had no real belief in the Christian faith. It is one of the paradoxes of life that a person who sets out to try and live as a good Christian often lives a life that is less Christian than that of a good pagan. Maddening, isn't it, to those of us who profess and call ourselves Christians?

I have already mentioned that we could have no children. But once I had got over that, life was good. I had taught her to drive a car, which her own family often twitted her with being beyond her powers, and this began to give her confidence to stand on her own. She kept a home beautifully, modestly in our younger days but on a larger scale after we moved into Esher's Clare Hill in 1957. Throughout the war she worked for the Red Cross, on hospital wards; and when the threat of invasion was real she learnt to use a .303 service rifle at Bisley and proved a better shot than I was. Later, when I used to travel a lot as Managing Director of BOAC, she made a point of getting to know the wives of our overseas managers wherever possible – a useful contribution to maintaining morale in a world-wide airline.

* * * * *

When the war ended Basil Green came back to us at Doulton's and we could start planning again. I recruited help from outside by bringing in Kenneth W Bevan, another chartered accountant who had gone industrial and had worked for most of the war in a large ordnance factory. We worked happily together. But in the matter of company policies Basil Green and I could make little or no progress. Eric Hooper seemed determined to block all change. And apart from Basil Green, who believed in waiting until personalities changed, there was no one else on the Board who worked in the business. So there was nobody to change Eric Hooper's attitude. I grew more and more restless. If there was to be no growth and development, there was – for me – no challenge left.

In 1948 I decided to look round for another job. And it chanced that an approach came from Reggie Wilson, whom I had met while working briefly in the Treasury in 1940, asking whether I would like to make a change and join him. He had recently been appointed comptroller of the newly-formed British Transport Commission, by Sir Cyril (later Lord) Hurcomb, the civil servant who had been made its chairman.

This was the period when the mining, transport, gas and electricity industries were first nationalised. At first I hesitated. But after a while I came to feel that nationalisation was here to stay, whether one agreed with the politics of it or not; that it was important for the country that the nationalised industries should be well managed; and that it didn't serve the country well if people who might have something to contribute stayed out of them. So I decided to join the commission as director of costs and statistics. On 1 May 1948 – eleven years to the day after I first joined Doulton's – I began working at 55 Broadway, where the BTC had its headquarters at that time.

When the Commission was set up by Act of Parliament shortly after the war it was entrusted with the country's five mainline railways, including their docks, hotels and road services. This was my first experience of transport management. The economics of transport are very different from those of manufacturing industry. But it was a science that could be learned. I soon learned, for instance, that one of the most important economic factors in any transport undertaking is the utilisation of its vehicles, both in hours used per day and in occupancy or load factor.

But the British Transport Commission was all so vast. It seemed impossible to get near enough to the basic transport job, and to those who did it, to do anything really productive. I would point out, for example, that on average a railway wagon was used only one day in thirteen. I would make suggestions. But there was no chance in such an organisation of having the authority to see that reforms were carried out properly and made to work constructively. I began to despair of ever being able to put my management-accounting skills to positive use.

At headquarters, of course, there was a mass of paperwork. But there was no integration between the financial accounts used for annual reporting to Parliament and the various costs and statistical ratios I was employing to test the efficiency of different operations. Reggie Wilson and I were always looking for ways to improve matters. But we could find few.

I also came to feel disillusioned with the basic ideas on which the Commission had been formed. They had taken root way back in 1928 in the years of the great depression, when Cyril Hurcomb was one of the senior civil servants in the Ministry of Transport. It was foreseen that the railways were bound to become less economic as more traffic moved to the roads. The solution was thought to be cross-subsidy by road transport. There was never any real prospect of road transport making sufficient profit for this to be possible. But when the opportunity came in 1946 to put these twenty-year-old ideas into practice, this elementary fact was overlooked.

This was a classic example of the faults H G Wells attributed to 'the delayed realisation of ideas'. A reformer in his youth or middle age evolves plans for overcoming the problems of the world as he sees them. Yet in almost every case it will be 20 to 25 years before he has the opportunity and the authority to implement his ideas. By then, with the passing of time, the surrounding circumstances will have changed materially; his pre-conceived remedies will no longer fit the new situation and will fail.

So, in one way and another, I felt very frustrated and ineffective. There seemed nothing else to do but look for another job. I still felt convinced by the ideas that had attracted me to accept Reggie Wilson's approach. Some of us ought to work in nationalised industry and help if we could. But, because of the scale of nationalisation, I saw no real opportunity anywhere.

It seemed sensible to go back into the private sector of industry. For one thing I would be more highly paid. But I wanted to help create something new. I felt that in private industry I would have only the challenge of repeating my management-accounting experience in a different set of circumstances. And I didn't find that prospect particularly exciting.

I mentioned my problem to a few friends who might be able to help. One of the first I saw was Sir Harold Howitt, a past-president of the Institute of Chartered Accountants and the embodiment of professionalism. He had been one of those who were most sympathetic to the reformers like myself who had gone into industry. It chanced that on the morning of the day I saw him – in the late summer of 1949 – he had been approached by Sir Miles Thomas, the new chairman of the British Overseas Airways Corporation. Sir Miles was after someone to head up BOAC's financial side. Would I see him?

I took an immediate liking to Miles Thomas, with his Royal Flying Corps tie. I met him at BOAC's headquarters office, then in Stratton House on Piccadilly. But I was still disillusioned with the prospects of working in a nationalised industry. After half an hour of heart-searching, walking round and round Green Park on a beautiful September afternoon, I turned Miles' offer down.

A month or so passed. After the next Council meeting at the

My mother and father – in England on quinquennial leave, 1914.

Myself when young, with my 'cobber' of those days – in Pernambuco, Brazil, 1911.

Start of the world's first jet service – a BOAC Comet 1 leaving London for Johannesburg, 2 May 1952. *(British Airways)*

The board's tribute to Capt O P Jones on his retirement from flying duties, 12 May 1955. From left: Ronald McCrindle, Sir John Stephenson, Sir Francis Brake, Sir Miles Thomas, Whitney Straight, OP, Lord Burghley (now Exeter), Hugh Newlands, Lord Rennell and BS. *(British Airways)*

Institute, Harold asked me whether I had thought any more about the job with BOAC. I told him about my disillusionment with the Transport Commission. But, I added, I was coming to feel that there might possibly be three things in favour of BOAC. First, it was a relatively small nationalised industry, employing only about 20,000 people compared with the half million or so in the Commission; this would make it possible to get to know and understand the people who actually did the work, and so give me a chance to make a contribution through personal contact. Second, a Conservative Government had originally set up BOAC as a public corporation in 1939, so perhaps it might not be governed by the same kind of thinkers who ruled in the postwar nationalised industries established by Labour. And, third, it would be very different under the dynamic personality of Miles Thomas.

'Do go and see Miles Thomas again,' Harold said. 'Because I know he hasn't yet found the person he needs – and I think you are that person.' Harold Howitt knew a good deal about BOAC because, apart from having been Finance Member of the Air Council, he had been chairman of BOAC for a short time after the resignation of the Pearson board in March 1943 and had remained a director until 1948.

I saw Miles Thomas again – Whitney Straight was with him on this occasion – and they won me over. But I didn't need much winning. I was half prepared to take the job before I went to Stratton House. The salary – £3,000 a year – wasn't what I would have looked for in the private sector. But as Miles engagingly explained, his own salary was fixed by Government and wasn't that much higher; and everybody else had to fit in underneath that.

So at the beginning of January 1950 – at the mid-point of the century – I started work as financial comptroller of BOAC. I was 43, and eager to take up this exciting challenge.

3 The Jet Revolution

The BOAC that I joined at the beginning of 1950 was in process of being transformed from a war-time organisation operating air transport services for Government into a profit-conscious corporation operating scheduled public services world-wide on accepted commercial principles.

BOAC was originally set up by the Conservative Government in 1939 as the country's chosen instrument to develop the whole of British civil aviation world-wide. But during the war there was obviously no opportunity to operate services into Europe. When the war ended the Government of the day decided to set up a separate corporation, British European Airways, to re-establish British short-haul routes to and from Europe and internal air services within the United Kingdom.

Then, when the new Labour Government embarked on its plan to nationalise some of Britain's essential industries, the Airways Corporations were ready-made instruments for the label of 'nationalised industry'. But it is an open question whether it was ever right to impose nationalisation, essentially applicable to internal domestic industries, on an industry working almost wholly in the highly competitive field of international aviation. Sir John (later Lord) Reith, BOAC's first chairman, told me that he always lamented the fact that the concept of a public corporation, which had worked so well in his beloved BBC, had been taken away from us; a public corporation enjoyed far greater independence of Government or ministerial influence than any nationalised industry ever has.

★   ★   ★   ★   ★

At the end of the war BOAC was desperately short of suitable aircraft for developing its long-haul services to all parts of the British Empire and across the North Atlantic to the United States. The Government naturally insisted that BOAC should buy British, to save dollars and to help our aircraft industry get back on to its peace-

A BOAC Comet 1, 1952.   *(British Airways)*

Presentation to Sir Miles Thomas on his leaving BOAC, 27 April 1956. From left: Sir Victor Tait, Ken Staple, MT, BS, Ronald McCrindle and Freddy Gillman.   *(British Airways)*

With Capt Bone on a Britannia 102 flight deck, January 1957. *(British Airways)*

Capt Jim Weir, newly appointed Chief of Flight Operations, at his desk, December 1956. *(British Airways)*

time feet. But what made this policy difficult to achieve was the fact that, during the war, the British aircraft industry had concentrated on fighters and medium-range bombers while America had developed long-haul combat and troop-carrying aircraft capable of operating across the Atlantic and the Pacific.

In any case, irrespective of defence, the accident of geography had a marked effect on the thinking of aircraft designers and manufacturers on each side of the Atlantic. Britain is a small country, and close to Europe. Short-haul aircraft such as the Airspeed Ambassador and the Vickers Viking and Viscount were all that were then required for air services to and within Europe. Even the furthest parts of the far-flung British Empire could be reached by medium-range aircraft with intermediate stops. Indeed the Brabazon Committee, set up to advise on the best types of aircraft for Britain to produce after the war, called for 'medium-range Empire' types. No one seems to have considered the importance of non-stop inter-city transatlantic range.

By contrast, America is a vast country in itself. Several of its major cities are some 3,000 miles apart. Thus, apart from national defence, it was commercially desirable to have aircraft capable of flying non-stop coast-to-coast. American aircraft manufacturers therefore had to meet the challenge of designing and developing long-haul aeroplanes.

The lack of a long-range aircraft requirement has bedevilled the British industry ever since the war. The de Havilland Comet and the Bristol Britannia were basically medium-range. Attempts were made to stretch them into longer-range aircraft, but without success. In fact, the British aircraft industry has never overcome the handicap of war and geography, and has never produced long-haul aircraft as good as those built in America. BOAC depended almost entirely on long-haul aircraft for its world-wide routes, but was obliged by Government to buy British whenever possible. This was bound to lead to endless difficulties and arguments.

The North Atlantic was one of the main threads in BOAC's route network, and long-haul aircraft were essential. Even the Empire routes demanded higher performance aircraft with better economics than those currently available to BOAC in Britain such as the Avro York and Solent flying boat. So, on Sir Harold Hartley's appointment as chairman of BOAC in July 1947, the search for better aircraft had been stepped up. Much of the drive was supplied by the able lieutenant he brought with him from BEA, Whitney Straight. In April 1948 BOAC's position was greatly strengthened by the appointment of Sir Miles Thomas to the board as its deputy chairman. Soon afterwards a coherent aircraft policy began to emerge in BOAC.

On the North Atlantic, the Boeing Stratocruiser was much the best of the aircraft then available. It was in service with Pan American. It had 50 per cent more carrying capacity than its nearest rival, the Lockheed Constellation 749, though its operating costs per seat-mile were no lower. It had sleeping berths above the seats for those who would pay for them. This was important because aircraft speed at that time was such that all transatlantic air travel had to be overnight; and it was equipped with a downstairs bar in its somewhat bulbous belly. The difficulty was to get any. Fortunately, the Scandinavian Airlines System, SAS, and the Irish airline, Aer Lingus, had options on ten Stratocruisers, which they were unable to take up. Arrangements were made for the orders to be transferred to BOAC.

For the so-called Empire routes to Australia, Africa and the Far East, the Government were persuaded to authorise the purchase of early Lockheed Constellation 049s and 749s for the routes. The number of these aircraft that could be obtained was, however, insufficient to carry all the traffic on those routes.

To supplement capacity, Miles Thomas and Whitney Straight succeeded in obtaining Government permission for the Canadian dollars to buy 22 Canadair Argonauts, provided the engines were Rolls-Royce Merlins paid for in sterling. These aircraft were the pressurised version of the Douglas DC-4 and were being built under licence in Canada for Trans-Canada Airlines with the type name North Star. Our Argonauts, together with the Constellations, would form the backbone of BOAC's fleet for use on the Empire routes until the Comets and the Britannias came into service.

So far so good. The position by the end of 1949 was that BOAC could confidently plan ahead with a fleet as good as any other. It consisted of too many different types, but BOAC was evolving and there was no other answer in the circumstances. The Yorks and the Solent flying boats would be withdrawn from passenger service during 1950, as the more modern aircraft from North America were introduced. The hopes of the top management I joined in January 1950 were high. For, as well as having a fairly competitive fleet, BOAC with its Comet 1s coming along would be the first airline in the world to introduce jet aircraft into regular passenger service. The pioneering spirit abounded.

★   ★   ★   ★   ★

But while plans had been laid to equip BOAC with the aircraft to run a successful airline in due course, the staff generally was very much over-size and required drastic slimming down. It was not an easy task, and it could not be accomplished overnight. But BOAC could not have had a better person to carry through the necessary re-organisation than Miles Thomas.

In the first two years after the war the staff was increased alarmingly by what seem to have been almost wholesale intakes from the RAF. On top of that, all staff of British South American Airways were brought into BOAC when that airline had to cease operations. Taking BOAC and BSAA together, the number of people employed in 1947 was as high as 24,100. To give an idea of the degree of overstaffing that this represents it is only necessary to compare the number of people employed with the total revenue earned in that year by the two corporations combined – £14.6 million. The total revenue earned for each person employed was therefore only £605 a year. Had this been private enterprise, that was all that was available to pay every employee's salary or wages, and all other operating, selling and administration costs. This is only a rough and ready yardstick, but it illustrates dramatically the extent of overstaffing. Had BOAC been in the private sector, it would have gone out of business. But, fortunately for the future of British civil aviation, BOAC had the temporary support of Government grants.

Miles Thomas set about dealing with the problem. He realised that he would get nowhere without the understanding and support of the seventeen trade unions with which BOAC had to deal. To win this, he started the practice of holding informal monthly meetings with national officers of those unions – people such as Jim Matthews, Anne Godwin, Denis Follows, Douglas Tennant, Ian Mikardo, Tom Williamson and Bill Carron. These informal meetings were held in the BOAC board room in Stratton House, Piccadilly, a few days before each board meeting. This enabled Miles, who always had his departmental heads with him, to explain why staff numbers had to be cut by one-third, to let the unions know when and where the next axe would have to fall, and to keep them informed of his forward policy. In fact, he led the union leaders to feel that they shared his problems so that they came themselves to want these cuts for the sake of BOAC's future.

I was immediately involved in these meetings when I joined BOAC, and was greatly impressed with the atmosphere of co-operation he had been able to generate. By the beginning of 1950, the total number of employees had been cut to around 19,500 – a reduction of some 4,500. By March 1951 a further 3,000 had been shed, bringing the total number to 7,500 – almost his one-in-three target. The staff was now down to about 16,500. And all this was achieved without a strike – a remarkable tribute to Miles Thomas's handling of a very difficult situation.

Partly as a result of this slimming down, operating revenue per employee had been raised from the abysmal £605 to some £1,500 a year, with a target of £2,000. This was in fact reached by March 1952, just one year later. At this figure, at money values of the early 1950s, it was possible for BOAC to look forward not only to making ends meet but also to making profits.

* * * * *

Miles Thomas became chairman and chief executive of BOAC in July 1949 after Harold Hartley retired. Miles was, without question, one of the best bosses I have ever had to work under. He was by any standard a successful businessman, having joined Lord Nuffield (then Mr W R Morris) in 1924 and been one of his right hand men until 1947. He had a highly developed commercial sense, and perhaps an over-developed personal sensitivity in the field of public relations – which is no bad fault, if fault it is. He recognised and respected expertise in fields that were not his. He did not tolerate ineffectiveness, which is why some people could not get on with him. But once he had satisfied himself that you were the man to do the job he wanted done, he would leave you to get on with it and make you feel that he had complete confidence in you – one of the best ways of getting someone to give all he has got. We must have taken to one another quite quickly, because I soon came to feel I was being ridden on a light rein and was being given my head to do what I thought best.

There was much to be done. When BOAC was released from its wartime role in 1946, the Government recognised that it would inevitably take a good many years before the airline could get itself into profitable operation. Accordingly, Parliament provided that the airlines could be given Exchequer Grants of up to £10 million in each of the ten years up to 1956. The Corporation received Exchequer Grants of £6.56 million in 1947-48, £5.75 million in 1948-49, and £6.36 million in 1949-50. When I joined BOAC at the beginning of 1950, a forecast was being submitted to the Ministry asking for a Grant of £6 million for the year to March 1951; and this was in fact paid.

The system of supporting BOAC and BEA with Exchequer Grants while they were establishing themselves as post-war international airlines was absolutely vital. Without it, neither airline would have survived against the fierce competition from other countries. Accepting it as a necessary evil, one of Miles Thomas's great ambitions was to end BOAC's reliance on Government financial support as soon as possible. But he could not achieve that ambition without the tools of financial control that any progressive manufacturing industry would have regarded as essential.

In this field of financial control, I found BOAC to be woefully lacking. Annual forecasts of results had to be made and submitted to the Government in order to obtain the needed Exchequer Grants. But these forecasts were not budgets in the management accounting sense. There was no budgetary control by cost centre as it would be understood in productive industry.

I could not see anything in the nature of transport which would make it impossible to apply the same methods of cost control that I had developed in other industries. After all, the essence of accounting for purposes of industrial management is simply that all expenditure incurred is analysed and broken down to the department, section or person that takes the decision to incur it. These are the units known as cost centres. There should be no difficulty in arranging for all expenditure involved in airline operations to be broken down in the same way to the cost centres where the decisions to spend the money were taken. That done, there could then be no reason why the various people in charge of those cost centres should not be required to submit a budget of what they felt it necessary to spend in the next financial year, for approval by higher authority; nor why they could not be held to account for any over-spending against budget. A thorough-going budgetary control system could be operated just as effectively in an airline as in any other industry.

So I started looking round the Accounts Department to see if there was anybody experienced in these matters. There were a number of able accountants in BOAC – people like Derek Glover and Geoffrey Pout, who had qualified as chartered accountants in 1937 and 1938, and Ken Reddish. But the war had interrupted their post-graduate accountancy training. None of them had so far had any opportunity to practise the art of modern management accounting.

I badly needed some experienced help. I could have undertaken the task myself but I did not want to get bogged down in the technical business of designing and installing a whole new accounting system. At the outset Miles Thomas had made me a part of the top management group of BOAC, and it was top management that really interested me.

I was reluctant to bring anybody in from outside at a time when we had to reduce staff numbers. Yet I knew the man for the job – Ken

Bevan, whom I had left behind me at Doultons. I soothed my conscience about enticing him from Doultons by explaining the position to my former boss, Basil Green, who understood and agreed to let him go if he wanted to. Ken Bevan was very attracted by the prospect of working in so different a field. The transfer was arranged, to the great benefit of BOAC.

Before he could join us I wanted to define something that anyone in manufacturing industry would regard as an essential, if simple, tool of management. This is the break-even point, the point at which revenue would equal expenditure, beyond which point we made profits and not losses. This was a concept of American origin, which I had first come across and learnt to use in my Hoover days some twenty years earlier. Miles Thomas knew well what I was after; in fact he wanted the same information himself.

Fortunately there was on BOAC's staff an airline stalwart called J B Scott, our chief economics officer. He and I soon concluded that the most telling way of presenting a break-even ratio, which nobody could fail to understand, was through the passenger load factor – the percentage of aircraft seats that we needed to sell to avoid a loss.

BOAC was at that time filling about 60 per cent of its seats. We were able to tell Miles Thomas and the management that, whereas in 1947 we had needed to sell an impossible 115 per cent to avoid making a loss, we had brought the break-even down to 100 per cent in 1948 and 90 per cent in 1949. It was currently down to 75 per cent in 1950. An airline operating scheduled public services day in and day out all round the calendar – charter operations are very different – cannot expect to get its aircraft more than about 63 per cent full on average over a year. So no one could fail to recognise that our immediate target must be to reduce our break-even to about 60 per cent as soon as possible.

Ken Bevan arrived soon after this in October 1950 and settled in very quickly. The target I set him was two-fold – first to produce monthly accounts for the board within 17 days; and second to produce for top management and the board a full budget, drawn up on industrial lines, before the start of our financial year 1952-53.

All this entailed a lot of intensive work. But both targets were met, and Miles Thomas was able to say at the board meeting in March 1952 that it was the first time the board of BOAC had ever had a complete budget for the financial year starting the following month.

Meanwhile, as a result of all the efforts made from 1947 onwards to reduce staff, total operating costs per ton-mile flown had been brought down from 24p (new pence) in 1948 to under 17p in 1951. Productivity per head had improved three-fold on average. And by that year, too, we had brought our break-even load factor – that is, the percentage of aircraft seats we needed to fill in order to cover all our costs, including interest on the whole of our capital – to a level that was just about capable of being achieved in a good year, 65 per cent. In fact, BOAC did achieve a load factor of 65.7 per cent in the year ended 31 March 1952 and succeeded in making a profit for the first time in its history – £1¼ million before interest of £1 million.

Miles Thomas felt confident enough to tell the Minister that BOAC would not be asking the Government for any further Exchequer Grants – four years ahead of the date set by Parliament for the grant scheme to end.

★　　★　　★　　★　　★

At the end of 1949, after I had accepted Miles Thomas's offer of the top financial post with BOAC, and before I actually joined, I used to wonder how I should be received by my colleagues-to-be. My doubts were soon dispelled. I had barely been in BOAC a month when Air Vice-Marshal Sir Victor Tait, who had been appointed operations director in 1945, had a word with me – perhaps sensing that my mind needed to be put at rest. 'We know all about operating aeroplanes,' he said, 'and we run a good airline service – or we shall do when we get the new aircraft now on order. But we just don't know how to run a business and make it pay. That is where we need your help, and if you can show us how to do that, that is the greatest contribution you can make to BOAC.' He couldn't have said anything fairer.

So in mid-1950 I set about taking some flights to see what modern passenger aeroplanes were like, what ground operations we had at airports, what sales organisations we kept in different places, and to meet people up and down the line. The last flight I had made in a passenger aircraft was between London and Paris in a Scylla operated by Imperial Airways in the 1930s. The first flight I made by BOAC in 1950 was in a Boeing Stratocruiser to New York. In those days it was necessary to make an intermediate stop at Gander in Newfoundland, if not one in Shannon also. Westbound flights would leave London Airport at around 8 pm and take roughly twelve hours to reach Gander, arriving there at the ungodly hour of 4 am local time. Then, after an hour in the terminal building while the aircraft was refuelled, we would take off with a new crew that had been resting at Gander for a day or two on the next leg of the journey to New York, where we arrived at around 8 am eastern standard time.

The Stratocruiser captain on my first flight into New York was

Ben Prowse and I was delighted when he invited me up to the flight deck to sit in the jump-seat. I expect he wanted to see what sort of queer fish their new financial comptroller was. I certainly wanted to meet the crew up front and learn a little of what work in the cockpit was like. After that I made a practice of going up front whenever I flew so as to get to know more about them and their work, and always seemed to be welcome.

I also made a practice of going down to the headquarters of each Line or aircraft fleet as often as I could. I would ask to be taken round the hangars and would stop and talk to people as I went. I not only wanted to know what was involved in running a fleet base; the maintenance and operation of our aircraft fleet accounted for more than half of all BOAC's expenditure worldwide.

No 3 Line, the Stratocruiser fleet, was under the management of Charles Abell at Filton, near Bristol. Once, when we were having lunch in the hangar building, Captain Denis Peacock, who was in charge of Stratocruiser flight operations, asked me: 'Why is your title spelt "Financial Comptroller"? Why the "mpt"? Why not "Controller"?'

'A good question,' I said, 'and I am very glad you asked it. It was in fact originally suggested that I should be brought in as financial controller. But I didn't want that. I took the view that, coming into an industry I knew nothing of, I didn't want anybody to think that I was going to set about controlling everything they did. Sir Miles took the point, and we discussed it for a while. The title had to be of greater significance than chief accountant because I was coming into BOAC at a higher level than that. I suggested to Sir Miles that my title should simply be "comptroller", as that was known and understood in management circles in the United States. But he didn't think that adequate; he wanted to include the word "finance" or "financial". So we agreed on financial comptroller which met both points of view.'

'All right,' said Denis, 'but I still don't see the difference between controlling and comptrolling. Isn't it just a question of spelling?'

'No,' I replied. 'A comptroller is someone who counts and compares. A controller controls – or that is what the title implies. I don't control what you or other managers in BOAC do. But it is my job to see that you are all provided with the financial information you all need so that you yourselves can control what you spend and keep it within the limits of an agreed plan for the Corporation as a whole. It rests with you, and with all managers in BOAC wherever they may be, to be your own controllers and control your own costs.'

Apart from my long-held belief that a man is a better manager if he knows how to control his own costs, it was essential to get such a belief widely adopted in a far-flung organisation like BOAC, with its routes reaching out all over the free world and many of its managers very far from head office supervision.

I had another opportunity of reinforcing my own thinking on this when I went to Alexandria on one of the last flying-boat services. This method of air travel was certainly leisurely and comfortable; passengers and crew were put up in hotels overnight. But it hadn't a hope of ever paying. It was just impossible, even with the aircraft absolutely full, for fares to cover operating costs. BOAC only kept the flying-boats in operation as late as 1950 because we had no other aircraft for our Southern Route. The final nail in the flying boat's coffin was the coming of pressurised landplanes which could get up to fifteen or twenty thousand feet; flying boats could not be pressurised and therefore could not fly above the weather.

At Alexandria, I saw a little of what was involved in having a flying boat base. We had to carry the whole cost ourselves because no other airline was then operating flying boats. I was then driven to Cairo, where we had just moved operations from Heliopolis to the new and larger Farouk Airport. Here we handled not only our own aircraft flying through the Middle East to India, South-East Asia, the Far East and Australia, but also the aircraft of our partners on the Kangaroo and Springbok routes, Qantas Empire Airways (as they were known at that time) and South African Airways.

Stations – which is what most airlines call their organisations at transit stops and terminal airports – incur considerable expenditure, something like one-eighth of total operating costs. In those days Cairo was one of our busiest stations. Control of station expenditure worldwide was obviously important, and I was lucky to find in charge of the local accounts department at Cairo an accountant with a good many years of airline experience, Eddie Weight. It was not long before I had him back in London, where his knowledge of what was needed by station management to control costs was of great practical help in devising our budgetary control system.

*   *   *   *   *

Back home, the main body of my accounts staff were quartered along with the supplies department of Air Vice-Marshal Sir William (Bill) Cushion in a building at Brentford on the Great West Road which had been bought in Sir Harold Howitt's day and renamed Airways House – the purpose being to bring our scattered UK staff back from Bristol and other places to which they had been evacuated in the war, and centralise them near London Heathrow Airport.

Board and top management, however, were still housed in Stratton House, Piccadilly.

Miles Thomas, I was glad to find, was a great believer in having his office 'on the works', where he could see what went on, and be seen. This was, as he saw it, an essential part of leadership in industrial management. It was very much my own philosophy, too. So I was delighted when he decided, a year after becoming chairman, that we should move our head office from Piccadilly to Brentford – though we should keep a board-room at Stratton House, together with our press and information office under Freddy Gillman (a good, self-effacing PRO if ever there was one) so that it should not be too far removed from Fleet Street and the BBC.

Even so, BOAC was still rather scattered. We did not yet have the buildings at London Heathrow Airport to house more than the Argonauts and the Constellations. Special larger hangars were to be built to accommodate the Stratocruisers with their broad wing-span and high tail-fins; but for another two or three years No 3 Line would have to stay down at Bristol. Still, we had at Brentford a substantial number of our headquarters or central staff, and our move there from Piccadilly was a beginning. It took only a quarter of an hour to get to the airport, where we could see flight crew as well as ground staff, and only about half an hour to get to Airways Terminal, Victoria, where our sales staff and central reservations system were based. Top management was no longer so remote.

Air Force terms lingered on well into the 1950s. The various staff canteens were called messes. There was an engineers' mess, a loaders' mess, a clerical mess and so on. But Miles Thomas embargoed the word in one case. The room where the chairman and top management lunched was never to be called the chairman's mess. 'People might take it too darned literally,' he said. And it has always been known as the chairman's dining room.

Again, anything not operational was lumped together as 'admin', and naturally regarded as dead weight. This we progressively changed, because in my view (and Miles Thomas's) all clerical staff had to be productive, in the sense of helping things to be done better and profits earned; otherwise, they weren't pulling their weight.

One of Miles Thomas's great contributions to the building up of BOAC was that he gave us a unified sense of purpose and made us into a team. He also gave BOAC back a healthy sense of commercial purpose and profit justification, which had been lost during the war years. And with the first Comets nearing completion at Hatfield and due to get their Certificate of Airworthiness late in 1951 or early in 1952, there was an air of suppressed excitement and expectation amongst the management down at Brentford, and indeed throughout the whole Corporation.

★   ★   ★   ★   ★

In 1951, BOAC received a real shot in the arm, which did much for morale throughout the Corporation. In October, we had the honour of being selected by The King's Flight to carry Princess Elizabeth and the Duke of Edinburgh on an official visit to Canada. It seems strange to recall now that the first charter of a BOAC aircraft for a royal flight came by chance – or rather, mischance. The King had become gravely ill. It had originally been arranged that Princess Elizabeth and her husband would travel by sea, leaving for Canada on the first of the month. But the King had to undergo a major operation at the end of September; and they decided to postpone their departure until 7 October and go by air instead.

I was told that Winston Churchill, then Leader of the Opposition, expressed to the Prime Minister his doubts (from the point of view of safety) about the wisdom of the heir to the throne flying the Atlantic. But Prince Philip and Sir Edward Fielden, the Captain of The King's Flight, had no such doubts and won Mr Attlee over. Captain O P Jones, who had done much to give civil air piloting the quality of a profession in the early days of Imperial Airways, was selected to command the flight; he had been one of the first to require aircrew to wear blue uniforms and to give up wearing riding-breeches and windcheaters.

A mid-morning arrival time was required for the reception in Montreal, and this allowed a later start than the normal departure times for westbound flights. When Princess Elizabeth and Prince Philip arrived at the airport, accompanied by Queen Elizabeth and Princess Margaret, Miles Thomas and Whitney Straight escorted the party aboard. Punctually at 11 the royal BOAC Stratocruiser, G-AKGK, started up its engines under the glare of camera floodlights; it taxied out through patches of mist to the end of the runway, where each piston engine in turn was run up and checked. Those of us listening in the dark to those sounds on the far side of the airfield heard the take-off run get under way. Suddenly the noise faded. What could have caused O P to abort the take-off? But all was well – he had seen patches of fog lying on the runway, and had decided to run the aircraft up and down to disperse them. He knew from experience this would keep the runway clear for a couple of minutes. Soon afterwards the royal aircraft took off into the blackness of the night towards the west and the North Atlantic.

Princess Elizabeth's visit to Canada that autumn was to be

followed early in 1952 by an official visit to Australia. Once again BOAC had the honour of being commissioned by The King's Flight to carry her and Prince Philip. As the Royal Party were going eastabout, the Argonaut fleet was selected to carry them to Nairobi on the first stage of their journey halfway round the world. From East Africa they would go on by sea in HMS *Vanguard*.

At the beginning of February Princess Elizabeth and the Duke left London. The King and Queen with Princess Margaret came to the airport to see them off. His Majesty looked drawn and far from well. After a transit stop in North Africa, the royal aircraft flew on to Nairobi, where it had been arranged that Princess Elizabeth would stopover for a few days' rest at the Royal Lodge, Sagana, not far from Nyeri. While there, the couple went to Tree Tops to spend the night in the furnished hut up in the famous ficus tree and to watch big game come down to the water-hole. That very night, in the early hours of 6 February, news flashed round the world that her father had died in his sleep. It was only later in the morning, after the royal party had been conducted back through the forest to the Royal Lodge, that the Princess could be told the news.

It fell to BOAC to fly the new Queen back to London as soon as possible. Fortunately, our Argonaut and its specially selected crew were still in the area. Shortly before midnight the same day, the aircraft took off from Entebbe in Uganda. The next afternoon, 7 February 1952, the Queen descended the aircraft steps at London Airport to set foot on English soil as Sovereign – and to be welcomed by her Prime Minister, now Winston Churchill, with Clement Attlee, Anthony Eden and a company of others.

The manner in which we discharged these responsibilities of state must have satisfied any misgivings Winston Churchill may have had, because from then on it came to be accepted that BOAC should be the chosen instrument for the Royal Family's long-distance journeys overseas.

★   ★   ★   ★   ★

Towards the end of her Coronation year, the Queen and the Duke of Edinburgh set off once more for Australia, to resume the journey which had been so sadly interrupted in 1952 by the death of her father. This time, however, it was planned to go westabout. BOAC was to carry the Queen and the Duke as far as Jamaica, where they would board the liner *Gothic* and proceed onwards by sea. As planned, Her Majesty flew out of London by Stratocruiser on Monday, 23 November.

The fact that BOAC was being commissioned to carry out these royal flights raised the standing of BOAC as a worldwide airline to an extent that it is difficult to exaggerate. People who might perhaps have used other airlines, simply because BOAC was labelled a nationalised industry, now came to feel that it was an airline to be proud of.

The reason why we were given this honour was entirely practical. There was no element of Royal patronage in it; nor was there anything in it of salesmanship on our part. The Royal Air Force didn't like it much, of course. After all, in seagoing days, it had always been the Royal Navy and not the merchant marine that had transported the Sovereign. So, now that the Sovereign was to be transported by air, why not use the Royal Air Force?

The Captain of the Queen's Flight, Sir Edward Fielden, was himself very much of an institution by that time. He had been pilot to the Prince of Wales as far back as 1929, and Captain of The King's Flight all through the reign of King George VI. An Air Commodore when I first met him, he was a committed RAF officer, soon to be promoted Air Vice-Marshal, and a perfectionist in all matters bearing upon flight safety. The Queen's Flight itself had never undertaken flights of the distance now required and was not equipped to carry them out. Whatever may have been his natural leanings towards the RAF, he knew that RAF pilots had little or no experience of civil aircraft operating procedures along the world's commercial air routes. Moreover, the RAF had no coverage of spares along those routes, as we had, in case of technical faults developing *en route*. So he felt that the task could only be carried out by BOAC.

BOAC was acutely aware of its responsibilities. Weeks of careful planning went into the preparation of each flight. Our staff received the closest co-operation from officers of The Queen's Flight. The chosen aircraft had to be taken out of service some weeks before departure so that the interior could be laid out differently. It was necessary to install a royal sitting room, dining room and bedroom, and to provide normal first-class seating for the staff of the Royal Household travelling with the Queen.

Moreover it was essential for a flight of this sort to arrive exactly on time, because of all the arrangements made for the Sovereign's reception. In those piston-engined days you could never be certain that a fault would not develop in some part of the engine or its control system at the last moment before take-off. Consequently, we used to take a second aircraft out of service and keep it on stand-by, prepared and ready to be rolled up on to the tarmac in case of need. As it happened, though, the stand-by aircraft never was called up – thanks to the thoroughness of our preparations and the devotion of the staff who handled the No 1 aeroplane.

Not to have given this work to the RAF must have been a hard decision for 'Mouse' Fielden. The Royal Air Force came to accept his point of view, even if reluctantly. He once told me that he had been under great pressure to allow an RAF squadron to act as a kind of guard of honour, flying abreast and astern of the Royal aircraft and escorting it for a hundred or more miles out or in – much as the Royal Yacht might be escorted by naval ships. He would have none of it. Even though the Royal aircraft would be allocated a special 'purple airway' clear of other civil aircraft, he was just not prepared to accept the risk of any other aeroplane, however expertly handled, within miles. And unescorted aircraft departures and arrivals have, thankfully, remained the standard practice for Royal Flights ever since.

★   ★   ★   ★   ★

Meanwhile great progress on the de Havilland Comet had been made in our Flight Development Unit led by Captain 'Rowley' Alderson. Captains Majendie and Rodley were the two pilots selected to work with him to develop the operating procedures and techniques for getting the best out of these first generation pure-jet aircraft. This was an entirely new and untried field, and they had no one else's experience to draw on. Never before had there been a passenger airliner which would fly at speeds of over 450 mph and at altitudes of up to 40,000 feet. Moreover, the nature of jet engines was such that aircraft consumed fuel at a higher rate, causing real problems if for some unforeseen reason it had to go into the normal holding stack at a much lower altitude while waiting to come in to land. This – and much else besides – required the mastering of new operating techniques. The best methods of using jet aircraft on civil air routes had to be tested and proved, and proved again. It was all done with the quiet competence and thoroughness which I had come to learn was so typical of BOAC's flight operations management.

The Comet 1 was due to go into passenger service on the route to South Africa at the beginning of May 1952. The planned schedule of training flights was well on time, and in April we took the press down to Rome for lunch and back the same day. That may not sound much of an achievement these days. But in 1952 it took the most advanced piston-engined aeroplane some 4½ to 5 hours, depending on the wind, to cover the 900 miles between London and Rome. But in the Comet, with a following wind, we reached Ciampino airport near Rome in under 2½ hours. Distances between places, as measured in time, were on the point of being halved.

Then on 2 May the first pure-jet passenger service in the world left London Heathrow Airport as planned, bound for Johannesburg. Miles Thomas had gone on ahead with the last training flight and joined the service at Livingstone (there was no trunk-line airport at Salisbury at that time) and went on with it to its destination at Palmietfontein airport (Jan Smuts airport was not then built). Two days later he left in the Comet on the first northbound jet service from South Africa to London, arriving on schedule – the culmination of countless hours of devoted effort by thousands of people in Britain and other parts of the world.

So another piece of aviation history was made – and BOAC was beginning to ride high.

4 Wings Across the World

When British South American Airways lost two of their Tudors over the mid-Atlantic and had to be merged into BOAC, we kept their route to Venezuela and Peru going with Constellation 049s. But their route down the South American east coast to Brazil, Argentina and Chile had to be abandoned. It was not until 1950 that BOAC were able to re-open the service with Argonauts; but it was a financial headache and lost a good deal of money from the start.

In 1951, Miles Thomas decided to go down the route to assess the position for himself, and he took me with him. As we went round, we had a good look at our station costs, including crew-slipping. (Crew-slipping is when the crew bringing in an aircraft go to a rest-house or hotel to wait for another aircraft coming down the same route in two or three days' time; meanwhile the crew that has been resting there takes the first aircraft on.) We also looked at our selling costs in each area. But we found nothing to worry about in any of these fields.

Our problem was simply that we were not getting enough traffic. There seemed to be various reasons for that. One reason, which naturally struck a sympathetic chord in my memory, was that the old staff-leave practices of the British companies operating in South America still lingered on. Expatriates were still not given home leave more frequently than once in five years. And when people did go home on quinquennial leave, the rule was that it did not start until they landed in England. If travel home by ship was treated as working time and paid for by the company, why should anyone going to England on leave use an aeroplane and sacrifice that extra month or so of paid holiday at sea? Moreover, with British air services relatively undeveloped down the South American east coast, the custom of flying children out to their parents in the school holidays had not yet begun.

Thus, the number of British people travelling to and from South America was limited to those travelling on urgent commercial or government business. And most South Americans visiting Europe would go to Paris or Rome before thinking of going on to London. We had Lisbon as a staging post on the route and we had traffic rights there. But, in spite of Brazil's Portuguese connections, it was nothing compared with Paris for attracting passengers.

BOAC had no traffic rights in Paris on this route (or on any other, for that matter). This was because, when governments traded traffic rights with one another, they each nominated one airline (or, in very rare cases, two airlines). France had only one airline operating to Britain – Air France. So, given the existence of two British air corporations, the British government could nominate only one of them for traffic rights in France. The obvious choice was British European Airways – and BOAC had no chance of getting rights in Paris on this potentially good South American route.

From that time, both Miles Thomas and I began to realise how much possible traffic Britain was losing through having two air corporations, of which only one could be designated in almost all bilateral negotiations. In terms of re-developing intra-European operations, it may have been right to set up a separate British European Airways Corporation – but Britain lost a lot of traffic on her overseas routes because of it. One of these days, we both felt, BOAC and BEA would have to be merged.

*   *   *   *   *

It was always an important part of BOAC's policy to operate its principal routes to Commonwealth countries in partnership with the airlines of those countries. It began when Imperial Airways and Qantas Empire Airways started in 1934 to operate what they called the Kangaroo route between England and Australia. In those days, Qantas flew its aeroplanes as far west as Singapore and Imperial Airways flews theirs eastwards from London to meet them there. This form of joint enterprise had its origins in the old concept of Empire, with the distant Commonwealth countries and Britain wishing to help each other to get air services linking them more closely together. But it also was bred out of the spirit of a great adventure which was not without its risks, so that those taking part freely shared all their knowledge and experience.

After World War II, both BOAC and Qantas flew their aircraft right through from end to end and the partnership took on a different form. This set the pattern for all other Commonwealth airline partnerships that followed. The joint revenues were pooled, which made it possible to provide the best schedule of services for our customers, because it made no financial difference to either partner which of them had to operate on the higher or lower traffic days of the week. And as each partner continued to bear his own costs, the incentive to keep costs under control was not lost by either airline.

One of the great benefits of this kind of partnership is that it enables both partners to make the greatest possible use of their traffic rights. In marked contrast to cargo shipping rights, which had come to be acquired by the maritime countries over two centuries, rules for sharing international air traffic rights had to be worked out towards the end of the 1939-45 war. There had been few long-distance international air services before the war. But the wartime development of long-range aircraft made it clear that worldwide air transport would begin in earnest immediately after the war. So rules had to be established quickly to govern who could fly where and carry what cargo.

The Chicago Convention of 1944 established five basic freedoms of the air. The first freedom is the right to overfly another country's territory, without landing. The second freedom is the right to land in another country's territory for the purpose of re-fuelling or repairs, but without discharging or uplifting traffic. These two basic freedoms are generally granted automatically by all countries of the free world, though there have been cases where they have been temporarily withheld.

The third freedom of the air is the right to carry traffic from your own country to another; and the fourth freedom is complementary – the right to bring traffic from another country into your own. These third and fourth freedom traffic rights are the foundation upon which any international airline exists; and they are granted by bilateral agreement between one nation to another.

To complete the picture, the fifth freedom of the air is the right of your country's airline to pick up traffic in a second country and carry it on to a third. Fifth freedom traffic proved to be of very great value in the 1940s and 1950s. Aircraft did not have the range they have now, and had to land half a dozen times between London and Sydney.

But the practice grew up of combining third and fourth freedom traffic – or rather fourth and third – picking up passengers in one country, carrying them to and through your own (often with a change of aircraft) and taking them on to a third. This came to be known as sixth freedom. Geography very much affects the extent to which an airline can exploit sixth freedom. For example, if a country is situated rather like a gateway to a continent or subcontinent, as Britain is to Europe in respect of traffic coming across the North Atlantic, there are considerable opportunities for gathering in valuable sixth freedom traffic.

Domestic traffic – that is, traffic within one's own country – is completely reserved, and is known as cabotage. Again, geography determines the value of cabotage rights. The enormous cabotage area of the USA between New York and Honolulu, situated on the route from Britain westabout to Australasia, reserves a very substantial volume of sector traffic to American airlines. This was a principal reason why, in the 1970s, Qantas had to give up the route. The present British Airways/Air New Zealand service westwards from Britain to New Zealand is conceived differently; it is a linking of two separate routes – a British route between London and Los Angeles, and a New Zealand route between Los Angeles and Auckland.

Under the international rules that govern cabotage rights, the territory of a colony is regarded as part of the mother country. For example, for the purpose of air traffic rights Hong Kong is part of Britain; all traffic between the two is wholly reserved to British airlines. In the 1950s it was the same with all Britain's colonies around the world before they became independent. The reservation of this Colonial cabotage traffic to BOAC, at a time when long-distance aviation was starting up, allowed Britain to open up worldwide air services to a far greater extent than would ever have been possible otherwise.

All this dry stuff of aviation politics was soon to enrich my life in ways I had not foreseen. Through the airline partnerships we developed against this political background I came to know many of the leading figures in civil aviation throughout the English-speaking world. To me personally the friendships that grew up between us were very rewarding.

On a similar basis to our partnership with Qantas, BOAC also went into partnership with South African Airways. By BOAC and Qantas pooling all their third and fourth freedom traffic on the Kangaroo route between Britain and Australia, and by BOAC and South African Airways doing the same on the Springbok route, those routes became almost cabotage areas for the two airlines concerned. And, as London was the hub from which these Commonwealth airline partnership spokes radiated, BOAC derived great strength from them.

This was a long-term benefit, of course, which could not be fully realised until the late 1960s and early 1970s, but the policy begun in the 1940s was expanded in the 1950s. At that stage our object was to add to the number of Commonwealth partnerships as opportunity offered, without being quite sure how far our policy would eventually take us, except that it seemed commonsense as well as good business. Thus, in 1953, a partnership plan was developed by Miles Thomas and Ellis Robins (later Lord Robins) of Central African Airways for bringing the Salisbury-based airline into the Springbok route with BOAC and SAA. This then became a tripartite partnership of the three airlines. Some years later, East African Airways under the chairmanship of Sir Alfred Vincent joined in too.

KLM Royal Dutch Airlines provides a contrasting example. KLM had been built up by the great Dr Plesman on the foundation of Dutch cabotage rights between Holland and her colonies in the Indies. But the Netherlands Government did not encourage the formation of reciprocal airlines in their East and West Indies colonies with the result that, when Indonesia became independent, KLM's traffic rights were greatly eroded.

The operation of worldwide partnerships was not without its difficulties. With the head offices of the partners thousands of miles apart, there was plenty of opportunity for misunderstandings and friction to develop. This was perhaps inherent in the different national aspirations and interests. There were also inevitable clashes of personality. The maintenance of good human relationships among the partners was of paramount importance.

In 1953 relations between Miles Thomas and Sir Hudson Fysh, the founder and chairman of Qantas, nearly reached explosion point. Until then the British airline operating across the Pacific from Australasia to the United States was British Commonwealth Pacific Airways, owned jointly by Britain, Australia and New Zealand. Its presence in the Pacific stood in the path of Qantas ambitions to operate the route in its own name and to move towards becoming Australia's round-the-world airline – ambitions which had not been properly appreciated by BOAC. This tricky situation, which could well have brought the BOAC/Qantas partnership to an end, was resolved by Britain and New Zealand agreeing to withdraw from BCPA so that it could be wound up to make way for Qantas; by way of compensation, New Zealand became the sole owners of Tasman Empire Airways Ltd (TEAL), at that time operating only across the Tasman Sea but later to become Air New Zealand.

Good relations were restored; and on 8 December 1955, we were able to celebrate happily the 21st anniversary of the start of the BOAC/Qantas Kangaroo partnership.

The trickiness of the situation at that time was not made easier by the fact that nobody in BOAC seemed able to get on with C O (later Sir Cedric) Turner, the dynamic but stubborn general manager of Qantas and deputy to Hudson Fysh. Probably because discussions with our partners were usually financial, I found myself getting more and more involved in holding our partnerships together. I made it my job to get on with C O Turner. After all, it was natural that there should be tension from time to time between two such thrustful operators as BOAC and Qantas. But out of tension can come great strength. I made it my business to find out what was really worrying him, and to get him to see our point of view.

We soon established a good understanding of each other's position, knowing where there could be give and where there was none. From then on, although there were often arguments we never failed to reach workable solutions. And C O and I have remained firm friends ever since.

★　★　★　★　★

In those days the developing long-haul carriers such as BOAC found it paid to own a number of local airlines to feed traffic on to their trunk-route operations. These airlines had in most cases started to provide purely local air services. But in those days there was generally only one airport in any one area at which long-haul airliners could land. In the West Indies, for example, BOAC could land only at Palisadoes Airport, near Kingston, Jamaica. Anybody in the West Indies wishing to fly to Britain or Europe had to get by local plane to Kingston to take the mainline aircraft on; similarly, anybody in Britain wishing to fly to Trinidad or Barbados had first to get to Kingston and then transfer to the local airline.

This meant that feeder services could be of considerable value to the long-haul airline, and this was particularly so in the British Commonwealth. But it was quite fatal to let the local airline managements feel that they were so valuable that they could trade at a loss and that their parent airline would be happy to foot the bill; they had to be made to understand that they had to make profits and stand on their own feet.

After the merger with British South American Airways, BOAC acquired the ownership of British West Indian Airways based in Trinidad. BWIA was then making losses and in the summer of 1950 Miles Thomas sent me to Port of Spain to look at its operations. I formed the opinion that the airline was not managed well enough and that the board needed strengthening. Fortunately, already in position was an able young assistant general manager, John Rahr; and I ascertained that Sir Errol dos Santos, a former financial secretary in the Trinidad Government, and Hugh Wooding, an eminent lawyer, were available for the board.

That reconnaissance completed, I returned to London. In 1950 this entailed taking the BWIA Viking back to Kingston, Jamaica, and then picking up a BOAC Constellation 049 to fly home along the former BSAA route via Nassau, Bermuda, the Azores and Lisbon to London. Nowadays, that's a very roundabout and tedious way of getting home from Port of Spain; but in those days there was no better way. On one sector of the flight, I was sitting in the cockpit jumpseat talking to the commander, Capt Maurice Aries, formerly of BSAA. A Scottish chartered accountant, he had been an RAF pilot during the war and had decided to make his postwar career in civil flying. I made a mental note that here was someone with experience and ability who could prove of great value when we reached the stage – which would have to come – of applying industrial methods of budgetary and cost control to the flight operations department.

Miles Thomas accepted my BWIA recommendations in principle. We went together to Trinidad in November 1950, so that he could confirm my assessment and give his personal authority to the new set-up – which, events were to show, greatly improved personal relations between London and Port of Spain.

On the way back from Trinidad we stopped off at Nassau to have a look at another wholly owned subsidiary inherited from BSAA – Bahamas Airways. This was also losing money, though not a lot at that time. It was a small local airline linking Nassau with the out-islands of the Bahamas, with six-seater aircraft.. Later, with the aid of Vikings released by BWIA, we added a service linking Nassau with Miami to exercise the British rights on that short route in competition with Pan American. But although Bahamas Airways was a useful feeder to our London trunk route service, it seemed that the Bahamian directors, headed by chairman Harold Christie, thought of the airline as a means of increasing the value of their properties in the out-islands, with BOAC making good its losses.

In addition to British West Indian Airways and Bahamas Airways, BOAC owned Aden Airways, which operated local Dakota services connecting with our mainline operations at Cairo; and we held varying degrees of interest in Gulf Aviation, the Jordanian airline, Malayan Airways and Hong Kong Airways (then dormant). It became evident to me and to Miles Thomas that we needed to set up a separate division to look after these associated companies and to delegate specific responsibility for their success to a senior manager.

The sort of person we needed was not easy to find. But at about that time, Vladimir Wolfson, who was doing this kind of work with Geoffrey Amherst in BEA, was not particularly happy and put out feelers to us. He was just the man we needed, and the chairman of BEA, Lord Douglas of Kirtleside, raised no objection to his transfer.

Vladimir Wolfson, known to his many friends as Vova, had come out of Russia in 1917 and had gone to Cambridge to complete his education. Before going into civil aviation his business life was spent with Shell, mainly overseas; and he was fluent in half a dozen or more languages. He was commissioned in the Royal Navy, and at one stage in the war was Naval Attaché in the British Embassy in Turkey. Not long after joining BOAC in 1951, he was promoted to Captain RNR.

★   ★   ★   ★   ★

In January 1952 Britain's troubles with the Egypt of Colonel Neguib started. Our offices in Cairo were burnt. We had to transfer our principal Middle East transit point from Cairo to Beirut. This could not be done quickly as Beirut Airport was still being extended to take trunk route aircraft. But we steadily built up our Beirut organisation in 1952, and it became apparent that Beirut would in fact be a more attractive connecting point than Cairo for off-line Persian Gulf traffic. The Sheikhs were beginning to exploit their new-found oil wealth. Miles Thomas and I started thinking, with Vova Wolfson, about a local airline to feed Beirut.

I went to Beirut on Wednesday 1 October, 1952, and took Kay with me. On our way to the Hotel Bristol I was seized with acute abdominal pains. There was nothing for it but to go to bed and cancel all engagements. BOAC's local Lebanese doctor diagnosed food poisoning. However, matters got worse instead of better, and on the Saturday night I had a high fever. Kay rang the doctor at 02.00, and on the Sunday morning I was carted off in an ambulance to the American University Hospital.

I was operated on with my temperature at 104°F as a case of emergency peritonitis. Fortunately, though I did not know it at the time, I had one of the best surgeons in the Middle East, Dr Jidejian. Instead of finding anything wrong with my appendix, he found a perforated caecum and had to remove, so he told me afterwards, about 350cc of gas gangrene before he started trying to close me up again. As it was, he had to leave me with a caecostomy, which I had to live with for the next three and a half months.

When I came to later that day, I found myself in what I learned later was a fourth-class Arab ward. I recall that across the ward a patient's bed was surrounded by female members of his family, all in black yashmaks, facing outwards and staring at me. I must have seemed a strange sight, with tubes coming out of me all over the place. And my neighbour on my right was sitting cross-legged on his bed making a dreadful noise blowing bubbles through water, and looking ghastly because he had no nose – only two holes in the middle of his face. Perhaps one of his forbears had had leprosy.

It was not until the Monday evening that they could move me into a separate room. After midday on the Tuesday I became very ill – the reaction, it seems, to one of the drugs. I lost consciousness for the next five days, and what I write now I learnt afterwards.

Next morning, Sir Harold Whittingham (BOAC's director of medical services) arrived in Beirut from London. To him I owe my life. The operation report received at Brentford on the Monday had caused a good deal of concern at BOAC headquarters. Miles Thomas had discussed the situation with Sir Harold, known as George to his friends, who caught the next plane to Beirut. When he arrived at the hospital he took samples from my several tubes and worked on them himself in the path lab – he wouldn't trust anyone else. He came back an hour or so later and quietly said that he had diagnosed the trouble; the perforation of the caecum was amoebic. He immediately put me on a course of emmetine, which meant I had to stay prone in bed for the next fortnight.

It seems that amoeba do not necessarily produce immediate dysentery. They may just lurk in the body and lie low for a year or two. The amoeba inside me were of a particularly violent type, probably picked up in West Africa. When they do start breeding they breed very fast and set about tearing down whatever is enclosing them. Their favourite haunts are the large intestine or caecum, and the liver which I am thankful to say they never reached.

Sir Harold greatly impressed the medical staff at the hospital. Bending over my bed with his pince-nez alternately on his nose or held delicately between his fingers, and with his well-groomed but thinning white hair, he had an air of in-born authority. One of the Arab doctors remarked admiringly (French being the common language in Lebanon): 'Quel aristocrat!'

He came with Kay to see me several times in the next two days and then had to leave on the Saturday to go back to London. During this critical period I had some 25 pints of Arab blood transfused into me – about three times the body's normal stock. But as a person's supply of blood renews itself entirely every six weeks or so, I cannot claim now to have Arab blood left in my veins, though it certainly helped to save my life.

Sometime during my unconsciousness, I must have dreamed that I was going to die. But then it came into my confused mind that when people were going to die they would be called by God. And I felt sure that I wasn't being called – I should recognise it, surely, if I were. So I decided that I wasn't going to let myself die and must start getting

better. This must have coincided with Sir Harold's visit and may
subconsciously have helped a bit – I don't know.

I began to come out of my coma on the Sunday. I remember being
greeted by smiling doctors who seemed very relieved at the
outcome. I was told later that I was the first case of this kind to have
survived in the 80 years' history of the hospital; the previous six cases
had not been diagnosed until autopsy.

My day-nurse, Mrs Arabi, was a refugee from Palestine. I
remember how she would go foraging in the hospital kitchen for
nice bits of food, instead of just taking what was brought round on
the trolley. One day she came back smiling with pride and gave me
what tasted like delicious sweetbreads. 'That was good,' I said, 'what
was it?' She burst out laughing. 'Sheep's testicles,' she replied. 'I dare
not tell you before you ate it; you might have refused it.' And I
remember, too, my little Lebanese night-nurse, who often kept me
awake at night by snoring herself.

Looking back on things, it must have been a dreadful time for
Kay. She had never been in an Arab country before, and had the
strangeness of that to cope with on top of the anxieties of wondering
what was happening to me. In addition, Britons travelling abroad
then were very restricted as to currency and at first she couldn't
afford more than one meal a day in the hotel. But BOAC staff at
Beirut were a tremendous help to her.

It was not until 12 December that I was fit enough to be flown back
to London. George Whittingham met us on arrival and took me
straight to Westminster Hospital for Sir Stanford Cade (an eminent
Polish surgeon with the RAF during the war) to have a look at me.
He quickly decided that it would be necessary for me to have a
second operation – the wound wouldn't close otherwise – but not till
after I had had another full course of emmetine to make certain there
could be no amoeba remaining alive. Kill or cure, I thought!
However, the course was finished by the 24th and I was allowed
home for Christmas.

After that, all went well. I went back to Westminster Hospital on
New Year's day, where I was again sterilised internally. Stanford
Cade operated on the 6th and closed me up; a fortnight later I was
released and allowed home. Early in February 1953 I started going
back to work.

★　　★　　★　　★　　★

Middle East Airlines was a local airline based in Beirut. It was owned
mainly by the Salaam family, but Pan American Airways had a
substantial minority shareholding and controlled policy. In 1953

Saeb Bey Salaam became Prime Minister of Lebanon for a short time and asked Sheikh Najib Alamuddin to take over as general manager.

Sheikh Najib had been at Exeter University, and wanted to develop closer links between Britain and Lebanon – but on the basis of mutual respect. Lebanon was not a quasi-colonial or mandated territory. This I understood and sympathised with. Najib and I became close friends, and we worked together to further his ambitions for Lebanese aviation and ours as a worldwide airline.

Sheikh Najib had the business acumen and political shrewdness to be expected of a Druse from the mountains of Lebanon. He had become disillusioned with Pan American's policy of providing MEA with aircraft; they seemed unwilling to let him have anything better than second-hand Dakotas. He knew of the Vickers Viscount and wanted it for MEA, but Pan American would have no part in buying British aircraft. Soon Najib asked us to take over PanAm's shareholding. We in BOAC had our own relations with PanAm to consider. But we cleared our yardarm with them, finding that they were not very interested in their MEA investment.

Buying into Middle East Airlines would fit in well with Miles Thomas's view of the relationships between BOAC and the British aircraft industry. He accepted an inherent obligation to help prove and develop British-built aircraft – nobody else would if we and BEA didn't – and to promote their sale. So, in addition to securing a feeder airline in the Middle East, he saw an opportunity for Britain to supplant American aeroplanes with a short-range type that we were good at producing, and in a part of the world that was about to become aircraft-hungry. So we started negotiations with the Lebanese. Eventually, in 1954, I signed the agreement for the purchase of a controlling interest in Middle East Airlines.

While this agreement had been in the making, an idea was taking root in the minds of Miles Thomas, Najib Alamuddin and myself. Might it be possible to establish a Beirut aircraft maintenance base to service British aircraft operating in the Middle East? The quality of MEA's engineering staff at Beirut Airport was higher than anybody else's in that area. At first the customers would probably be our own associates; but we felt sure that there would be considerably more in time.

The idea appealed to us also because the overheads of MEA's engineering department (which would need to be separated off from the airline) could be spread over a larger output, thus benefiting MEA financially. The new base ought to appeal to airlines in the Middle East who would otherwise have to send their aircraft and engines across Europe for overhaul; and, by holding spares in

Lebanon for British aircraft and employing certificated engineers, we could also help the UK aircraft industry to export in that area.

Later, after Miles Thomas had left BOAC and I had become its managing director, responsibility for our associated companies was placed in the hands of Sir George Cribbett, a deputy secretary at the Ministry of Transport and Civil Aviation whom the Minister had appointed to the board of BOAC. Unhappily – for a variety of reasons, including lack of support from the British aircraft industry and lack of interest by Cribbett – this imaginative Middle East project died in infancy.

Meanwhile, until Miles Thomas left BOAC in 1956, losses by local feeder airlines in which we had a financial interest were carefully contained. In fact, in the three years up to March 1955, losses for all our associated companies around the world came to no more than £80,000 a year on average – a figure which we considered was amply justified by the value of the feeder traffic they brought to us. In 1955/56, the costs of introducing Viscounts into British West Indian Airways service ran up a loss of £360,000; but the rest of our local airlines did not cost us more than £40,000 that year in total – again, a sum amply covered by feeder revenue.

★ ★ ★ ★ ★

The re-shaping of BOAC under Miles Thomas's leadership was making good progress. The major staff redundancies were behind us. Commercial realism was beginning to prevail. All nine de Havilland Comet 1's – the Ghost-engined version – had been delivered by October 1952. And the prototype Bristol Britannia had first flown in August of that year.

The Comets were in fact doing well commercially and matching all our hopes. Encouragingly, breakeven passenger load factor proved no more than about 75 per cent, or three out of every four seats filled. This was high by any normal standard, but better than expected for the introduction of the world's first jet airliner – an aircraft which doubled the speed of air travel and halved point-to-point flight times. We were carrying average payloads of almost 80 per cent. This was also higher than normal. But the Comet was everybody's first choice along the routes concerned. It overcame its higher costs with its passenger appeal, and was turning in a modest profit.

All our aircraft fleets had moved into London Airport, except for the Stratocruisers which had to remain at Filton, near Bristol, for another couple of years. The centralisation that had already taken place helped us to start building, under Charles Abell when he could be spared from No 3 Line, a unified engineering department for aircraft maintenance throughout BOAC.

Meanwhile Ken Bevan had been making good headway developing BOAC's accounting along lines that provided our managers everywhere with the financial information they needed to control their costs. I had given up taking any part in designing our accounting system. I was more than happy to leave all that to Ken. I knew what I wanted it to do for BOAC and I knew that he was the person to produce it.

But one financial matter I dealt with personally was the operation of the Airways Corporations' Joint Pension Scheme. I had been horrified to find that a substantial part of its funds had been invested in 'Daltons' – undated 2½ per cent Government stocks. Unless we got out of them and adopted a more imaginative investment policy, there might not be enough money to meet our existing pension commitments, let alone improve them. With the help of Sir Jack Keeling, BEA's deputy chairman, I recruited the services of Hugh Recknell as the fund's investment adviser. Hugh had been general manager of a leading insurance company and had just retired. He recommended to the BOAC and BEA boards major changes in the fund's investment policy and practice. Since then the Airways' Pension Fund has grown very greatly in strength.

On 1 October 1953 I was appointed to the board of BOAC and made a member of the corporation by the Minister, Mr Alan Lennox-Boyd (later Lord Boyd of Merton). Miles Thomas took advantage of this to expand my duties considerably. In addition to my existing job I was made into a sort of chief planner, responsible for getting the best financial results by seeing that the most suitable type of aircraft was used on each route. It was a daunting task, but challenging. I was fortunate enough to have the assistance of such airline stalwarts as John Douglas, operations planning officer, J B Scott, chief economics officer, and Derek Glover, my personal assistant at that time.

In 1953 there was a considerable re-organisation of BOAC's selling side. Miles Thomas had, I think, long been restless about its lack of a good cutting edge. Apart from anything else, it suffered from being double-headed. In 1952 John Brancker left to take up a senior post in the International Air Transport Association, and it became possible to weld the commercial and sales organisations together under Keith Granville as sales director.

Of our traffic revenue on scheduled services 77 per cent came from passengers, 15 per cent from mail, and the remaining 8 per cent from freight. In the three years since 1950, we had almost doubled our passengers – from 150,000 to 290,000. And these were not passengers merely flying across the Channel; each flew over 3,000 miles on average. In winning this increase in business, the numbers of staff we employed had been held down to 17,000.

Over the same three-year period the retail price index in Britain had gone up by 20 per cent. Yet we had raised first-class fares by only 10 per cent. And when we introduced tourist class travel across the Atlantic in 1952 we brought down the cost of air travel by 25 per cent.

BOAC's general management was still based at Airways House at Brentford, away from our operating base. In 1953, Miles Thomas and I persuaded the board that our new hangar block, nearing completion at London Airport, should have office accommodation built on at both ends and in the transepts. This would allow us to transfer our headquarters to the airport and to sell off our building in Brentford. With our offices on the airport we would be seen working with everybody else. We could just walk out of our offices and spend half an hour in the hangars, seeing for ourselves what was being done. And we would not be so cut off from our aircrews. That would provide us with the chance to exercise personal leadership at the place of work and give a badly needed feeling of togetherness to all in BOAC.

5 The Comet 1 Tragedy

In spite of being the first of the two Airways' Corporations to start making profits – something a private-enterprise Conservative Government should have blessed us for – BOAC found itself constantly under political attack in the early 1950s. Perhaps because BOAC had been converted by Labour in 1946 from the Conservatives' 'chosen instrument' into a nationalised industry, the impression was continuously put about that BOAC was a monopoly and needed the competition of British private-enterprise aviation to keep us efficient. Yet nothing could have been further from the truth. BOAC was all the time in intense competition with the airlines of other nations, and had always to provide the highest standard of operation and service to hold its own.

In the early post-war years quite a number of small independent aviation companies had set themselves up in Britain with war-surplus aircraft sold off cheap by the Government. These companies naturally wanted work to do; but they found themselves barred from scheduled operations by the fact that Parliament had established BOAC and BEA for that purpose. To further their interests, the independents joined together in a trade association and set up the British Independent Air Transport Association (BIATA).

BOAC welcomed the independents in fields that did not conflict. A conspicuously successful example of such an operation in the early 1950s was 'Taffy' Powell's Silver City Airways, ferrying cars across the Channel from Lympne and later from Lydd. Another example was Eric Rylands and his Skyways cargo operation based at Stansted and Coach Air passenger service based at Lympne. Rylands was one of the few members of BIATA who believed that the proper role of the independents was to supplement and strengthen the role of the corporations rather than to take work away from them.

This sort of complementary activity was obviously limited in scope and was nowhere near large enough to satisfy the ambitions of most independents.

In those days Britain had substantial numbers of troops based in

Hong Kong, Singapore and other places far afield. All were originally transported by ship. Although the air transfer cost might be no lower than by sea, the saving in time was enough to reduce the number of troops required to maintain the necessary British presence. By 1953 almost half the movement of British troops overseas was by air; and all trooping contracts went to the independents to provide them with work.

Now that the Comets were in service alongside our Stratocruisers, Constellations and Argonauts, BOAC had no work for the fleet of Handley Page Hermes, ordered in 1946 and now delivered years late. We therefore asked the Minister for permission to tender for trooping contracts.

But the pressure on the Conservative Government by the political lobby for the independent airlines was too great. Permission was refused. Air trooping was wholly reserved to the independents. This at once robbed us of the opportunity to use our Hermes. It also ensured that the independents could buy them off us for a song; we had no other market.

Pressure for new independent openings reached its height when Alan Lennox-Boyd was Minister for Transport and Civil Aviation. He decided in October 1953 that cargo services should also be reserved to the independents in addition to trooping. Then, because Britain's cabotage rights between the United Kingdom and her colonies required no agreement from any other country, the independents were allowed to apply for 'Colonial Coach' services at fares below the internationally agreed tourist level. Miles Thomas was encouraged, with the help of not a little arm-twisting, not to oppose these developments.

Matters reached such a pitch that the BOAC board took the unprecedented step of asking as a body to see the Minister. This was in early March 1954.

In the previous few years I had come to appreciate the value of an outside non-executive director. Roland Thornton, of the Liverpool shipping firm Alfred Holt, had taught me most of what I came to know about transport economics. Frank Brake had brought Sheikh Najib Alamuddin, Miles Thomas and myself together. But of greater importance was the fact that such people were independent of political favour. Their great value was that they could stand between the management of a business and the pressures on it from outside. In a nationalised business such as BOAC those outside pressures could be exerted by Ministers and their civil servants whenever it suited them. When conflict arose, the presence on the board of people prepared to resign was worth a lot. Not all outside directors would be prepared to go to this length, but Roland Thornton and Frank Brake certainly were – as was Lord Rennell later.

At the board's meeting with the Minister in March 1954 it was Roland Thornton who put our case. He argued forcefully that to bar BOAC from trooping contracts and all-cargo services was imposing unreasonable and wholly uneconomic restraints. He emphasised also how damaging it would be to the British scheduled overseas airline, obliged to provide its services day in and day out irrespective of the traffic, to have a British independent operator flying alongside at cut-rate fares and at full-load times. This was just skimming the cream off the market we had created. Of course the independent could under-cut our fares if he didn't have to operate to a regular schedule, as we did; it didn't mean that he was any more efficient.

But it was all to no avail. The Minister went ahead and granted these privileges to the independents. BOAC had no option but to co-operate with the independents most directly concerned, namely Airwork and Hunting-Clan. In the outcome, Roland Thornton was not re-appointed to the board by the Minister when his term of office expired in 1955; and BOAC thereby lost its most valued outside director.

Accounts can, if properly prepared and presented, give a true and fair view of what a business accomplishes. But they do not, and they never can, show what the business would have accomplished had it been allowed to go ahead without political interference. It is Government's privilege in dealing with nationalised industries that it can meddle with the conduct of a business without the cost of that interference ever being revealed or brought to account.

And how profitless the Government's policy has been. Airwork gave up its transatlantic freight service in December 1955 because of their losses. Hunting-Clan's colonial coach services gradually ceased to have a genuine basis as more and more African colonies achieved independence. Meanwhile BOAC was forced to sell off unwanted Hermes at knockdown prices and to carry the resulting capital losses in our accounts – all because we ourselves were not allowed to use them for trooping.

★   ★   ★   ★   ★

As if political pressures were not enough, things began to go markedly wrong with our aircraft plans.

Although the prototype had flown in 1952, the Bristol Britannia – on which many of our hopes for the future were built – soon began experiencing serious teething problems. After a while it became obvious that it would be at least two years late. This presented us

Capt Tom Stoney, Flight Manager Comet 4s and (later) Boeing 707s, during Comet flight training, 1958. *(British Airways)*

de Havilland deliver the first two Comet 4s, 30 September 1958. *(Associated Press)*

The Queen and Prince Philip return by BOAC Comet 4 from Canada, to be met by Prince Charles and Princess Anne, 3 August 1959. *(British Airways)*

with a major problem when our international competitors had the latest models of Douglas DC-7s and Lockheed Super Constellations joining their fleets – on schedule.

Although usable for trooping, the Handley Page Hermes was commercially uncompetitive and uneconomic. It was a civil adaptation of the military Hastings, but it had been converted from a 'tail-dragger' to nosegear type (like all modern airliners). But the centre of gravity was in the wrong place and it flew tail down. This gave it added drag, which reduced speed and increased fuel consumption. It was consequently uncompetitive in range and uneconomic in both running costs and payload. There was no alternative but to phase it out as soon as we could.

The one new British aircraft which had been delivered on time and had lived up to its specification was the de Havilland Comet. It was the focus of most of our hopes. But as early as October 1952, when I was in hospital in Beirut, I heard news of an incident – fortunately without casualties – at Rome. The aircraft was starting to take off from Ciampino Airport but it never left the ground and slid to a stop beyond the end of the runway. It was found that rotating the aircraft through 6° caused the wing, which had a symmetrical section aerofoil for the new high-speed cruise regime, to stall and lose its lift. The pilot was blamed and transferred to York freighters.

Then in March 1953 there was a fatal accident to a Comet 1A at Karachi. It was on a delivery flight to Canadian Pacific Air Lines, and it was easier to deliver the aircraft in Sydney than to fly it across the Arctic to Vancouver. As at Rome, the aircraft had failed to lift off at Karachi. For some reason which it is difficult to understand, the lesson had not been learned, and all 11 CPAL crew and de Havilland staff on board were killed. Pilot error was again imputed; but by now the manufacturer was very worried. Ground-stall, a new phenomenon, had been discovered in an aircraft which had clearly been inadequately developed by its makers.

The Comet 1 had been the first jet airliner in the world to enter public service. By a tragic coincidence, on 2 May 1953 – exactly one year after the start of jet travel – a Comet on service from Singapore to London was destroyed with all its passengers and crew. I was waiting in Rome to join that particular service and was rung up at my hotel to be told that air traffic control had lost contact with it soon after take-off from Calcutta.

I feared the worst – and so it proved. This was in the days before weather radar was fitted in civil airliners, and it had flown into the core of a tropical storm without the pilot knowing. The aircraft was torn apart and the wreckage strewn over a wide area. The Indian

Government set up a court of inquiry, which reported 'pilot error' only 24 days after the accident occurred – far too short a time to establish scientifically whether there had been any cause other than the extremes of force in the thundersquall.

Comet operations continued normally for a time. By the end of the year de Havilland had delivered all 21 Comet 1s and 1As – nine of them to BOAC, three to Air France, and nine to other lines. There were 35 Comet 2s on order, of which we in BOAC were expecting to take delivery of twelve in 1954; and eleven long-range Comet 3s had been ordered – five by BOAC, three by Pan American, and two by Air India. 'As 1953 closed jet propulsion had been firmly established in the world, by one aircraft only, the Comet, of which there was an accumulated experience exceeding 30,000 hours. The Comets were then flying 177,000 miles a week.'[1]

But then, on the tenth of January 1954, one of our Comets, homeward bound from Singapore, took off from Ciampino Airport, Rome, and exploded in mid-air near the island of Elba. It was a Sunday morning, the sky was clear and blue, and the aircraft had just climbed through 30,000 ft. The wreckage fell into the Mediterranean. Twenty-nine of its thirty-six seats were occupied by passengers, and they and the crew of six were all killed. This was a tragic, shattering blow to all involved in Comet production and operation.

It was horrifying to think of people for whom we were responsible, falling 30,000 ft through the air into the sea. But experts assured me that the sudden decompression from an explosion at that altitude meant that all thirty-five people in the Comet would have suffered an instant death and not known what was happening – which was some comfort, but not much.

To me, it brought personal grief as well; among the passengers was Vova Wolfson, who had become a great friend and colleague in the two years that he had been with the corporation.

BOAC immediately withdrew all its Comets from service, pending a decision as to the cause of the explosion. The difficulty was that the sea into which the wreckage had fallen was some 600 ft deep, and at first there were no bits and pieces of the aeroplane to give the experts any worthwhile clues. Some sixty modifications were made to all Comets to cover any imagined contingency – and Comet services started again on 23 March.

Within two and a half weeks, disaster struck again. On 8 April 1954, one of our remaining Comets on charter to South African

[1] *DH* by C Martin Sharp, p 319 (Faber & Faber. 1960).

Airways took off from Ciampino Airport, Rome, *en route* to Johannesburg. Again, after climbing to about 30,000 ft it exploded in mid-air south of Naples and the wreckage fell into the sea. All passengers and the South African crew were lost. For the second time BOAC discontinued all Comet operations immediately. Four days later, with Miles Thomas's willing concurrence, the Comet's Certificate of Airworthiness was withdrawn.

Meanwhile the Royal Navy had been carrying out a remarkable salvage operation near Elba. Over three-quarters of the wreckage of the lost Comet was recovered. All four engines had arrived back in England towards the end of March, a centre-section of wing in early April, and the front part of the cabin in mid-April. All this was passed to the Royal Aircraft Establishment at Farnborough, whose director, Arnold Hall (now Sir Arnold) was conducting the official investigation.

After exhaustive reconstruction and examination of the salvaged wreckage, a Court of Inquiry was held in public in London in October and November 1954. It published its report the following February. The cause of the explosions was accepted as metal fatigue in the skin of the aircraft at the corner of a window. The skin of the fuselage had not been strong enough to stand the repeated pressurisation – double previous levels – of the cabin after each take-off and climb to the jet's high altitude. Again, the aircraft had been inadequately tested by its makers, and we the operators found ourselves doing the tests in passenger service.

This was disastrous enough for de Havilland, who had to give up all the orders they had won for Comet 2s and Comet 3s. It was disastrous, too, for Britain in that it robbed us of a world lead in the manufacture of civil jet aircraft. To us in BOAC, it was a real body blow. It stopped us dead in our tracks, and looked like halting all progress until the next generation of jets came along. Perhaps the feeling within BOAC was best summed up by Victor Tait, our operations director: 'Overnight four year's work on planning, training and operational development fell into shambles through no fault of that work, and the planning for at least two years was rendered abortive. We were left, among other major problems, with 400 flying staff sitting on the ground with no job for months ahead; during this time they could not be told their future as we ourselves did not know it.'

The task of getting BOAC back on its feet would be a massive one.

6 Punch-drunk

It is difficult to recapture now, over a quarter of a century later, the full extent of what the Comet disasters meant to BOAC. Of the nine Comet 1s we had so proudly put into service, we had lost three – one near Calcutta, one over Elba and one south of Naples. The remaining six were grounded, and out of service. On top of that we had to assume that the twelve Comet 2s we had ordered for our Empire routes, and the five Comet 3s we wanted for transatlantic operation, would never come.

Our current operations were completely disrupted, and our plans for the future had collapsed.

The first step was to help ourselves as much as possible. We cut out our two least profitable routes – to the east coast of South America and to Israel – and distributed the Argonauts thereby released to help cover Comet operations. Then by better planning we increased flying hour production – Argonauts by 15 per cent and Stratocruisers by 10 per cent.

But there was still the problem of finding other aircraft to fill the large gap left by the Comets. This was not easy. First of all, there were not many suitable aircraft about, the only types being Boeing Stratocruiser and Lockheed Constellation. Secondly, our competitors would release them only when better aircraft came into their possession. And thirdly, our need was plain for everyone to see and our bargaining position correspondingly weak.

By 1955 we had managed to buy an extra six Stratocruisers which United Airlines were phasing out, increasing our fleet from 10 to 16. Qantas, then taking delivery of new Constellation 1049s, released six of their old Constellation 749s. And there was a single, almost brand new, Constellation 749 in the ownership of Howard Hughes, then chairman of TWA. He had kept it for his personal operation, but he had never used it and he said he was willing to sell. He was a difficult man to get hold of. Charles Abell, by then our chief engineer, spent many fruitless days tracking him down. In time he was run to earth in the hours before dawn in a hotel lavatory near Los Angeles, and a deal was made – an incident used but unattributed in a novel called *The Carpetbaggers*.

All this patching up of our aircraft fleet was weary, unsatisfying stuff. Compared with our main competitors, we had become, overnight, a second class fleet rather than a world leader.

In June 1954 Miles Thomas appointed me deputy chief executive to free deputy chairman Whitney Straight to concentrate on replacement aircraft, and to enable me to devote more effort to the continual replanning that we needed.

Bristol's delay in delivering Britannias, coming on top of the Comets' withdrawal from service, created another huge gap in our planning. Whitney Straight went to America and reported that the only fully competitive aircraft available to us was the new Douglas DC-7C. It was piston-engined, but it was the only aircraft capable of flying nonstop both ways across the North Atlantic. Fortunately, the Government were sympathetic and agreed to allow us the US dollars and to buy 10 DC-7Cs ('Seven Seas') free of duty – provided we sold them for dollars when the Britannias came into service. Our order for 10 Douglas DC-7Cs was placed in March 1955; all were delivered on schedule between October 1956 and April 1957.

However creditable it was to make these stop-gap arrangements and keep the airline going, the fact remained that we had lost all our frontline aircraft. I sensed that this had a considerable effect on Miles Thomas. For the time being, the zest for new achievement seemed to desert him. The spark of adventure seemed to have been quenched and his hand seemed to have lost some of its sureness of touch.

Yet, when de Havilland came forward with definite proposals for a Comet 4 early in 1955, he did not hesitate. Miles's faith had kept de Havilland going. We had stayed in close touch with them all along. We knew that, with the more powerful Rolls-Royce Avon engines now available, the Comet 4 had considerably better performance than the Comet 3. Even so, it could not fly the North Atlantic westbound without an intermediate stop. But later it could be used to great advantage on other routes. So, that March, we placed an order for 19 Comet 4s, and for one Comet 2E for development flying.

But should the new aircraft be called a Comet, in view of the disaster-laden reputation of the first Comets? Again, Miles did not hesitate. It must be called the Comet. If we or de Havilland changed the name, it would be thought we were trying to hide short-comings under a guise. The faults in the first Comets had been established and corrected; and all the world should know that this new Comet was proved beyond doubt.

★   ★   ★   ★   ★

There were other problems in the offing. One of them was already on my plate – the high level of our engineering costs. (The term 'engineering cost' in airline parlance means the cost of maintaining aircraft in service in first-class condition.) Roland Thornton had drawn my attention to the fact that our engineering costs were markedly higher than those of our principal international competitors, and we discussed from time to time how to tackle this problem. He raised the matter in the board; and I discussed it personally with Miles Thomas, because his support as chairman and chief executive was essential if we were to overcome all the natural resistances to change.

For some reason I have never understood, Miles Thomas was not convinced that anything needed doing, or was reluctant to take the necessary action, or a bit of both. Perhaps he felt that, in having reduced staff numbers from 24,000 in 1948 to 16,500 in 1951, he had already been ruthless enough – I don't know. At any rate, I got no top-level backing for an attack on engineering costs, either before Roland Thornton had to leave the board in June 1955 or for the remainder of Miles Thomas's time as chief executive.

Then there was the longer term but crucial question of choosing the best aircraft for BOAC for the 1960s, because the Comet 4 did not have nonstop transatlantic range against the prevailing westerly wind. A Vickers project for a long-range military transport – known as the V.1000 – had been on the drawing boards at Weybridge since about 1952. Later on, a civil version of this aircraft – known as the VC7 – was designed and presented to us on paper. For a time we were seriously interested – Miles Thomas was always conscious that a secondary role for BOAC was to help develop British civil aircraft for the aircraft industry. Our order depended on the RAF first ordering the military transport version and shouldering an appropriate part of its development costs. As time passed, the design weight increased beyond the forecasts; range and performance were thereby reduced, and for us became very marginal.

Eventually matters came to a head. In September 1955 there was a top level meeting between Miles Thomas, Whitney Straight and myself for BOAC and Sir Ronald Weeks, Sir Charles Dunphie and George Edwards for Vickers. We were told that the RAF had decided not to take the aircraft. That left only us. We were asked if we would take it on our own. We gave the only conceivable answer.

The following month Whitney Straight left us to take up an appointment as deputy chairman of Rolls-Royce. Lord Rennell of Rodd was appointed part-time deputy chairman in his place.

In mid-1955 there were signs of trouble among the pilots. There was no spectacular evidence, but there were a number of near-incidents which we interpreted as indicating a trend towards some undefined uneasiness. Perhaps it was engendered by a lack of faith in our future. Accordingly in October 1955 the board set up a 'select committee' under the chairmanship of John Wells Booth, one of our directors who had been chairman of BSAA before it was merged into BOAC. This committee reported two days before Christmas.

Meanwhile, Miles Thomas had been thinking about the best long-range aircraft for the future of BOAC. Whether or not he allowed himself to become influenced by Peter Masefield of Bristol, he seemed to have espoused the view that the future lay with long-range jetprops, or turboprop aircraft, rather than with the jets Boeing and Douglas were beginning to produce.

Masefield had left BEA a year or so earlier to go to Bristol Aircraft and was naturally trying hard to interest airline chiefs in the virtues of the projected third version of the Britannia, to be known as the Britannia 430 – even though we were only then about to take extremely late delivery of our first Britannia 102. But surely, I thought, a medium-paced turboprop could never be a match for a straight jet.

At the end of February 1956, while Miles Thomas was absent overseas, I had an embarrassing and unscheduled visit from two 'barons' of the pilot establishment – Capt Ben Prowse and Capt Tommy Farnsworth. They came into my office in the late afternoon, on their own initiative, to tell me that the senior pilots in general had lost confidence in Miles Thomas as head of BOAC. They no longer had faith in his judgment about future aircraft nor in his attitude towards the organisation of our flight operations management. I told them that he was in the process of dealing with the latter, following the report from the select committee, which they knew about. For the rest I could only listen and say nothing.

I never reported this meeting to anyone, because events soon overtook it.

★   ★   ★   ★   ★

By the beginning of 1956 I came to feel that Miles Thomas had really lost heart. Perhaps he was punch-drunk after all the hard knocks BOAC had received. But Harold Watkinson had succeeded John Boyd-Carpenter as Minister a month or two before. Having now experienced four changes of Minister in the six years I had been in BOAC, I knew well that the chairman always seemed unsettled and unsure of himself until an understanding relationship had been established with the new Minister. This time, too, I was beginning to sense that Miles's relationship with Harold Watkinson was not developing as well as it should.

The Queen and the Duke of Edinburgh flew by BOAC from London to Nigeria on 27 January, returning on 17 February. But on 9 February Miles left for a three-week holiday in America and the Caribbean, leaving me in executive charge. It surprised me a little that he had decided to go on holiday before the Queen's return. He arrived back at London Airport on the morning of Saturday, 3 March. The following Tuesday we had a meeting about Proteus engines for the Britannia; on the Friday he and I had a meeting with Peter Masefield on the same subject, which was becoming a vexed one. On the morning of Monday the 12th, the Minister, Harold Watkinson, came down to the airport. I didn't know why at the time, but from what happened later it seems a safe guess that in the previous week Miles had told the Minister of his intention to resign.

The following Sunday, 18 March, Miles Thomas flew off again, this time to Southern Africa. There was no business reason that I knew of, but he had a property in Rhodesia. I began to feel that there was something in the wind.

On the Thursday the Prime Minister, Sir Anthony Eden, called a meeting of the chairmen of nationalised industries in the Cabinet Room at No 10 Downing Street to discuss their finances and ways and means of providing them with capital. In Miles's absence abroad I represented BOAC; and it seems that I made some remarks which led to my being asked to see the Chancellor of the Exchequer, Harold Macmillan, at the Treasury the next Monday afternoon. I explained to him as best I could that although an expanding airline needed repeated injections of capital to finance new aircraft, the capital was quickly recovered because an airline turned its capital over once a year. If we used hard currency to buy competitive American aircraft, Britain would recover the dollars in the first twelve months of the aircraft's life. In terms of the nation's balance of payments, we would either earn the dollars from foreign passengers or keep British travellers from flying foreign. Macmillan remained inscrutable as ever, but I think the point was taken.

Next day, Tuesday 27 March, Miles returned. I then learnt from him (and from the *Daily Express*) that he was to leave us at the end of April to become the UK chairman of the American-owned Monsanto Chemicals. I said I was terribly sorry. He said that he would be too, but that he had finally decided it just wasn't worth the candle; he was only being paid in 1956 the same amount as the managing director of Imperial Airways was paid before the war – £7,500 a year – whereas he could get three or four times that outside.

This made him feel even more that the constraints under which the chairman of a nationalised industry worked were not worth putting up with.

I asked him who was going to be appointed in his place, and he said he didn't know; the Minister had not told him yet. Next Sunday, Easter Day, he left again for the United States.

Francis Rennell returned a few days later from his annual visit to Australia and we had a long talk about it all. The situation was pretty shattering, as can be imagined, and we had no power under the Act to put forward our own proposals. Everyone in top management was wondering anxiously who would be inflicted on us by a Minister who had only taken office recently and knew little about any of us. The Minister always appointed the chairman and other board members, but we took comfort from the fact that the board had the right under the Act to appoint its own chief executive.

Miles came back from America on Tuesday 10 April to preside on the Thursday at what we all realised would be his last board meeting. Still no word from the Minister.

On the Wednesday evening of the following week, Francis Rennell rang me at home. 'The Minister asked me to see him late this afternoon,' he said, 'and he wants to see you at noon tomorrow. You are not going to like what he tells you. I am going to resign. If I were you I should take a good sleeping pill tonight. I had better not say any more now, but come and see me at Morgan Grenfell tomorrow afternoon after you have seen him. At any rate, sleep well – and good luck.'

I duly presented myself in Harold Watkinson's outer office shortly before 12 next day, Thursday 19 March. In private in his own room he told me that he had decided to appoint Gerard d'Erlanger as the next chairman, but on a part-time basis. I did not then know 'Pops' d'Erlanger, though I knew of him. Whatever he proves to be like, I thought, BOAC ought to be able to live with that; and, after all, it is the Minister's prerogative to appoint whom he likes.

Then came the bombshell. He was also going to appoint Sir George Cribbett, deputy secretary at the Ministry in charge of Civil Aviation, as chief executive of BOAC.

I asked for time to think. He said there was none. He had to make a statement in the House of Commons that afternoon and then release a press announcement. The discussion began to get heated. I said that, however good Sir George's services had been at the Ministry, he didn't know how to handle people, let alone trade unions, and he was not cut out to be the chief executive of a major airline.

Watkinson said he didn't agree. I retorted that, whatever anybody else in BOAC decided to do, I was not prepared to work under George Cribbett. 'And,' I said, 'you haven't the power to appoint him. The Act reserves to the board the power to appoint the chief executive.'

Harold Watkinson was obviously taken aback, and the temperature rose further. At one point he said: 'Well, you needn't be so bloody rude.' I said: 'I am sorry if you think I have been. But I am afraid I've had to speak bluntly. It's the only way I can make you realise how strongly I feel about it all.'

After rather more than a hour, he asked me if I would go to Pops' office at Erlanger's Bank in Moorgate, before he had to go to the House, to work out a top structure for BOAC that included Cribbett in some capacity. Soon after half-past-one I reached Pops' office, where we had sandwiches and beer. I found him eminently reasonable and anxious to find a solution.

Before long we agreed to recommend to the Minister that George Cribbett should be appointed deputy chairman of the Corporation with responsibility for international relations and associated companies, but not for the running of BOAC itself – other than as deputy for Pops in his absence. In due course the board would be asked to appoint me as managing director – a title Pops preferred to chief executive.

We phoned this solution to Harold Watkinson, who immediately accepted it and amended his proposed statement to the House accordingly. The Ministry, however, did not retype the press release; they merely blacked out the words about George Cribbett being appointed chief executive. But as is now well known, with modern methods that sort of blacking out can be seen through, and there was no hiding the change of mind that had taken place.

I got to Morgan Grenfell's by about 4 o'clock and told Francis Rennell what had happened. He seemed relieved and pleased. I told him how sorry I was that he was leaving and, while I understood his determination not to continue as deputy chairman, asked him whether he wouldn't reconsider his decision to leave the board altogether.

He replied that he had told the Minister he would resign from the board and its deputy chairmanship; this had had its effect; and he would not withdraw from the position he had taken. But he would willingly rejoin BOAC and me on the new basis, if Harold Watkinson was prepared to re-appoint him to the board on the day after his resignation took effect. And so it happened. Francis Rennell left the board on 30 April 1956, and was re-appointed the next day, 1 May. The next time we met as a board at London Airport, Francis –

rather deliberately I thought – took his seat, not on the chairman's right as before, but directly opposite him in the centre of our half-dozen outside directors.

Meanwhile top management foregathered in the chairman's dining room at London Airport on Friday evening, 27 April, to take a fond but sad farewell of Miles Thomas. And on Tuesday, 1 May, Pops d'Erlanger held his first board meeting as chairman at Stratton House, Piccadilly, and I was appointed managing director of BOAC.

7 New Management

For the second half of that April I had not fully committed myself in my own mind to staying with BOAC for long. I felt deeply the impending loss of the leadership given us by Miles Thomas. I was unsure how I would be able to get on with our new chairman and deputy chairman, both imposed on us from outside. I had met d'Erlanger only once, on that famous nineteenth of April, but he seemed the kind of person it would be easy to work with, though perhaps unlikely to give BOAC much in the way of personal leadership. It would fall to me to provide that, if I had it in me.

I was much more worried about Cribbett. He had the arrogance of a man who, when you went to see him in his office at the Ministry, would lean back in his swivel chair, put both his feet on his desk, and talk at you as though you were no better than the furniture. And, to make matters worse, he knew perfectly well that the board had blocked his appointment as chief executive. In any case, the civil service is often the worst field from which to recruit people to be heads of industry. With too few exceptions, the civil servant has never managed anything in his life, and has little or no idea of how to handle people. His job does not require that quality, and tends to stifle creativity. He comments, criticises and reports from his ivory tower in some Ministry building, far removed from the real world. And he is never held to account for the result of his recommendations, nor held responsible for making ends meet financially.

We had arrived at an arrangement with Harold Watkinson under which Cribbett would not be allowed to interfere in any way with the management of BOAC itself. As the days passed, I came to feel that his position as no more than deputy to a non-executive chairman would not prove any obstacle to the executive job that lay ahead of me. I talked to friends who knew the people and would understand the problems – including my mentor and former colleague, Roland Thornton, as well as Francis Rennell. All urged me to stay. I didn't need much persuasion, really. I think I just wanted their assurance that I wasn't rating myself too highly. I certainly wanted the job, and welcomed the great challenge it offered.

The money I never bothered about. As deputy chief executive I. had been paid only £5,000 a year – but then Miles Thomas was getting only 50 per cent more as full-time chairman and chief executive. Not having been blessed with children, I have never had to worry about the expenses of bringing up youngsters. I was getting enough for my needs at the time, and that was all I thought about. If you worked in a nationalised industry, you had to accept the fact that salaries had a ceiling imposed by Government – the rate set for the chairman. You either accepted less than in private industry, or you got out.

I was much more interested in the chance to run BOAC, and to help it back on its feet after the great setback it had suffered through the failure of the Comets.

* * * * *

The responsibility I had accepted was far from easy. In the normal course, when a man is promoted to be managing director of a business he has worked in for some years, he will carry with him the support of a continuing board. But in BOAC in May 1956 neither the new chairman nor his deputy was of the board's own seeking. Sensing that it was not an easy situation, Harold Watkinson and his Parliamentary Secretary, Airey Neave, came to BOAC headquarters at London Airport on 14 June 1956 and lunched with the board.

There were a couple of aspects of d'Erlanger's appointment that were bound in time to bring us trouble with the trade unions. To begin with, he had been chairman of British European Airways from 1947 to 1949 but had been removed from office by a Labour Minister, Frank Pakenham (later Lord Longford) to make way for Sholto Douglas (Lord Douglas of Kirtleside). Whether his departure from BEA was right or wrong, this was not the best recommendation for his being made chairman of BOAC, Britain's premier airline. But on top of that, his appointment to the chair of BOAC was not only part time; it was also unpaid. To the unions – who believe fervently in the principle of a man being paid the rate for the job – the inference was obvious; if he wasn't worth paying, he wasn't worthy of the job.

For the next couple of years we were to suffer on these two counts, and because the outlook for BOAC was so bleak, from a continuing rash of unofficial strikes at the airport. After he had been knighted and became Sir Gerard, he started being paid – thereby removing part of the sting.

This was something which management would overcome in due course. But within the board it was the part-time nature of our chairman's appointment that was more significant. In a nationalised industry, the Minister frequently wants to talk to its chairman; too often ours and his Minister would meet in central London. Because d'Erlanger was by no means always at our London Airport headquarters this exposed us to the risk of our chairman having his arm twisted by the Minister without management being aware of it or having a chance to brief him fully.

★   ★   ★   ★   ★

In the top management of BOAC, changes were coming thick and fast. This was both a problem and an opportunity. Not only did Miles Thomas's resignation follow only seven months after the departure of Whitney Straight to Rolls-Royce, but our chief personnel officer, Hamish Blair-Cunynghame, had left us to go to the National Coal Board as its director general of staff. Victor Tait, our operations director – who amongst other things had introduced flight simulators for pilot-training and had greatly improved our worldwide telecommunications system – was 64 and coming up for retirement; so also was supplies manager Bill Cushion, by then 65; and in September George Whittingham, director of medical services, then 69, would also be leaving. All three were retired air marshals who had served BOAC well since soon after the end of the war. On top of that, with George Cribbett coming in from the Ministry, where he had carried responsibility for intergovernmental negotiations, our own Ronald McCrindle, a noted authority on international relations in the airline world, thereby became partly redundant.

The departure of all these senior people left major gaps in our top management group. A business consists of people; and business management is about how these people are led and how they can be got to work together most productively in their different technical or specialised fields. My task was not going to be easy. The part of our top organisation that needed the most urgent attention was flight operations management. The pilots' restlessness, which had led to the appointment of the Booth Committee some eight months before, underlined the urgency.

Victor Tait had been operations director for nearly ten years. The organisation under him had been governed by the geographical distribution of the fleets in the late 1940s and early 1950s. Each aircraft type had a fleet manager who was responsible for both maintaining and operating the aircraft. The fleets were based in Filton, near Bristol, and at Hurn, near Bournemouth, as well as at London Airport. Centralising maintenance became possible when the first new Heathrow hangar block was ready for the Boeing Stratocruisers in 1955. Bringing Charles Abell from Filton to London, and setting up aircraft maintenance as a centralised unit under the operations director, left the fleet managers responsible for flight operations – a responsibility for which the existing managers were not necessarily the best choice.

It was already evident that they lacked the confidence of the pilots and other flying staff. This was not a criticism of their ability as managers – it arose quite simply from the fact that none of them had command experience of their new aircraft. There was a feeling among the operating crew that their chairborne managers were out of touch with their problems and lacked understanding. Not altogether fair, perhaps, but the feeling existed and had to be recognised.

I came to the conclusion very early on that I must break down the operations department into halves and pick someone with current operating experience to head flight operations, to parallel the appointment of Charles Abell as chief engineer.

To our great distress one of our Argonauts crashed after take-off from Kano Airport in Nigeria on Sunday, 24 June, killing many of the passengers and crew, including the captain. I went immediately over to movement control at London Airport headquarters. Victor Tait was in his last week before retiring, so I decided to send his deputy, Owen Houchen, to the scene of the crash with our accident investigation team.

It was possible to establish what had happened. A tropical storm near Kano was thought by the local weather people to be moving away from the take-off flight path, and the captain was given permission to taxi out. Piston engines have to be run up separately at the end of the runway before take-off, and four of them take time. While this was going on, the line squall changed direction and moved rapidly towards the far end of the runway. It seems that the duty met officer did not appreciate the full significance of this; it was a week-end and the senior met officers were not rostered for duty that Sunday. The aircraft took off and had climbed to only about 200 ft when it ran into the windshear. Instead of having a strong headwind giving added lift to the wings, it suddenly had a strong tailwind giving no airspeed at all. It fell like a stone, with tragic results.

This was a terrible baptism into my new job. And it was sad that this accident should have occurred in Victor Tait's last week with us. I learnt much from it. I have always carried with me an awareness of the top man's ultimate responsibility for safety. In the nature of things, human errors will be made from time to time. But the procedures to prevent error or failure must be such that the chance of accident is reduced to as near to nil as humanly possible.

I checked through our incident-reporting and accident-investigation procedures, and found they were comprehensive and thorough. I then looked at our Air Safety Committee. It was the practice for our operations director to preside over this committee. Thus he could find himself as judge in his own case. It seemed to me that BEA had better arrangements. Their Air Safety Committee was presided over by Harold Balfour (Lord Balfour of Inchrye). He was not part of BEA management though he had been made a part-time member of their board in 1955. A distinguished member of the Royal Flying Corps in the first world war and of the Royal Air Force until he went into Parliament, he had been Parliamentary Under-Secretary of State for Air from 1938 to 1944.

I talked to Balfour about the problem and decided I must try to find somebody outside the operations department, and if possible outside BOAC itself, to chair our own Air Safety Committee. Ronald McCrindle now had time to spare, and temporarily took on this added responsibility, for which his legal mind and long airline experience fitted him well. Later on I was able to secure the valuable services of Freddie Guest (Air Marshall Sir Charles Guest) who had retired as Inspector General of the RAF in 1956.

Meanwhile, we were looking among our pilots for a chief of flight operations. Civil airline pilots are not the easiest group of people in which to find qualities that add up to human leadership. By the nature of their work they are in charge of single aircraft with a small crew for hours on end, and at slip-crew stations they are simply the senior officer among the same crew from whom they probably want to escape while resting. Moreover, the composition of each flight crew changes each time they go down a route. This tends to breed individualists. While in the air they are very much alone with their fellow crewmembers, and are required to conform meticulously to the detail of laid-down operating procedures and radio instructions from air traffic controllers. This produces nothing like the leadership qualities of the Guy Gibsons and the Dam Busters, or of the Don Bennetts and the Pathfinders.

Before long, we reduced a longish list of possibles to a short list of about seven most likely candidates. I chaired the selection board and saw them on Tuesday, 26 June. I decided in my own mind that Capt J N Weir was the best man for the job, and was glad to find that the others agreed. I wanted someone, in this first phase of bringing pilots into management, who was experienced and expert but who would not exert his authority too much. Weir seemed to me to fit that bill well.

The board approved my recommendation two days later. That weekend I phoned Jim at his home at Christchurch and told him I was going to offer him the appointment. Typically, he countered by asking: 'Are you joking?' 'No,' I said, 'I am absolutely serious.' There was a pause. 'Well, that's wonderful,' he said. 'I can hardly believe it. But when do you want me?' 'Now,' I replied. 'Can you come to my office on Monday morning at 10, and we will go over all the arrangements then?' 'I certainly can,' he answered.

We soon established a good understanding and easy working relationship. The first organisation question I wanted to talk about was aircraft fleet management. He had, as I had, nothing but respect for our fleet managers. But he felt as I did that they should be captains with current operating experience. The main problem was to ensure that they kept their pilot licences valid and flew a reasonable number of hours down the routes, in command of the aircraft type they were managing.

How could we achieve this? In 1956 the average pilot flew about 600 hours a year. In the end we decided on a deputy manager as well as a manager for each fleet; one would always have to be at headquarters in office hours, and they would divide flying duties so that the manager would fly at least 200 hours a year and the deputy manager about 400 hours.

The existing fleet managers would suffer redundancy – never a pleasant or an easy matter to handle. But Ernest Hessey went to West African Airways from the Hermes fleet when it closed down; Jackie Harrington went to one of the independents from the Argonaut fleet; and Denis Peacock was transferred from the Stratocruiser/Constellation fleet to operations headquarters at London Airport.

Allied to the operational side of BOAC were the medical services. Medical services in a worldwide airline are of far greater importance and significance than they are in almost any other industry. There is, first of all, the necessity to put all active pilots through a medical test every six months in the interests of flight safety. Again a worldwide airline has aircrew continually on the move up and down its routes, through the tropical zones or touching the Arctic circle, stopping off for two or three days at a time at slipcrew stations. Their health is in itself a responsibility; but from the commercial point of view, an airline needs to ensure that its flight schedules are not upset by aircrew sickness along a route.

Again, in 1956, BOAC operated to some 58 stations around the world, and at all of them food or drinking water could be taken on board. We had to be absolutely satisfied in the interests of both passengers and crew that the highest standards of hygiene were maintained at all times, day in and day out.

Twenty-five of these stations were manned with our own staff in places as different as Basra, Keflavik, Khartoum and Rangoon. Medical services were not available to those staff in the manner provided by the National Health Service at home, so suitable local arrangements had to be made and supervised. On top of all this, a most important commercial point in our service to the public was the care we could offer to invalid passengers in flight.

These comprehensive but varied medical services had been built up and presided over by George Whittingham since 1948. He had been Consultant in Hygiene, Pathology and Tropical Medicine to the Royal Air Force from 1930 to 1939 and Director General of Medical Services, RAF, from 1941 to 1946. With his retirement from BOAC in 1956, we might have been in a difficult situation were it not for the fact that his chief assistant, Dr Kenneth G Bergin, was ready to take over. Aged 45, he had served with the RAF Medical Branch from 1939 to 1946 and was known to be acceptable to the pilots. George Whittingham, I am glad to say, stayed on as consultant until he reached the age of 70 in 1957.

★   ★   ★   ★   ★

In January 1957, Miles Thomas asked me if I would like to join him at Monsanto Chemicals. I remember the occasion vividly. We were lunching together in the old Berkeley Hotel on the corner of Piccadilly and Berkeley Street. Monsanto needed, he told me, someone with my abilities; he and I had found it possible to work well together; he could guess that I had a difficult row to hoe, with the two new appointments to the board; and he knew only too well how underpaid I was in BOAC. He wondered if I would like to throw my hand in with him again in another and more financially rewarding field.

I was greatly touched by what he said. But I didn't think about it for more than a few moments. Much as I would have liked to team up with him again, I felt an overriding commitment to carry on the work that he himself had started in BOAC. I felt this commitment even more in view of BOAC's sorry state with no front-line aircraft. The rebuilding of the airline would take years. This was certainly not going to be at all easy in BOAC. But there was so much for me to do there.

So we left it at that. I was very grateful for his approach, and yet perhaps even more dedicated to my work in BOAC than before. Miles and I remained good friends ever since.

★   ★   ★   ★   ★

The creation of a new top management team to fill the gaps left by those who had retired, or were about to, was immensely important and urgent. As I have shown, we had already centralised the 'production' functions of engineering and flight operations under Charles Abell and Jim Weir. We had also ensured that the 'service' functions were in capable hands; Ken Bergin, Ken Bevan and Harold Spear had taken charge of the medical, financial and personnel departments, while Kenneth Staple and Freddy Gillman remained in charge of legal and press and information services respectively. There remained the question of how best to organise our 'merchandising' functions.

Since the time a year or two earlier when John Brancker left to go to the International Air Transport Association in Montreal, Keith Granville had been in charge of the whole of the commercial and sales side of BOAC's business. At 45 Keith had been in Imperial Airways and BOAC ever since leaving Tonbridge in 1929. Considering all the setbacks in introducing new British aircraft into service, it is no small tribute to him and his team that we had won and retained as much business as we did.

But I thought that some people were wrongly cast. For instance Winston Bray was in 1955 occupying the post of sales manager under Keith. But that position did not enable him to develop his real powers. He was a thinker more than salesman, a thinker with a commercial bent. Soon after being appointed deputy chief executive at the end of 1954, I wanted to supplement the two able planners I had in the operations and economic fields – John Douglas and J B Scott – with someone from the commercial field. Keith Granville took the point and saw the advantage to the commercial side of having a senior representative in our central planning group. So Winnie was appointed, at age 45, to be sales planning manager. That trio of Bray, Douglas and Scott proved to be one of the best planning groups in the airline world and was to serve BOAC well for the next 15 years.

The post of sales manager thus vacated was given to Gilbert Lee. Like Keith Granville, Gilbert had been an Imperial Airways trainee, starting in 1931, and staying with BOAC right through. In that time, he had seen overseas service in India and Pakistan and had been seconded to West African Airways as general manager from 1949 to the end of 1952. Now, at 44, he was just the sort of person I thought we needed to be our next general sales manager.

Responsibility for our 58 stations around the world was now in the hands of Ross Stainton. He, too, had been an Imperial Airways trainee, joining straight from Malvern in 1933. Apart from a short spell in the RAF from 1940 to 1942 he had been in BOAC ever since. In 1954 I persuaded Miles Thomas to transfer him to London from New York to strengthen our headquarters team. Now, at 41, he had charge of all our stations round the world as general manager, stations and traffic. He was organisationally neither fish, flesh nor good red-herring. He was regarded as part of operations more than anything else. Route stations are an important part of aircraft operation. But in my view the handling of passengers is essentially a part of after-sales service, capable of generating goodwill or ill-will, depending on how they are looked after, and consequently influencing repeat business. In any case, we had sales managers at all ports of call. I had no doubt that the local sales tasks outweighed in commercial importance the operating and engineeing work, which could be supervised from London.

A change in sales organisation was needed. And there is something in a name, too. I didn't like our valued customers being classed as 'traffic'. So I altered Ross Stainton's title to chief of ground services to cut out the word 'traffic'. A small point, but psychologically significant. Convinced that group services would be more sales-minded and more productive of business if made part of the commercial side, I placed Ross and the stations for which he was responsible under our commercial director, Keith Granville.

This was in the third quarter of 1956. By then I had got the basic overall pattern of management organisation sorted out. By the end of September I felt able to announce this new top management structure to all headquarters staff. So, apart from an hour's meeting with the trade unions, to whom I explained what I was doing and why, and another hour's meeting with Bristols about the Britannia 102, the whole of Friday, 28 September, was given over to a series of private 15-minute meetings with those personally affected, culminating in a general meeting of senior staff. After that, I was thankful to be taken out to dinner by my old friend and co-director Frank Brake.

I was still not satisfied with the commercial organisation. An airline is basically selling movement along routes, or along combinations of routes. 'Merchandising' must be based on the market potentials of the regions served by those routes. But there was so much else to handle in 1956 that I was prepared to wait a while before further re-arrangement of the commercial side. Apart from relieving me of immediate pressure, this pause would give time for the new organisation to settle down and for me to think more about further changes.

Fortunately, the accident of my being put out of action early in 1957 for a gall-bladder operation helped to bring matters forward. Because of my ten-week absence the board appointed Keith Granville as deputy managing director, though the Minister had not yet made him a member of the corporation. I welcomed this move, not only for its own sake, but also because it would enable us to work out together the next stage in the development of our commercial organisation.

*　　*　　*　　*　　*

Meanwhile Gilbert Lee had taken a firm hold of his new job as general sales manager, and had organised a world sales conference in London starting on Monday, 29 October, 1956. The object was to attract the maximum traffic with the outdated aircraft then at our disposal, but with the prospect of the DC-7C and the Britannia 102 coming at the end of 1956 or early in 1957. It was my first chance as managing director to meet our sales managers from all over the world. It was their first chance to get to know my thinking and hopes for the future.

To appreciate the nature of our marketing task at that time, picture the product we then had to sell and our competition. In October 1956, after the tragic withdrawal of all the Comets in 1954, we were entirely dependent on 16 Boeing Stratocruisers for our transatlantic services and on 21 Canadair Argonauts and 16 Lockheed Constellation 749s for the rest. All these aircraft were of 1949 vintage. In these days of jumbo jets carrying some 400 passengers each, it is easy to forget that the Stratocruiser, which in the early 1950s was the largest aircraft in civil airline service, was only big enough to carry 60 passengers. The Argonaut and the Constellation 749 could carry only 40 and 44 passengers respectively, though with the introduction of tourist class their capacities were enlarged to 54 and 60. By 1956, all our international competitors were equipped, or being equipped, with more modern and more spacious aircraft. But in spite of this competitive disadvantage, we had succeeded in selling over 63 per cent of all our seats – a relatively high percentage for a common carrier, with the obligation to operate scheduled services day in and day out all round the year.

The sector lengths which our aircraft could fly were also generally less than those of our competitors' newer aircraft. The Stratocruisers, for example, could not fly the Atlantic non-stop from London to New York and had to put in to Gander and sometimes Shannon. But in spite of that, something like 40 per cent of the total transatlantic passenger traffic was now crossing by air, and we felt confident that we could overtake the ships in 1957 or 1958 at the latest – especially now that the DC-7Cs could offer non-stop travel both ways.

In the longer-voyage market, although air travel was growing steadily, our penetration of the total travel market had not been so successful – understandably I think. A flight from England to South Africa or Australia was still something of an undertaking in those days. The limited range of our aircraft required at least four landings between London and Johannesburg, and eight between London and Sydney. At sea, there was plenty of sun and air to enjoy on board ship.

In 1956, airlines were carrying only about 10 per cent of all passengers to and from South Africa, and no more than about 5 per cent of end-to-end traffic to and from Australia. For that reason a worldwide airline such as BOAC had to rely very largely on picking up sector traffic. Much of this was fifth-freedom in character, and this made the negotiation of international traffic rights of great significance to us.

To hold our position and even improve on it, our passenger service in flight and on the ground had to be of the highest possible standard, and our selling had to be very keen at all points along our routes. At the same time the cost of both passenger service and selling had to be kept within strict limits.

It helps to understand the nature of BOAC as an airline at that time if one keeps in mind that our passengers' average journey was as much as 3,500 miles. We were very much a long-haul airline. Moreover, each round trip passenger was worth £160 to us. That may not seem much in today's inflated currency, but in those far-off days, before money had lost so much of its value, a passenger was still not asked to pay more than 2½p a mile. By way of comparison, a round trip passenger was worth only £15 to a short-haul airline such as BEA. With the average customer bringing in more than ten times that amount to BOAC, it made good commercial sense to spend money and effort attracting him and ensuring that he was well looked after.

In the autumn of 1956 I had been reluctant to introduce further changes in commercial organisation. But now I had made up my mind that the organisation pattern could and should be improved. If change was for the good, what was the point of waiting? The sooner people could settle down to their new responsibilities, the better.

All 'merchandising' functions, including ground services, ought to be grouped together in separate regions or routes. There would be a general manager in charge of each. He would rank as a full member of the board of management; and he would be responsible for making a profit with aircraft that the central planning group, and I as managing director, agreed he might have from our total fleet. In this way, we should get financial criteria and commercial realism down into the decision-making of the route managements themselves.

Well, inevitably, it took a little time to work out the details. But by the autumn of 1957, we had the new organisation established – a pattern which has served the airline well ever since. Keith Granville continued to act as commercial director in addition to being deputy managing director. Three regions were established: Western Routes, to cover all operations from Britain across the North Atlantic and beyond; Eastern Routes, to cover all operations to Asia, the Far East and Australia; and Southern Routes, to cover all operations to Africa, and also across the South Atlantic to the east coast of South America when we were able to return to it.

Gilbert Lee, who had been general sales manager under Keith Granville, was appointed general manager western routes. Ross Stainton, who was then chief of ground services, was appointed to take charge of eastern routes – the ground services department being dispersed at the same time into the three commercial route managements. Derek Glover, who had been my personal assistant for a couple of years and on whom I could rely, was put in charge of southern routes.

This is a good pattern of organisation for a worldwide airline such as BOAC. We do not sell a uniform product. An airline sells movement along routes; the requirements for movement vary in the different regions depending on their character; and meeting those varying requirements demands not only considerable local knowledge but also differing marketing techniques.

This completed the management team to put BOAC back among the top world airlines. The team became the management board of BOAC – though in deference to other people's susceptibilities I did not call it anything so lofty. All the same, we really had a two-tier board at the apex of the corporation's structure – the board of members appointed by the Minister, all of them (except myself) part-time and non-executive; and the equivalent of the board of management, all full-time executives. I was the only member of both and provided the essential link between the two.

Looking back on it all from a distance I am struck by the debt we in BOAC owed to George Woods Humphery and his Imperial Airways team. They were responsible for recruiting so much good material through their trainee scheme of the 1930s. Many business commentators often make the mistake of crediting or blaming the man of the moment. It hardly ever is so. I would almost say it never is, except in the exceptional cases of mushroom growths. Businesses are continuing enterprises. Current events are influenced greatly by what previous generations of management have done and planned in the preceding years and decades. An incoming chairman, or for that matter a chief executive brought in from outside, can in time influence the trend and the image of a business. But he is inevitably the beneficiary, for better or worse, of what has gone before.

The members of the new top management group I had constructed were changed as the years passed. Basil Bampfylde (a former personal assistant of mine and another Imperial Airways trainee) was to join it shortly as a route general manager. But this top group was the team, derived wholly from within the corporation, that was in fact destined to carry BOAC into the period of its great expansion and profitability in the 1960s and early 1970s.

8 New Aircraft

While we had been building up the new management team, we had also made a good start selecting our future aircraft. The Minister, Harold Watkinson, was fully aware that BOAC had no non-stop transatlantic jet aircraft on order. He was determined to do all he could to help us. He asked for our 'shopping list' as quickly as possible.

It was to be in two parts. The first part was to cover our requirements for long-range aircraft for our western routes across the North Atlantic. This he needed urgently by September 1956 at the latest, because dollars would be needed to buy American aircraft and he would have to put our case to the Cabinet in the early autumn. The second part could follow in 1957 and was to cover our requirements for shorter-range aircraft to supplement and eventually replace Comet 4s. How slow to die was the old medium-range-Empire concept so beloved by Ministry officials!

Early in May, Pops d'Erlanger decided to establish an aircraft requirements committee and asked me to select appropriate members from BOAC's top management. A key member would be Alan Campbell Orde, our development director. Pops was aware of our pilots' concern that BOAC was inclined to favour turboprop rather than straight-jet aircraft. He was going to ask BALPA, the pilots' union, to recommend an experienced non-management pilot for this committee. Campbell Orde and I welcomed this very much. In no time BALPA nominated their chairman, Capt Anthony Spooner. The full committee met for the first time on Tuesday 8 May, and weekly thereafter for the next couple of months.

A newly-appointed chairman, for the first four to six months of his term, is in a strong position in relation to the Minister who appointed him. That is the period in which he can ask for almost anything he wants – within reason – and know that the Minister will have to try to get it. After the honeymoon period, the Minister can afford to disagree with the chairman he has appointed. Pops d'Erlanger saw a great opportunity – possibly the greatest we should ever have – for BOAC to establish itself as a front-rank air carrier and dollar-earner across the North Atlantic.

He felt that Britain and the United States ought to aim at sharing 50/50 the traffic between their two countries. In practice, however, that could never be achieved because there were airlines of other countries operating on the routes with fifth freedom traffic rights. But he considered that we should set our sights on 40 per cent of the traffic by 1960, and work out the number of aircraft accordingly. So we got our commercial planning people to check our traffic forecasts.

Concurrently, we had to assess the relative merits of the different aircraft that could be available in time. The choice of aircraft was not wide. Theoretically, the Britannia 430 was one. But even if its operating costs proved lower per seat-mile than the straight-jet, none of us on the aircraft requirements committee believed that a propeller-driven aircraft could compete with the faster jets in passenger appeal. And from bitter experience of delayed deliveries, we knew we could not rely on getting Bristol aircraft when we needed them. Time was of the essence.

This left us with only the American industry to look at. We felt that insufficient work had yet been done on the Douglas DC-8. On the other hand the Boeing 707 was well advanced, and we believed the claims made for it. But to be as certain as possible, we sent a twelve-man team to the West Coast during July. It was led by Alan Campbell Orde and included two of our senior line pilots, Capt Tom Stoney and Capt Tommy Farnsworth. On returning at the end of the month they reported unanimously that the Boeing 707 was the best aircraft for our purposes – particularly when powered by Rolls-Royce Conway engines. These would help its performance and reduce the amount of dollars needed.

Our commercial planning team had finished reviewing our forecasts of traffic expected on western routes in 1960. The aircraft requirements committee met twice during August to complete our report and recommendations to the Minister.

The one unknown factor in the equation was the number of flying hours that we could expect to get from a Boeing long-range jet in a year. This was an uncharted field. There was no experience anywhere to draw on. True, we in BOAC knew what we had achieved with the Comet 1 in the first two years of jet airliner history. But the range of the Comet 1 was far shorter than that of the Boeing 707 and it had to make a good many stops along a route. By the beginning of 1954 we had only been able to get the Comet utilisation up to 2,400 hours a year. We could get 2,550 hours a year from piston-engined aircraft on long-sector routes.

We were convinced we could do better with the long-range Boeing jets. But how much better? We didn't want to be over-optimistic, but we thought it safe to bank on some 3,000 hours a year. With that productivity, we calculated that we should need 17 ₁Boeing 707s to carry our forecast traffic for the early 1960s. And that is what we asked the Minister to seek Government approval for, with delivery between December 1959 and December 1960 – the earliest positions we could then get in the delivery queue.

Parliament was in recess at that time, but towards the end of September things began to move in earnest. We were very fortunate in that our Minister, Harold Watkinson, was a member of the Cabinet – the Minister responsible for civil aviation was not always so. Because of that, he was able to argue our case himself in Cabinet. It was not long before we got his reply to our submission. The Government had approved our request, but for 15 and not 17 Boeing 707s equipped with British engines. The necessary dollars would be made available. But we were to understand that we would get no more dollars at all for whatever aircraft we might need for other routes than the North Atlantic.

This was really great news for all of us in BOAC. By getting this decision from the Cabinet, Harold Watkinson had done more for the corporation and the place of British civil aviation in the world than any previous Minister.

★   ★   ★   ★   ★

While we had been establishing the new management team in BOAC, and also making arrangements for the supply of fully competitive aircraft for the 1960s, the current business of the corporation had to be carried on without interruption.

Among the many things to be dealt with, perhaps the most important and the most urgent was the task of getting the DC-7Cs and the delayed Britannia 102s into service. Moreover, the Britannia 312 was due to enter service in December 1957. And then de Havilland were due to start delivering the Comet 4s to us in September 1958. All this constituted an exceptional programme of putting new types of aircraft into service – greater than anything we had undertaken before. Four new types in 21 months called for intensive retraining of pilots and engineers – and thanks to Paul Adorian of Redifon we were able to get early delivery of British-built flight simulators in good time.

With the DC-7Cs everything went well. The Douglas Aircraft Corporation of California delivered all 10 of them on schedule. In

January 1957, they enabled us to start genuinely non-stop transatlantic services. By June of that year, the DC-7Cs were providing as many as 20 services a week from London to New York. Of these two a week were extended onwards to San Francisco to connect with the Qantas services across the Pacific to Sydney.

With the Britannia 102s things were very different. Back in 1954 the second prototype, G-ALRX, had had to be crash-landed by Bill Pegg, Bristol's chief test pilot, on the banks of the Severn. This was a considerable setback as the first prototype, G-ALBO, had been far from representative of the production aircraft. Although much basic performance work could be evaluated from it, more than one aircraft was needed, and one with representative systems. Not until the first production aircraft, G-ANBA, was built could the certification and customer tests be completed.

On 12 March 1955 Walter Gibb, a Bristol test pilot, took an aircraft down to Johannesburg in 17 hours 24 minutes with only one stop at Nairobi. This was very impressive. Nine months later, on 30 December 1955, the Britannia 102's Certificate of Airworthiness was signed by Jack Profumo, then Parliamentary Secretary to Harold Watkinson. Within 90 minutes of his signing it, Capt Sigfrid Rendall and Capt Frank Walton took off from Filton with our first two aircraft, G-ANBC and G-ANBD, and brought them to London Airport.

Even so they were two years late. We began flying training out of Hurn airport. Only three months later, on 3 April 1956, one of our Britannias, with our 102 flight manager, Capt Rendall in command, experienced a new type of engine trouble over the Rift Valley about 200 miles south of Nairobi. All four engines stopped within about five minutes. Capt Rendall and his crew managed to get them going again and the aircraft did not lose much height. (Subsequently, the entire starting system for all four engines was found to depend on a single fuse!) Rendall was known to his many friends by the nickname of Flaps. Not that he ever got in a flap – and certainly not over the Rift Valley.

Incidents of this kind recurred, and came to be known as flame-outs. Flame-outs occurred only in tropical zones. Flying in the temperate zones of Europe, North Africa and the Middle East presented no problems. But the routes the aircraft were designed for, and on which we wanted to operate them, were our eastern and southern 'Empire' routes, all of which passed through tropical zones.

Although no pilot myself, I was anxious that the pilots knew that I shared their concern. Until the flame-out trouble was cured, there was to be no question of our putting the aircraft into passenger service. Training had to be carried out in the tropical as well as temperate zones, and it became necessary for us to pay 'danger money' to the crews under training. Having had sufficient aircraft delivered for flight training, I refused to accept any more aircraft until further notice; and I refused also to make any more progress payments in respect of the whole order for 33 aircraft. This caused the Bristol Aeroplane Company a great deal of concern and involved us all in an endless series of meetings with their chairman Sir Reginald Verdon-Smith, Peter Masefield, Dr A E Russell, Sir Alec Coryton and others. But I was determined not to budge until we were satisfied.

The Britannia's Proteus engines were originally intended for use in the abortive Princess flying boats. As the wing of a flying boat is in water spray when on the sea, the air intakes of a normal engine scoop up a lot of water on take-off and alighting. The engine designers had therefore arranged for it to take in air through a duct round the turbine to the back of the engine and feed it in forwards from behind. On test-beds and in temperate skies the engines ran perfectly well.

But the designers had unknowingly produced a highly efficient ice-making machine at altitude in certain tropical cu-nim cloud conditions. As the slushy ice particles taken in through the air intake quickly built up round the bend at the back, the engine became starved of air, and the flame went out. Out of cloud, warm air came in again, the ice melted, and it proved possible to relight the engine in flight. This was no laughing matter – very far from it.

In August 1956, the situation in the Middle East erupted over Egypt's claim to the Suez Canal. Prime Minister Anthony Eden decided to send troops to re-inforce our Cyprus bases. Our Britannia 102s were based at Hurn for training and were suitable for this purpose. They could each carry some 90 officers and men, and reach Nicosia non-stop. On Sunday, 5 August, I went to London Airport soon after 05.00 and was flown to Hurn in one of our light training aeroplanes. When I got there the troops were boarding and, punctually at 07.00, the first Britannia taxied out and took off. With turbine engines there was no need to run up each one at the start of the runway, as there had been with piston engines.

Britannia trooping operations to and from Cyprus continued without incident for the next two or three weeks. On 19 August I was able to join one of our Britannias returning empty to Hurn under the command of Capt Frank Taylor. This was the first flight of any length I had been able to make in a Britannia 102. It was a good aircraft and handled well in the air. But, in spite of having been nicknamed by Peter Masefield 'the Whispering Giant' because of its quiet take-off, the noise and vibration inside in flight seemed every bit as bad as in the piston-engined Argonaut.

As time passed we came under increasing pressure from the Bristol Aeroplane Company to take delivery of more aircraft and release more money. But we still were not satisfied that the modifications were foolproof, and would prevent ice forming in the bend at the back of the air-intakes in tropical zones. At one meeting to discuss delivery a top Bristol executive actually suggested that our pilots didn't want to get the aircraft into service quickly because they had a vested interest in continuing to receive 'danger money' while training. This slight on our pilots made me so annoyed that I broke off the meeting there and then. A couple of days later Reggie Verdon-Smith himself came to pour oil on troubled waters, assuring me that what had been said wasn't meant. It probably hadn't been – the person who said it had merely taken momentary leave of his senses.

Reports reaching us in August and September 1956 about the latest Bristol 'mods' seemed more encouraging. On 14 August, we made our first Britannia transatlantic flight (with no payload) from London to Montreal non-stop in 10 hours and 52 minutes. Then in September Walter Gibb of Bristol took a Britannia to Australia for demonstration. As there were to be test flights on the way, in monsoon conditions near Calcutta, our new chief of flight operations, Jim Weir, went with the aircraft too.

Back home at London Airport, the BOAC board were considering on Thursday, 13 September, how to respond to Bristol's pressures for further payments. Up to that time we had received no reports of anything untoward, beyond having been told that the Bristol demonstration flight to Australia was delayed at Singapore. We decided that we must meet Bristol's request to some extent. But later in the meeting a telephone call from Singapore was put through to me in the board room.

It was Jim Weir on the line. It was about seven in the evening in Singapore. Typically calm, he told me that at one point in the flight out of Calcutta all four engines were flamed-out at the same time. One after the other had gone out before any could be relighted. As the aircraft glided without power into warmer air, it proved possible to relight all four turbines one by one. But as he knew we were having a board meeting, he thought he ought to let me know that all the Bristol people in Singapore agreed that the engine modifications to date were wholly unsuccessful.

· I learned later that, out of Calcutta, Flaps Rendall had been in the left hand seat. As he laconically recorded in his log-book he had a situation in the monsoon where 'one engine was bumping, another autorelighting, a third being manually relit and the fourth feathered, all at the same time'. They had taken the aircraft back to Calcutta and talked matters over in the old Great Eastern Hotel which they had left a few hours earlier. Next day they set off again. By flying low, they reached Singapore without incident. Further flying was cancelled while Weir and Rendall discussed the problem at the Sea View Hotel with Walter Gibb and the senior Bristol Siddeley engine representatives who had been on board.

Well, that settled it. We reversed our earlier decision. Until Bristol's aero-engine people could guarantee that these things could not possibly happen, the board decided that there could be no question of taking more Britannias from Bristol, or of making more progress payments, or of putting the aircraft into passenger service.

Fortunately for Bristol, and for us, much was learned from that incident. The group of experts on board happened to be about the best there could have been to sort the problem out. Certainly, their personal experience of it in flight concentrated their minds wonderfully. By mid-November Reggie Verdon-Smith was able to tell me that they were sure they had solved the problem. Exhaustive flying tests showed that they were right. By the end of December the unrestricted Certificate of Airworthiness was restored, and we could plan for the start of services on 1 February 1957. Even so, this was over three years later than Bristol quoted when we had ordered these aircraft.

★   ★   ★   ★   ★

But the way ahead was still not clear. In the middle of November Douglas Tennant, the general secretary of the Merchant Navy and Airline Officers' Association (MNAOA), had warned me of serious trouble brewing: there was no work-station in the Britannia's cockpit for a flight engineer.

In the late 1940s and early 1950s the flight deck of a long-distance passenger airliner generally had work-stations for five people – two pilots, a navigating officer, a radio officer and a flight engineer. By about 1950 the radio officer became redundant, as the pilots were now able to talk to ground control and *vice-versa*. Soon afterwards navigating by taking sights became unnecessary over most routes: ground-to-air navigation facilities were developed apace and specialist navigating officers also became redundant.

The pilots had their own union, the British Air Line Pilots'

Association (BALPA); our flight engineers belonged to MNAOA. When the Britannia cockpit layout was originally settled with Bristols some years earlier, Whitney Straight believed that, when the aircraft went into service, it would no longer need a flight engineer. Consequently no provision was made for a flight engineer's work station, though the layout contained all necessary control panels and dials.

In 1956 my antennae had picked up indications of difficulties ahead in this respect. When I asked about it I was told it was only an inter-union squabble; it was simply that the MNAOA resented the prospect of aircraft flight-decks becoming the preserve of BALPA and the pilots alone. When Douglas Tennant came to see me on that November day of 1956, I realised that there was much more to it. He told me frankly that he didn't care a damn about a possible monopoly on the flight deck for BALPA, except that naturally he didn't want to lose members from his own union. His sole concern was with flight safety, which his members considered would not be as good without an engineer's station in the cockpit. They felt so strongly about this that they would go to great lengths to prevent that station from being abolished.

Jim Weir and Harold Spear were with me and heard what Douglas Tennant said. We had a long talk about it after he left. Jim Weir himself had never yet flown a four-engined airliner with no engineer officer on the flight deck and he would personally have preferred a different cockpit layout in this respect. But BALPA's official view was that they did not accept the MNAOA fear of lower safety standards.

I had to go to Southern Africa the following week for meetings in Johannesburg, Pretoria, Cape Town and Salisbury. I left the two of them to assess the relative merits of the two contentions, and to reach an agreement with the unions which would at least permit the aircraft to go into service as soon as possible after the flame-out problems had been cured.

On the way down and back I went forward as usual into the cockpit at various times and tried to judge the situation myself. But I was a layman, and didn't reach any conclusion. From observation, though, it did seem to me that the engineer was fully occupied during climb and letdown, and I wondered how the pilots would get on without him.

It was around this time that I started the practice of holding periodic meetings of captains as a means of improving communication between management and pilots. Of our 900 pilots we employed, some 300 would be at home on stand-off until their

A royal cabin in a BOAC DC-7C.   (British Airways)

A BOAC Comet 4, 1958.   (de Havilland)

With Sir George Edwards (centre) and Keith Granville (left) at the signing of
the contract for 35 VC10s, 14 January 1958.   *(British Airways)*

Capt A S M ('Flaps') Rendall, Flight Manager Britannia 102s and (later)
VC10s, on a VC10 flight deck, 1963.   *(British Airways)*

next tour of duty. If a quarter of these 300 attended I felt it would be well worthwhile.

What I said at those meetings helped, I believe, to keep our pilots in the picture about what the management of BOAC was doing and planning to achieve. To me the really valuable part was the longish informal buffet supper afterwards when I could move around among them as I pleased, trying to answer questions thrown at me and, more important, asking them what I wanted to know.

At one of these first captains' meetings in January 1957 I soon came to realise that the BALPA attitude over the Britannia cockpit was not supported by a number of senior pilots. Apart from the question of workload during climb and letdown, which I had noted, they wanted a flight engineer to diagnose troubles and explain them to the ground engineers at transit stops while the pilots were busy dealing with flight-planning for the next sector. This was very much in line with Jim Weir's view. (Whitney Straight had been years ahead of his time; avionic science was still in its infancy.) I felt I now knew where management would have to take its stand.

The official views of the two unions still differed, and there was no sign of give on either part. In this sort of conflict no one party will give way an inch until the very last moment. I reckoned that, if we were going to get the Britannia into service on the first of February, that last moment would be before dawn on Thursday 31 January. We needed the whole of that Thursday to make whatever last-minute alterations were agreed upon. Jim Weir, Harold Spear and I made our plans accordingly. In the meantime MNAOA were still saying that flight engineers would not fly as crew members without a proper work-station; BALPA were still saying that they would not fly with an engineer officer. The stalemate positions had not changed – and would not change until the final crunch.

On 30 January, talks were being held on and off all day between BOAC management and the two unions. The Government felt strongly, we were told, that nothing should prevent the Britannia being introduced into service on schedule, no matter who had to give way to ensure that.

In the afternoon, therefore, those directly involved were all called to a meeting at the Ministry of Labour in St James's Square by Sir Wilfred Neden, the Chief Industrial Commissioner. No progress was made by the early evening. At that stage Wilfred suggested that the management representatives should withdraw so that he could talk separately with each union. Our people were to remain on call, so that they could go back to the Ministry quickly if it seemed that there was a chance of reaching an acceptable decision. About six o'clock that evening Jim Weir and the management team moved to the boardroom we still retained in Stratton House, Piccadilly, and made that their headquarters for the night. I joined them at about half past seven.

Things dragged on late into the night. We did not like to go out for a meal in case we were called, so we refreshed ourselves at frequent intervals with sandwiches, beer and coffee. Nor did we want to get caught in the street by the press – there were a good many reporters around all night outside the Ministry of Labour. Fortunately, although the BOAC press officer was also in Stratton House, the press never cottoned on to the fact that BOAC management were there too for the night.

I have always liked to be direct and honest in talking to the press; but, in situations like this, with delicate industrial negotiations in progress, it is often best to avoid making off-the-cuff statements. If pressmen meet you you have to talk to them, otherwise you spoil your relations for all time. But it is only too easy, not being in the negotiations themselves, to let fall an unguarded word which, when reported back, could easily upset the talks at a tricky stage.

As the night dragged on into the small hours of 31 January, we were getting very little information from St James's Square. At one stage, the BALPA representatives asked if they could come and join us as they wanted to get out of the Ministry and had nowhere else to go. Chivalrous as ever, we agreed. They didn't want to talk shop, and we felt it wiser not to question them. At long last, at about 04.00, we were summoned. Wilfred Neden had a possible solution to put to us. He thought it best if I would hold myself in reserve in case he needed to bring me in later.

Before 05.00 that Thursday morning they were back. It seemed very good. BALPA accepted that an engineer work-station should be fitted on all Britannia flight decks as soon as practicable; the MNAOA would allow their engineer officer members to work from a temporary but securely fixed seat behind the captain and the first officer.

We all wanted to know, of course, whether such a temporary arrangement was physically possible. Could the aircraft earmarked for the inaugural service be modified during the Thursday now beginning, ready for take-off at noon on the Friday? Charles Abell, who had remained with me at Stratton House, said that it could be done. I phoned our agreement through to Wilfred Neden. At about 05.30 we all dispersed to our various homes, except for Charles Abell who had to go to the airport and arrange for the necessary modification work.

Thus, at long last, all was now set for the inauguration of the Britannia 102 into passenger service at noon on Friday 1 February 1957, on the route from London to Johannesburg. Reggie Verdon-Smith, Bristol's chairman, met me at London Airport about eleven o'clock and, after the usual business of seeing the press and having photographs taken, we boarded the aircraft together to make the round trip to South Africa and back. It was a good moment for both of us, after so many trials and setbacks.

My pocket diary tells me that our flight time to Rome was two hours and fifty-five minutes, chock to chock. That was half an hour slower than the Comet 1 had achieved some five years earlier, but more than an hour faster than a piston-engined aircraft. The sector from Rome to Khartoum was a longish one by the standards of those days, and we didn't reach the Sudanese capital till after midnight local time.

On the way I had begun to feel distinctly unwell. Before descent into Khartoum I felt considerable pain in my middle so I did not go ashore (it is strange how the language of the sea and flying boats stayed with landplanes) but remained on board.

Before the aircraft took off again I was in such discomfort that I was persuaded to be off-loaded (without delaying the aircraft to collect my baggage from its hold) and taken to the house of our manager in the Sudan – Dick Cole, whom I had first met when I flew to Alexandria in a flying boat in 1950.

By next daylight the pain had gone, but Dick insisted on calling in the local doctor BOAC retained at Khartoum. She pooh-poohed my suggestion of 'flu, and thought that, in view of my colour (which I had not noticed) I might well have jaundice or something like that; she recommended me not to stay and have treatment in Khartoum but to get back to London as soon as possible.

This was welcome advice. It meant that I could rejoin Reggie Verdon-Smith and the Britannia next day, Sunday, on its way back north. I should then get in to London on the Monday morning with the first northbound Britannia service as originally planned.

Sunday afternoon came and the Coles took me to the airport well before the Britannia was due to arrive under the command of Capt Tommy Farnsworth, with Reggie Verdon-Smith and Alec Coryton on board. We took off for Rome, which we transitted at first light, and London.

Once there, I was driven home as soon as I could escape the attentions of the press, and went straight to bed. Tests showed that I was suffering from gallstones, which mercifully would release themselves after a while and pass on their way. A week later I was operated on for removal of my gallbladder by Mr Denis Ellison Nash of Barts. I was back home early in March but had to have a longish period of convalescence. In fact, I could not get back to work again until the Tuesday after Easter, in mid-April.

Quite a few things had been developing during my absence, which I needed to catch up with urgently. But at least I had been able to see both our new types of aircraft, the DC-7C and the Britannia 102, successfully brought into service.

★   ★   ★   ★   ★

In the latter part of 1956 we had been thinking about new aircraft for routes other than the North Atlantic. For these so-called Empire routes we were not to be allowed any hard currency, despite what had been said at my meeting with Harold Macmillan. We had to get what we needed from the British aircraft industry. We already had 19 Comet 4s on order from de Havilland for delivery starting in October 1958, and with the 15 Boeing 707s now ordered for delivery in 1960, that made a total of 34 jet aircraft. We estimated, however, that we should require another 26 jets, making 60 in all, by the time the Britannia turboprops became outmoded in the 1960s.

We looked round to see what might be available. There was nothing building in Britain except the Comet 4. Its range was not long enough and its operating costs were not low enough for us to order more. There was therefore no possibility of ordering a proved aircraft, as we could have done in America. But de Havilland had a larger Comet, called the Comet 5, on the drawing board. Handley Page had a civil version of the Victor bomber, again only on the drawing board. And Vickers-Armstrongs, who were in Harold Watkinson's Parliamentary constituency of Woking, had a proposal for a passenger jet aircraft about the size of the Boeing 707.

Two of the three fell out of the running quite soon. To begin with, the Handley Page Victor's tail unit was suspect, in Alan Campbell Orde's judgment; and we in BOAC would not touch it. Then, at a meeting in the House of Commons set up jointly by the Minister of Supply and the Minister of Transport and Civil Aviation, Aubrey Burke of de Havilland told us all that they could not go ahead with the Comet 5 without firm orders for 50 – an assurance they knew we could not give – and that they were therefore withdrawing the project. That left us with Vickers Armstrongs.

We told Vickers and the Ministry of Supply that we wanted an English version of the Boeing 707, which had better economics than any other aircraft then being built or planned. Word came from on high – reputedly from the Cabinet – that the British industry must not demean itself by merely copying an American design; we had first-class designers of our own and ought to be able to produce something better. In any case, the Ministry of Supply added, there were very few airfields on the 'Empire' routes with runways long enough for the Boeing 707; it would therefore be much better, surely, for Britain to design an aircraft with a shorter take-off run than the Boeing.

Well, this set off a good argument. Alan Campbell Orde pointed out that our competitors would certainly devise ways of operating the Boeing 707 off shorter runways – for instance, by reduced fuel uplift and shorter sectors out of particular airports. In any case, we all thought it a safe bet that countries on the main world air routes would soon enlarge their airfields and runways to receive the new American jets – with the help, if necessary, of American finance. This in fact happened all round the world in the next four or five years.

Towards the end of 1956, we were forced to break away once and for all from the outdated concept that the 'Empire' routes needed only medium-range aircraft. At that time we were having great difficulty with Air-India and the Indian Government. With Boeing 707s coming on to the Atlantic in 1958 or thereabouts, J R D Tata, Air-India's dynamic chairman, asked Britain for fifth freedom traffic rights beyond London to New York. Not unnaturally, we demurred. They retorted by reminding us that we enjoyed many fifth freedom traffic rights east of India, and threatened to withdraw all our landing rights on routes to and from Australia and the Far East. This issue was eventually settled by bartering. But it was a serious issue, and we included in our specification to Vickers the capability to fly non-stop with a full load from Singapore to Karachi (that is, against the prevailing winds) without having to land in India.

So George Edwards had to produce something that was not a Boeing 707 but had performance characteristics that were not a whit less good. As he was to say later: 'If you know that the American design is bloody good, probably the best of which present knowledge is capable; and you are told you have got to design something different, what on earth can you do but put the engines in a different place?' Which is what he did. After all, the Caravelle's twin engines at the tail of the aircraft had been pretty successful, even if its unsilenced engines made it very noisy to people on the ground.

The new Vickers design needed four engines – the Caravelle was only a short-range aircraft. And it was a very different problem to mount four engines at the rear of the aircraft, compared with only two. At the rear, all four engines have to be in line abreast – two on each side of the fuselage. Engines of the power required are very heavy, and this in turn meant that the cantilever or crossmember had to be made of steel – a weight penalty of some 12,000 lbs, which the aircraft had to carry all its life. But that was not all. Because of the greater weight in the tail, the wings and fuselage had to be strengthened; this added a further 5,000 lbs and brought the total weight penalty up to about eight tons.

But when we received the outline specification and performance figures from Vickers at the end of the year, we found that there were offsetting advantages to compensate in part for the tail-heavy nature of the aircraft – by now known as the VC10. Its speed on take-off and approach over the airport 'fence' was some 20 knots less than that of the Boeing 707. This was a material consideration from the point of view of flight safety, since the high take-off and landing speeds of the Boeing had been causing us and the Air Registration Board some concern. With its engines at the tail, too, the VC10 would be quieter for the passengers inside it. And, as we were to learn with experience, there was something in George Edwards' design of the aircraft that gave its passengers a very comfortable ride.

Inevitably, the eight ton weight penalty worked its way through into higher costs per passenger-mile – or per ton-mile, the accepted unit of cost measurement in the airline world. On figures we worked out jointly with both Vickers and the Ministry of Supply, VC10 direct operating costs would be at best 14 old pence per ton-mile compared with some 12 pence for the Boeing 707 – some 17 per cent higher.

We therefore re-stated our desire for an English version of the Boeing 707 design. Would it not be possible to negotiate an agreement with Boeing which would enable Vickers to manufacture the 707 in England under licence? It seemed that there was as much aversion in high places to adopting an American design as to copying it.

The Ministry of Supply, claiming support from the Royal Aircraft Establishment at Farnborough, would not accept Boeing's performance claims, and maintained that our estimate of the 707's operating costs were far too low. We believed we knew differently, on the basis of information coming to us from Boeing and our long experience of dealing with them. But we could not prove it at the time.

The Ministry contended that the apparent advantage of 17 per cent which the Boeing 707 seemed to have in lower direct operating costs would disappear if their performance claims were not achieved. But it was a big 'if'. We contended that, while the VC10 was still paper, the 707 prototype had already been flying for more than two years. We added that the performance of the Vickers VC10 could equally fall short of claims.

However one looked at it, the VC10 had that built-in weight penalty, created by the different siting of the engines, which nothing could remove. In the middle of all this argument I was removed from the scene by that gallbladder of mine which had to be removed.

When I returned to work in April 1957, I found a *fait accompli*. Pops d'Erlanger on behalf of BOAC had agreed with the Ministers of Supply and of Transport and Civil Aviation, and with Vickers, that we would order 35 VC10s off the drawing board – nine more than we estimated we might need. One might ask why the BOAC board approved of what their chairman had done; but by then the agreement had the seal of Cabinet approval, and nothing could alter that.

Thirty-five was said to be the smallest order Vickers would take to set up a production line; and even then, from the drawing board to the earliest possible first delivery would be more than six years – a far longer period ahead than any other airline in the world had to order its aircraft.

I have always felt that Britain lost a remarkable opportunity at that time by insisting on developing an aircraft of different design on its own. Aerodynamically speaking, in the state of the art at that time, the optimum design for a long-range aircraft had already been achieved in America. Had Vickers negotiated an agreement to build the Boeing 707 under licence in this country, Britain would have acquired the capability to build long-range aircraft and its aircraft industry assured of substantial work for 20 years to come. British-built 707's could have been sold readily to most Commonwealth countries interested in long-range aircraft – and to others besides. All ended up buying American-built ones.

Moreover these British-built 707s would probably all have been equipped with Rolls-Royce engines. Admittedly, Vickers would have lost design office work for the VC10. But that loss could have been offset by the gain to Britain in designing short- to medium-range aircraft – in which we have specialised – and in our turn granting the American industry licences to build them. In the event, because we lost the opportunity to build 707s under licence, when de Havilland produced the Trident design Boeing went ahead on their own and produced a virtual spit-image of it in the shape of the 727.

But, in April 1957, we were committed up to the hilt by

d'Erlanger's agreement with Vickers and the two Ministers concerned.

★　　★　　★　　★　　★

Throughout 1957 we continued to be plagued by Britannia troubles. We had started services with the 102 to Australia in March, only a month after putting it into service to South Africa. On the route to Sydney it earned a very bad name for irregularity and unpunctuality due to repeated mechanical troubles. By August, Charles Abell reported that certain provisos we had made in accepting the aircraft from Bristol at the end of 1956 had not been met.

We had stipulated (a) that we should never encounter engine damage through ice ingestion so that it was necessary to shut down engines in the air; (b) that the engine relighting system provided by the glowplugs would never require manual operation by the crew; and (c) that the aircraft could be used over all our routes without temperature or altitude limitations.

In Capt Rendall's absence his deputy, Capt Trevor Marsden, held a meeting of pilots to consider the matter. It was agreed that, until mid-October, we must accept a height limitation and operate at low level between Karachi and Hong Kong, and between Karachi and Darwin; after mid-October, operations on all sectors would have to be reviewed in the light of experience and information gained from the Burnley tunnel.

Meanwhile, Flaps Rendall re-assured his pilots that 'the whole matter is being pursued at the highest possible level. The Prime Minister has asked to be kept informed at short intervals of how things develop, and to this end a combined report by MOS, MTCA, BAC[1] and BOAC is submitted twice every week to the Minister of Transport and Civil Aviation and the Minister of Supply.'

The long-range Britannia 312 also ran into trouble, but of a different kind, after a promising start. At the end of June 1957 our first 312, G-AOVA, made the first ever non-stop flight from London to Vancouver, taking 14 hours 40 minutes to cover the distance of 5,100 miles. But on a proving flight which took off at 24.00 hours on Friday, 27 September, our second aircraft, G-AOVB, had two engines fail almost simultaneously after flying for about four minutes in cloud at altitude. Bristols thought that the quenching effect of the moisture in cloud caused a contraction in the compressor casing which resulted in the stator blades rubbing on the

---

[1]Ministry of Supply, Ministry of Transport and Civil Aviation, Bristol Aeroplane Co.

spaces between the rotor blades and causing destruction. This had not happened in the 102 engine; so what had gone wrong? It transpired that the stator blades in the 312 engine were made of a different material, which expanded more under heat.

No other airline in the world was liable to encounter such snags in aircraft recently delivered by the manufacturers. The matter was so serious – particularly against the background of the 102's history – that I felt I had to report personally to the Minister, Harold Watkinson. Then on Tuesday, 8 October, I was asked to receive a deputation from BALPA consisting of Capt Merrifield, their chairman, and Capt Wellwood of BOAC. Our pilots were now concerned about flying the 102 in service, let alone the 312 under training. We tried to reassure them with information not yet in their possession. Next day Flaps Rendall wrote to all his flight deck staff in the Britannia 102 fleet, explaining what had happened in the 312 engines and assuring them that it could not occur in the 102 engine.

Matthew Slattery had only recently joined the board of Bristols, and he brought a breath of fresh air into it all. Bristol's Aero-Engine division ran tests at full take-off power, with water injected at a rate several times greater than could be expected in the tropics. It seemed incredible to us that Bristol had not run such tests many months before, and had left us, the first operator, to discover the defect ourselves. That was a part of the price we had to pay – in contrast to all other airlines – for carrying the responsibility of proving British-built aircraft for service. We have never received thanks or financial compensation.

At long last the Britannia 102 improved its performance in service, and there was no longer any question of grounding it. Modifications were made to the 312 engine to increase the clearance of the stator blades. To test their effectiveness Jim Weir and Walter Gibb took an aircraft out to Singapore again. The final test flight on 30 November lasted 7 hours 38 minutes, starting from and returning to Singapore. After evaluating its results Walter Gibb took the aircraft on to Sydney to demonstrate it to Qantas, while Jim Weir returned to London Airport and reported that all was well. I in turn reported this to the Minister. And on 19 December 1957 we put the Britannia 312 into service on the route between London and New York. But, being delivered years late by Bristol it was only 10 months ahead of straight-jet services on the same route. For all that, it was the first British-built aircraft ever to fly the North Atlantic in commercial airline service.

Deliveries continued to be made by Bristol throughout 1958, being completed on the last day of that year. By March 1959, all 33 of them (eighteen 312s and fifteen 102s) had been put into service.

In the financial year to March 1960, the 33 Britannias provided some 58 per cent of our total capacity and the DC-7Cs a further 18 per cent in non-stop services across the Atlantic. Thus these two propeller aircraft produced three-quarters of our total output. All Stratocruisers were retired from service by May 1959 and our last Argonaut service was in April 1960 – truly the end of an era.

★   ★   ★   ★   ★

As we moved through the first half of 1958, reports on the Comet 4 from Hatfield were more and more encouraging. In the light of the Comet 1 explosions, its airframe had been submitted to rigorous static tests under the supervision of the RAE at Farnborough. It passed satisfactorily. In other respects, too, production was well up to schedule and it looked as though de Havilland would repeat its 1952 performance and deliver the aircraft on time.

But then we ran into difficulty over the Comet 4 with the authorities in New York, who would not authorise us to land the aircraft because of the noise it was alleged to create. We produced evidence that the noise level in 'perceived noise decibels' was not materially higher than that of large piston-engined aircraft and was lower than that of the French Caravelle. But the Caravelle had never flown in New York, which was unimpressed by that particular evidence. We brought as much pressure to bear on the Port of New York Authority as we could, through the Ministry in London and the British Embassy in Washington. As a first stage we succeeded in getting approval for Comet 4 training flights but not – repeat not, they emphasised – for commercial service flights.

PONYA's willingness to meet us to this extent was, I feel, greatly influenced by the fact that Pan American Airways were also hoping to put the new Boeing 707 jet into service in the autumn of 1958. Americans would not stand in the way of PanAm or a Boeing product. The Port Authority in New York also feared that, if they were too difficult, Pan American might encounter retaliatory action from London. The New York authorities were also aware that the jets – both Comet and Boeing – would be welcome at Boston.

I had had my first flight in a Boeing 707 in January 1958. I was in Seattle with Gilbert Lee on my way to New Zealand and Australia. That flight was in fact the first 707 flight ever made with other than test crews and engineers on board. It was laid on for the benefit of Bruno Velani and his colleagues from Alitalia, to whom Boeing were trying to sell 707s; but as I was visiting Seattle at the time,

Wellwood Beall invited us to go for the ride, along with Robbie Trench-Thompson, our manager United States.

The aircraft was naturally full of recording instruments and test equipment. 'Tex' Johnson, Boeing's chief test pilot, was in command and submitted us to the experience of a high-altitude stall, whereat the aircraft started behaving like a bucking bronco reminiscent of his native Texas. The aircraft's performance was most impressive. Thinking about New York's reluctance to admit the Comet 4 on noise grounds, I was certain they would never keep the Boeing out. They would be bound to give way on our Comet 4 application in due course – but probably not until the fifty-ninth minute of the eleventh hour. So we went ahead full speed with our Comet 4 pre-service flight-training and other preparations as though there were no obstacles in our path.

In early September 1958 I was in Hong Kong with Ross Stainton, by now our general manager eastern routes, to review our arrangements with Jardine Matheson & Co, our sales and handling agents there, and to be present at the opening of the new airport runway by the Governor, Sir Robert ('Robin') Black. The old runway at Kai Tak airport on the mainland was extremely restrictive. In one direction it headed straight into the mountains, though at some distance. The new runway, capable of taking the largest jets, was a most imaginative project. It was built out into the harbour for virtually the whole of its length in a line from Kowloon towards The Gap, the narrows to the south-east between the island of Hong Kong and the mainland. The climax of the opening ceremony on 12 September was the flypast by the Governor in Comet 4 G-APDA, which John Cunningham had taken out to the Far East for the overseas flight experience required by the Air Registration Board for airworthiness certification.

I returned with John Cunningham to London in that aircraft, and the flight showed off the Comet 4's capabilities to perfection. It was two days later – the fourteenth of September – and we took off from Hong Kong at 07.00 as the sun came up over the horizon. We flew non-stop to Bombay, where we spent an hour refuelling. We then flew on to Cairo, where we again took an hour to refuel and complete the inevitable formalities. From there we flew right through to Hatfield, and arrived at 17.30 BST in the light of the same day's sun – the sun we had seen rise over Hong Kong only 18½ hours before, when we had been 7,295 miles away

John Cunningham took the aircraft off for more overseas flight experience, and worked off another 50 hours flying round Canada, Central and South America and back by way of New York on 27

September. Aubrey Burke told me that de Havilland would be delivering our first aircraft on Tuesday 30 September, ahead of schedule. When the day arrived, de Havilland delivered not just one aircraft but two – a great achievement.

I was already determined to get to New York in our first aircraft as soon as possible. I wanted to see what I could achieve with the Port Authority with a BOAC Comet 4 actually sitting on the ground in New York – previous Comet 4 visits having been made with aircraft still belonging to de Havilland. The Ministry did not rate very high my chances of success in getting early PONYA permission for scheduled public services, but I decided to go all the same. Aubrey Burke and Jim Weir would come with me.

On the Wednesday we alerted the press and took them across on Thursday, 2 October. For their purpose we dubbed our westbound training flight to New York that day a pre-inaugural flight. Next morning, I met the Port Authority. After the meeting, there was nothing to do but return to our office on Fifth Avenue, and try to possess ourselves in patience until we heard the results.

On the Thursday before leaving my home in Esher, I conceived the idea that, as we now had two aircraft, we could inaugurate the world's first transatlantic jet service with a flight in both directions on the same day, passing one another in mid-Atlantic. Pops d'Erlanger liked the idea, and said he would accompany the westbound flight.

While waiting in New York on the Friday for the Port Authority decision I was turning over in my mind the organising complexities of a double inaugural, when suddenly, about 5 o'clock, word came that a letter was on the way. It was 10 o'clock at night in London. There was still time to alert them for a possible flight next day.

Shortly afterwards, waving the Authority's letter in my hand, I stood on a chair in the Speedbird Club and told everybody that we could at last start New York services with the Comet 4 – and would do so next morning.

After the initial excitement we had to get down to work preparing for the service to leave New York in the morning. The DC-7C and the Britannia 312 still had to operate overnight eastbound because of their long flight times. Only the jets made it possible to schedule daytime flights from west to east. If we were to leave early from Idlewild (as Kennedy Airport was then called) and if the flight took no more than 6½ hours, we could reach London shortly before dark.

Operationally, there was no problem. The aircraft in New York was fully serviceable, as was its sister aircraft in London, and both crews were on standby.

So, on Saturday, 4 October, 1958, BOAC made aviation history by operating the first transatlantic jet service ever – and, to cap it, both ways on the same day. Capt Tom Stoney, our Comet flight manager, in command eastbound, took the aircraft up to 1,850 ft while still inside the perimeter fence of the airport, at which point he throttled back to reduce the noise level within limits acceptable to the authorities.

Out over the Atlantic we passed the other aircraft, out of sight, with Pops d'Erlanger on board and Capt Roy Millichap in command. Our eastbound flight to London took only 6 hours 12 minutes, thanks to a tailwind of 92 mph and the priority given us by Air Traffic Control over the UK. The aircraft glided in to a beautiful touch-down. A warm welcome was given us on the tarmac, and it gave me a particular glow of pleasure to find Miles Thomas among those who had come to greet us.

Not until nearly three weeks later were Pan American able to introduce their own transatlantic jet service with their newly delivered Boeing 707. Our team had scored another BOAC first.

9 The Importance of Being in Earnest

In the 1970s we were all brought face to face with a major change in the industrial balance of power. The 'workers' came to appreciate what enormous power they had through their ability to stop working without the risk of being fired. They could literally bring a works, a company, or an industry to a standstill by simply not working. By contrast, management are powerless to enforce their wishes because in general they can no longer terminate the employment of a worker for disciplinary reasons.

Modern management, understandably, has been slow to admit the change. Too many still assume that, because they own the means of production or because they possess professional skills, they can tell those who actually do the work what to do and have their instructions obeyed without question. But with this latest shift in the balance of power those who actually do the work will only do what they are told if they believe it to be right and in their own interests.

Management has got to change, therefore, and adapt itself to the new circumstances in which, like it or not, it has to work. It will have to recognise that its main function is that of human leadership, and that it may have to devote much more time and thought to the practice of this art than to any of the professional techniques from which it formerly drew its authority.

I know of first-class engineers and scientists who regard this as a great waste of their valuable time. So it is, in one way. But in this day and age the leadership of people in industrial groups is every bit as important as the planning and devising of technical processes or the designing of a new product, and in many cases more so. It is no use being a good manager technically if you cannot induce people to work together willingly to produce your product or service. Managers at all levels have to accept that a main part, if not *the* main part, of their job is to lead and inspire those they are managing.

I had had to come to terms some thirty years ago with a forerunner of this shift in the balance of industrial power. Under the 1946 Act which nationalised BOAC and BEA, a National Joint Council for Civil Air Transport was established, and management was obliged to bring to this industry-wide Council all disputes affecting their employees. The unions had equal standing in the Council with management.

When faced in 1948 with the necessity to reduce staff by one in three, from 24,000 to about 16,000, Miles Thomas felt the problem to be so special to BOAC, without parallel in BEA or the independent airlines, that he started the practice of personal monthly meetings with the union side of the National Joint Council. This was continued after the staff-reduction programme to keep the unions informed of our plans for the development of the airline.

I found the practice so valuable that I continued it after Miles Thomas left in 1956. In our dire straits after the Comet 1 disasters, it was more than ever necessary for management to have the confidence and full support of the unions in the measures we were taking to put BOAC back again in the front rank of the world's airlines.

★　　★　　★　　★　　★

I found irksome our inability to get to grips with the problem of our high engineering (aircraft maintenance) costs. Maintenance was then costing us almost a quarter of total expenditure. Soon after I was appointed managing director in May 1956 our chief engineer, on whom I was dependent in this respect – Charles Abell – had to go into hospital for major surgery, and his recovery took a long time. Had I tried to tackle this problem before he returned I should have got nowhere, because his chief lieutenants and indeed most of our engineering management could not see or would not admit that there was much of a problem. And then I was out of action early in 1957 to have my gall-bladder removed.

But before that I was able to make good headway in one specialised field, that of engine overhaul. In terms of money and manpower, engines then accounted for one-fifth of an aircraft's maintenance. BOAC's engine overhaul factory had been located since 1939 in the Treforest Trading Estate in South Wales, as part of the Government's plan to bring work back to the depressed areas after the appalling unemployment in the Welsh valleys in the 1920s and 1930s.

Piston engines needed stripping down and completely overhauling after only three or four hundred hours. In 1956 we used up some 650,000 engine hours a year. We thus had a planned throughput at Treforest of some 2,000 engines a year. But inevitably there were more to overhaul than that. Because piston engines are reciprocating in type and subject to continuous vibration in use, engines could break down anywhere; and then had to be ferried home to Britain and taken to Treforest.

With the coming of the gas turbine engine for jet aircraft such as the Comet and turboprop aircraft such as the Viscount and the Britannia, fewer engine overhauls were needed. For one thing jet aircraft travelled faster and covered distances in fewer hours. On top of that, turbine engines were virtually free of vibration – apart from that produced by the propellers in turboprop aircraft – and there was already some evidence that turbine engines could safely run at least twice the hours of a piston engine without overhaul. The work available at Treforest looked like being cut by two-thirds before long.

This would have serious consequences for our skilled employees at Treforest. Something must be done to make good the shortfall in work. Control of our own spare engines and the rate at which they were overhauled was very important to us. It was essential to keep Treforest going as our engine overhaul factory. And by the early 1960s the expansion of our services would bring a lot more work to Treforest. So we had to bridge the five year gap that lay ahead.

It was basically a question of attracting other engine-overhaul business. During this period, and indeed for long afterwards, I used to fly to Cardiff at least once a month in one of our training Doves to encourage and discuss plans with Charles McGibbon and the management and shop stewards at Treforest.

We won through by securing a good deal of business from the RAF and from other airlines. With the prospect of an assured volume of business to cover the gap, our shop stewards gave us all possible help. They believed in what we were doing. By 1957 we had improved our methods of working, and the time taken for an engine overhaul was almost halved; costs per overhaul began steadily to come down, and engine reliability slowly but surely improved

★   ★   ★   ★   ★

Charles Abell returned to work in the spring of 1957. At last we had a chance to find the reasons for the high level of our aircraft maintenance costs. But even Charles Abell himself was not all that convinced that there was a real problem. This was the first act of conversion I had to undertake.

I set out to show him that, even though our methods of aircraft maintenance had proved successful in the past, the comparable costs published by other airlines of similar type or scale indicated that the methods they were using cost them far less than ours cost us; and yet their standard of operation was as high as ours. He agreed with me that we must find out how other airlines had succeeded in bringing down costs without lowering safety standards.

I knew well by now, from my knowledge of the airline industry, that other airlines would probably be only too willing to show us the whole of their maintenance methods as well as their detailed costings. One of the more remarkable things about the world airline industry, despite its inherent commercial competition, is its strong feeling of comradeship and technical collaboration, born of the fact that flying is an occupation not without risk and that all knowledge and experience in reducing that risk should be shared. We decided to approach the Royal Dutch Airline (KLM), Pan American World Airways, and United Air Lines of Chicago. The latter was the largest and one of the most efficient of the American domestics.

At my next monthly meeting with the union members of the National Joint Council, I explained the problem frankly, told them what our objective was, and how we were trying to achieve it. At the same time, I said, I thought we should be able to absorb through natural wastage and expansion any surplus staff that the enquiry might reveal we were carrying. The news was well received, but Ian Mikardo – representing Asset, the Association of Supervisory Staffs and Executive Technicians and forerunner of ASTMS – asked 'whether we could include two or three shop stewards in the team. If we could, he said, the men on the shop floor would not feel that this was just another management exercise; they would feel themselves a part of it. That would make it far easier afterwards to implement whatever changes it was agreed were necessary.

This was a good point. And in anything like normal circumstances I would have been only too glad to arrange it. But circumstances were not normal, in the sense that our engineering management was not yet convinced that we had a problem. I wanted the management team to have open minds when they visited the other three airlines, so that they would readily take in any new ideas. To include shop stewards in the team at this stage would have the effect of making the managers close their minds in self-defence. The first and essential step was to let the managers convince themselves that their own methods could be improved; unless they themselves were converted, we would not make progress.

So I said that I felt it inappropriate to include shop stewards in this particular instance, and I gave my reasons. My refusal caused a temporary raising of the temperature in the relations between BOAC and the trade unions, but it did not come to an open breach.

It was essential to secure the co-operation of the unions if we were ever going to get anywhere, because in aircraft maintenance there are almost limitless possibilities for inter-union demarcation disputes. So I decided to have a frank talk with Ian Mikardo, while not doing anything that might be regarded as letting management down. A difficult man to deal with, and a management consultant before entering politics, I felt he could be led to see reason. On 5 June 1957, and again some five weeks later, I met him privately. I said that I accepted his point entirely about the advantage of a joint team. But we were not ready for it yet; after all, he knew perfectly well that management were not perfect, any more than anyone else. We needed his help in making BOAC a more efficient airline, and for this to happen management must be allowed to convince themselves first of any shortcomings. Would he help? Understandably, he hesitated. But at our second meeting we agreed on a formula: the first visits to other airlines would be made by managers only, but we would include shop stewards on any later return visits to elaborate on first impressions.

This was the green light I wanted. Charles Abell had received friendly and welcoming responses from all three airlines we had approached; and his investigating team, led by our chief planning engineer, Harry Pearn, was on its way as soon as possible.

The team got on with its work quickly and reported on 16 December 1957. Charles Abell brought me the report and said: 'Well, here it is, sir. And I think I ought to offer you my resignation.' 'No, Charles,' I replied, before I had even read it. 'That's not what I want. I don't want your resignation. I want you to put matters right, and I know you can do it. As soon as I have studied the report, we will talk about how you and I are going to handle this situation.'

The team consisted of high level people in our engineering department. In addition to Harry Pearn, it included our chief inspector, assistant supplies controller, senior technical officer (Argonaut/DC-7C Fleet) and engineering manager (Constellation Fleet). What they reported was not likely to be critical of their own department unless they were really convinced.

Their findings were unanimous. The cost of maintaining the corporation's fleet was indeed substantially higher than that of the other three airlines. Our high costs arose mainly from fundamental defects in the engineering department's organisation, practices and procedures; in fact, the BOAC engineering department employed about three times the staff per aircraft or per flying hour as the airlines visited – including about four times the supervisors and six times the inspectors.

What a shattering report! And how right we had been not to have shop stewards in this first investigating team; if they had been included management could not have come so clean. Although the report was more damning than even I had expected, it did not shake my belief that Charles Abell was the person to put things right.

So far the investigating team had not had time to do more than collect and compare facts. But they had established that the way in which the other three airlines organised their aircraft maintenance was very different from ours. We were still governed by history, going back to the time when there was no room at London Airport for all our aircraft – with flying boats at Hamble, Stratocruisers at Filton, Hermes at Hurn, Argonauts at London Airport and so on. Each base had to maintain its own aircraft, so that our engineering was managed in separate small units – each with only ten or twenty aircraft. Each fleet had to carry its own reserve of manpower to deal with crises, holidays, peak workloads and so on. By contrast, KLM were fully centralised at Schiphol, United Air Lines at Chicago, and Pan American at New York and Miami; and all three treated their different aircraft types as one big fleet. The economies of scale were very impressive.

The other airlines had been able, because of centralisation, to separate 'engineering' from 'production' – to separate the determination of overhaul and maintenance standards from the production process of preparing aircraft for service. Moreover, they had organised inspection so that much of it was done by licensed supervisors. This reduced the number of inspectors.

The investigating team had returned convinced. Now Charles Abell and his people had to implement their report. This would require the willing co-operation of the staff. Inevitably it would involve lengthy and delicate negotiations with the unions. The whole operation was bristling with potential trouble over demarcation lines between unions. Moreover, as soon as the unions knew the tenor of this first report, which Charles Abell and I had promised them they would see, they would be sensitive to redundancy and could well block any changes we wanted to make.

Understandably, I was getting impatient. We were not getting on with things, being held back by all the talking. I sometimes wondered whether to impose an arbitrary cut on the engineering department's budgeted expenditure and manpower. But this would have produced a head-on collision with the unions in the National Joint Council and led to hardened defensive attitudes which would have taken far longer to break down. The safety of our passengers and crew was at stake. Cost savings would have to take second place and could be achieved only when agreement had been reached with the unions and the engineering department was satisfied with safety standards.

★   ★   ★   ★   ★

Only a week after we had successfully put the Comet 4 into service in October 1958, all our maintenance staff at London Airport came out on strike and our services came to a standstill. Underlying it all was a groundswell of resistance to our intended changes. The shop stewards seemed uncertain of the attitude of their union leaders, and wanted to test management determination to carry its proposals through.

At that moment too there was another element in the situation – the composition of the shop stewards committee. Of its seventeen members, fourteen were known to be card-carrying members of the Communist Party. If, as many believed, the Communist Party was set on disrupting Britain's civil air communications, they were well placed to do so at London Airport. There were a number of relatively minor issues to be exploited at the expense of management, which would conceal the underlying purpose.

At mass meetings outside our hangars they could be sure of good press, radio and television coverage. The media had representatives based full-time at London Airport for interviewing arriving or departing notables. Shop stewards, like many people, welcome the limelight that publicity brings. It is almost always one-sided, because a responsible management is seldom free to speak publicly during a dispute. And the resulting shop stewards' prestige makes the task of national union officers very difficult when they try to persuade a mass meeting back to work.

Because human relations are so intricate, every now and then a situation will build up in which confrontation with shop stewards is unavoidable. During the previous two years we had had a number of unofficial stoppages in the engineering department. Each time we had been on weak ground, and it had not been possible to take a stand. At some point, though, we would have to show that shop stewards did not always win. Those who stopped work would have to go back to work with nothing to show for it.

I remember talking about such a situation with Sir William Lyons, then chairman of Jaguar Cars. He had had his fair share of labour troubles. We agreed that management's worst mistake would be a trial of strength with shop stewards without being absolutely sure of winning. It is a question of choosing your ground very carefully when you decide the time is ripe for a showdown.

Such a situation had in fact opened up in September 1958. We had a good issue to take a stand on, even though it would mean postponing the Comet 4's introduction into service. Alas, word came from 10 Downing Street, reputedly from the Prime Minister himself, that nothing, repeat nothing, was to be allowed to delay the start of Comet 4 services or to take the shine off this great British achievement. I couldn't help being personally sympathetic to this order, embarrassing though it was to have to give way when we were on good ground. But it's an ill-wind that blows nobody any good. We got the Comet 4 quickly into service – the first airline in the world to operate jet services across the Atlantic.

The shop stewards were not to know that we were under orders from Downing Street; they thought we were a weak management. It soon appeared that their heads had been turned. Before mid-October they slapped in another claim, this time for night-shift overtime pay. But their unions did not support them; and at last we were free to stand our ground.

In the first two or three days of the stoppage Jim Matthews, one of the most responsible trade union leaders, urged a mass meeting at the airport to go back to work. He was shouted down; and Sid Maitland, the chairman of the Shop Stewards' Committee, promptly got a motion carried to continue the strike. But after about a week, the men returned to work without having gained anything at all.

The only sop offered to them by the Ministry of Labour's conciliator, which we welcomed, was a Government Court of Inquiry into the dispute – with the usual stipulation that there should be no victimisation by management. The Court, presided over by Professor D T Jack, found that the strike was unconstitutional; and among other things urged the trade union side and the employers' side of the National Joint Council to review its machinery and re-establish its authority at the airport.

★   ★   ★   ★   ★

Thus, at long last, in January 1959, we were in the clear to launch the grand attack on our aircraft maintenance costs.

In July 1959, however, BOAC was sharply criticised for the time taken to improve engineering productivity. The House of Commons' Select Committee on Nationalised Industries, with Sir Toby Low (now Lord Aldington) in the chair, complained 'that a state of affairs . . . proved to be unhealthy in 1956 may not be healed until the middle of 1960'.

That was true enough. And I could well understand MP's feelings of annoyance at the slow progress we had made. I shared them. But while I knew full well that the situation was unhealthy in 1956, we could not complete the study of other airlines until the end of 1957. And the trade unions – to whom Parliament had given statutory rights to be fully consulted on such matters – did not agree to co-operate fully until after the October 1958 strike and the ensuing Jack Inquiry. We could not make progress faster than the unions would agree to.

MPs seemed unable or unwilling to understand this. It was no longer possible, in the industrial power situation they had themselves created, for management to act arbitrarily.

But from January 1959 we had really begun to forge ahead. While increasing our output of aircraft capacity by 65 per cent we reduced the number of aircraft maintenance staff by 1,245 and more than doubled their productivity per man. In 1957-58 aircraft maintenance in Britain had cost us about 4.2 new pence per capacity ton-mile. In 1959 we brought it down to just over 3p – and we would bring it down still further to 2½p in 1960. At that time each penny per capacity ton-mile represented £6½ million a year. Thus by the end of 1960, only two years after getting clearance from the unions, we reduced BOAC's aircraft maintenance costs by £11 million a year.

Had we charged bull-headed at the problem without carrying staff and unions with us, we could never have achieved such savings. I suppose we should have blown our own trumpet more over this dramatic accomplishment; but, somehow, in writing reports to Ministers for submission to Parliament, one tends to be formal and underplay one's hand, expecting facts to speak for themselves.

★   ★   ★   ★   ★

Management had come out of the October 1958 strike without conceding any ground. To prevent recurrences I decided to improve communications with all our staff, in the air and on the ground, including our shop stewards.

For the staff generally, I felt we must break new ground – new for us, that is. I asked Freddy Gillman, our chief press and information officer, to start publishing from the beginning of January 1959 a weekly news-sheet for free distribution to all staff at London Airport, to keep them fully informed about what was going on in the airline. Copies would be posted each Friday to all flying staff at their home addresses, and distributed to all offices in Britain and overseas. By keeping everyone continuously in the picture about what we were doing and why, it should do much to promote a better sense of common purpose and a better team spirit throughout BOAC. This was the beginning of *BOAC News*, edited with distinction for many years by H P (Bill) Macklin.

Improvement in staff communications was not enough in itself. There was at least one other immediate step to be taken. As managing director I had to be known to be taking an active part in the work of the National Joint Council, so I nominated myself as one of BOAC's five representatives on the employers' side of the NJC.

Harold Spear, our chief personnel officer, decided early in 1959 to move to the Central Electricity Generating Board. His departure would leave a gap in our top management group. I did not want to appoint another professional personnel officer. We already had good professionals in the No 2 positions, of whom the more outstanding were L E (Jim) Atherton and Oliver Hinch. I wanted someone to look after BOAC staff who was more interested in people than in the intricacies of industrial relations procedures.

I knew we had such a person in Dr Bergin, our chief medical officer. At the same time I was unwilling to let him give up his direction of our medical services, perhaps the best of any airline in the world. He had an outgoing personality and could walk breezily into an informal shop stewards' meeting when trouble was simmering, ask them for a cup of tea, and then persuade them to tell him what was really biting them. This was the kind of person I needed to achieve better human relations throughout the airline.

I appointed Ken Bergin a member of our executive management as director of personnel and medical services, with effect from the middle of March 1959. This gave him a useful six-week overlap before Harold Spear left.

At the end of 1958 the Minister had to fill two BOAC board vacancies, caused by the retirement of Ronald McCrindle and Frank Brake. One of the two Harold Watkinson appointed was Sir Wilfred Neden, who had that year retired as chief conciliation officer in the Ministry of Labour. This proved to be an inspired appointment. He was to help me greatly in our work on the National Joint Council, and in fact readily agreed to become a member of it with me. For the next four or five years, BOAC's team of five on the NJC consisted of us, Ken Bergin, Jim Atherton and Oliver Hinch. We gradually achieved a tremendous improvement in relations between the corporation and our seventeen trade unions.

10 Common Carrier –
Uncommon Problems

By the early part of 1959 the new top management of BOAC had been working as a team for almost two and a half years.

Despite the delay of several years in the delivery of Bristol Britannias and the full certificates of airworthiness, we now had them in service. We also had the added capacity of all ten DC-7Cs and the Comet 4s as they arrived month by month from Hatfield. In the process we had been able to shed the various outmoded aircraft we had been forced to buy second-hand to keep our essential services going.

Much had been achieved. Apart from the North Atlantic, where we would have to wait another twelve months for our Boeing 707s, we were now equipped with fully competitive aircraft – at any rate until the turboprop Britannias became outpaced and outclassed by the growing number of jets.

Morale was budding over all branches of the corporation after the long hard winter of uncertainty ushered in by the 1954 Comet 1 disasters. Thus, five years after the pride of our fleet was grounded, temporarily dashing all our hopes, BOAC began to grow again.

But the growth had to be very carefully planned. It was not only a matter of re-introducing BOAC on routes we had to abandon in 1954. It was also a question of building up the frequencies on the routes we had kept going. Moreover, there was the added problem of trying to find profitable employment for all the 35 Vickers VC10s ordered for delivery in the mid-1960s, and not just for the 26 for which we had foreseen a need.

An airline operating commercially would have felt out the market first and then ordered off the shelf the number and type of aircraft it wanted. But the Government had refused to make any more hard currency available and had thereby forced us to buy in Britain. Not that we didn't want to buy British, but there were no suitable aircraft in production, let alone on the shelf. We had had to order more than six years ahead of deliveries. On top of that the order was based not on our requirements as customer, but on the needs of the manufacturers to set up a production line.

No one in their commercial senses would put the cart before the horse like that. But, being a nationalised industry, we had to do what the Government wanted. We now had to try to create markets for the extra nine VC10s forced on us. We could not leave that problem to solve itself. We must plan a series of steps.

First of all, I had to make some changes at the top of BOAC's commercial side. Since George Cribbett took over responsibility for our associated companies in 1956, a number of them had run into difficulties. Keith Granville had to devote more and more of his time to helping Cribbett handle them. It was no longer possible for Granville to double the role of commercial director with that of deputy managing director.

The route general managers I had appointed in 1957 had by now had some 18 months' experience of welding together the selling and traffic-handling sides of our business. So I decided to take Gilbert Lee away from western routes and put him in charge of our commercial side. Ross Stainton was brought across from eastern routes to become general manager of western routes. Next I appointed my former personal assistant, Basil Bampfylde, to be general manager eastern routes. Derek Glover I was able to leave unchanged as general manager southern routes. These four would work exceptionally well together as a team, together with Winston Bray as chief planning manager.

★ ★ ★ ★ ★

There were no particular problems in the way of re-starting BOAC services to eastern South America or to Israel. The traffic rights were still in existence. We would resume services with the new Comet 4s as soon as we had received enough from de Havilland.

Back in 1954 our London-Tel Aviv Argonaut service had had to terminate in Israel. We could not overfly Arab territory with aircraft that had landed in Israel. But with Jewish business spread throughout the world, and with Christian interest in the Holy Land, there was extra traffic to be won if we could surmount this barrier. And it now proved possible, with the greater range and speed of the Comet 4, to route services to the east from Israel by taking them back over Turkey and then out through Iran.

★ ★ ★ ★ ★

The main impediments on our existing routes were, first, the privileged position granted to the British independent airlines. They had been given rights by the Government to operate Colonial Coach services at special low fares to British colonies in Africa and Asia. Second, we could not persuade IATA (the International Air Transport Association) to agree to a lower economy-class fare, which would have widened the world air travel market.

As distinct from the British independents, BOAC had all the obligations of a common carrier: we had to operate the services as scheduled throughout the year. Any airline obliged to operate a public service day in and day out, week in and week out, cannot expect to fill its aircraft to more than 60 per cent on average. This means that fare levels have to be based on that proportion of seats filled.

The independents asked for weekly or fortnightly services at specially low fares which would prove profitable with 100 per cent of the seats sold. If an independent airline could choose to fly its aircraft when fully booked – and it could do this only because there were frequent and regular BOAC flights operating alongside – it could afford to cut fares by 40 per cent. Placed in this privileged position, the independents had been granted the ability to syphon off a lot of traffic from BOAC – as much as £5½ million in the first full year of Colonial Coach services.

It always irked us in BOAC that we were not allowed by successive Ministers to introduce a third tier of fares to match those of the independents for traffic between Britain and the Colonies. Because the traffic was cabotage these fares would not have had to be negotiated with IATA. With recollections of Hoover vacuum-cleaner marketing twenty-five years earlier, and of the lessons learnt from E A Filene of Boston, I knew well that air travel, just as much as any other product, would have to be offered at not less than three price levels to tap the widest possible market.

Under the IATA unanimity rules of those days we could offer travel only at the highest price (first class) and middle price (tourist). This let interlopers undercut us if they could, and held back the development of air travel to some extent.

As a matter of fact, we had persuaded IATA to agree to economy-class services from the beginning of April 1958, but only on the North Atlantic. Economy fares there would be 20 per cent lower than tourist, the reduction being made possible by giving less leg room and simpler meals. These new services proved so popular that by March 1959 half our North Atlantic capacity was economy-class. This was not all additional traffic; there was a substantial switch from tourist-class. But in all classes on our western routes that year we increased BOAC's transatlantic business by 30 per cent at a time when other airlines only increased theirs by about 5 per cent.

At the IATA Traffic Conference towards the end of 1958 we again pressed for the introduction of economy-class fares on services to Africa and the Far East. But there was considerable opposition by other international airlines and our proposals were defeated.

At the next IATA conference, in Honolulu in October 1959, Gilbert Lee tried yet again to get our policy of lower Atlantic-type economy fares adopted for routes to Africa and the Far East. Even though this time we had the support of Pan American, the opposition in IATA was still too great. But in October 1960 we did succeed in breaking down resistance a bit. New low 17-day excursion fares were brought in on the North Atlantic and lower propeller fares on the mid-Atlantic; economy-class fares were introduced to Australia and the Far East; and Sky-coach fares to Africa and the Caribbean. But these were only limited applications of the policy.

We were, I suppose, years ahead of our time; and, truth to tell, aircraft were not then large enough to carry three different classes in one aircraft. But the extra traffic these third-tier fares could have generated would have produced work for more aircraft.

The rigidity of IATA's opposition to the introduction of lower third-tier fares was not in fact broken until the late 1970s. The enterprising and barnstorming tactics of Sir Freddie Laker were by then so successful that Ross Stainton and British Airways were at last able to force their views upon IATA so as to be able to compete on equal terms.

In 1959, however, there was nothing for it but to consult the Minister and seek his help in finding work for our extra VC10s. As a result, on 15 December that year, we were allowed to match on our regular scheduled services the fares quoted by the British independents on their relatively infrequent Colonial Coach services.

It had taken a long time, but at last we had won a point. Having now lost their monopoly of cheap fares to Africa, the independents – and by this time Hunting-Clan and Airwork had merged to form British United Airways (BUA) – had to review their position. They asked for talks with BOAC (denying this to the press when, inevitably, the news got out).

There was really only one possible way of handling this remarkable new situation. For political and other reasons we could not seek to drive BUA out of business, so we set about working together in our own and the national interest. In the end on 5 April 1960, the Minister gave his agreement to the formation of a revenue-pooling partnership between BUA and BOAC.

Finally, the Civil Aviation (Licensing) Act was passed by Parliament and became law in June 1960. The Act brought to an end BOAC's statutory right to be the chosen instrument, as it used to be called, or the sole British operator on world-wide routes. From then on, the independents could apply for licences to operate scheduled services on any route. These applications would be heard by an Air Transport Licensing Board.

Although apparently to our disadvantage, all of us in BOAC welcomed this development. It brought to an end the transparent pretence of the Government under the old Act that British independents operating on the corporations' routes were 'associates'. The position in future would be clear-cut. The independents would be straightforward competitors on level terms; and we were not afraid of fair competition.

$$\star \quad \star \quad \star \quad \star \quad \star$$

Next there was the question of making greater use of existing traffic rights. We had not been able to do this for five years. One area in which British traffic rights were not being properly developed was created, without it being realised at the time, when British European Airways was separated off from BOAC.

That was in 1946, when BEA was set up by Parliament as a separate and independent corporation. I have already mentioned how in the early 1950s Miles Thomas and I came to realise that Britain lost much potential air traffic on the South American route because BOAC was unable to operate via Paris.

Britain's failure to exploit potential sixth-freedom traffic rights between North America and Europe was far more serious. Sixth-freedom traffic rights can be created simply by combining third- and fourth-freedom rights to both sides of the country concerned. Placed as Britain is at the principal air gateway into Europe from North America, we held in our hands a wonderful opportunity to earn large sums of foreign currency by carrying via London part of the substantial through traffic between the two continents.

This benefit could have been obtained quite simply by an equipment inter-change (that is, by BOAC aircraft flying on into Europe on charter to BEA) or better still by merger of the two airlines. It was in fact for this reason – the chance of exploiting Britain's sixth-freedom traffic rights – that Miles Thomas and I over the years had been consistently in favour of merging the two British airways corporations. But it could not be accomplished then.

In the 1950s and 1960s BEA refused to contemplate getting closer to BOAC, other than by each having a representative on the other's board. BEA claimed that they gained more by their interline selling arrangements with Pan American – from whom they derived traffic for onward carriage into Europe, and vice-versa – than they would from working more closely with BOAC. (This argument, of course, ignored the potentially far greater gain to BOAC; but BEA were not concerned with that.)

Perhaps, too, there was a fear at the back of their minds that a takeover by BOAC might eventually follow closer co-operation. Understandably they valued their independence. And, as always, personalities entered into it. Sholto Douglas was a very strong character. So also were Miles Thomas and Matthew Slattery. Neither side could be expected to give way to the other.

So the matter was left in limbo. No Minister responsible for civil aviation ever sought to influence matters in the national interest until the appointment of the Edwards Committee in the late 1960s. Traffic rights are not just operating rights; they are rights to earn foreign currency – rights of great value to Britain in terms of the national balance of payments, and rights which Britain failed to make the most of for more than a quarter of a century.

Fortunately, Edwards recommended merging BOAC and BEA together, and the Government agreed. But it had taken nearly thirty years to reverse the decision made in 1946 to split BOAC into separate corporations. And only in 1975, after the merger of the two into British Airways, could Ross Stainton demonstrate the extra traffic and the financial benefits won for Britain in this way.

It also proved possible in 1959 to start making greater use of rights in the UK/US bilateral for transatlantic services to points in the United States other than New York – hitherto our only port of entry. Combining two or more points on one service made it possible gradually to break into new markets. For instance, Chicago and Detroit were added to our London-Montreal service. Washington and Boston were brought on line with New York in much the same way.

This was important, increasing the earning power of our 15 Boeing 707s at little extra cost.

★   ★   ★   ★   ★

Reports reaching us from airlines which had already put the 707 into service were highly encouraging. In performance the aircraft was substantially achieving all Boeing's claims.

But Boeing's test pilots felt that handling the aircraft in flight could be improved by some design modifications. Our chief engineer,

Charles Abell, discussed the matter fully with Boeing. It was agreed to modify the aircraft in four respects: extending the fin some three feet; providing full rudder boost; improving the yaw damper; and fitting a shallow ventral fin below the tail. Boeing also agreed to incorporate the modifications free of charge at the end of the first year.

The Boeing 707 had of course been granted an American certificate of airworthiness, and for BOAC it would have to have a British C of A as well. When the time came for the Air Registration Board test pilot, D P Davies, to subject the aircraft to the full range of flight-testing, he agreed with what was being done to improve it. But Dai Davies was concerned about the effect on its handling in flight of the heavier and more powerful Rolls-Royce engines being specially fitted in BOAC's 707s. So he refused (rightly) to let our aircraft have a British C of A until the mods were actually incorporated.

The first 707 for BOAC had been due to be delivered in December 1959, but delivery was now deferred for several months. This stopped us temporarily in our tracks. It was a nasty setback; we were bound to lose a good part of 1960's summer traffic. But it was a penalty well worth paying in the long run.

BOAC's first Boeing 707 arrived at London Airport on 29 April 1960 under the command of Capt Tom Stoney, by now manager of the 707 Flight. The incorporation of special 'hand-made' mods had delayed delivery by only four months. We began to put them into transatlantic service on 27 May. The modified 707 proved a much better aircraft to handle – and indeed when the mods were retrospectively introduced into PanAm's aircraft, their senior pilots expressed great appreciation of the contribution to flight safety thus made by the British ARB and BOAC.

*   *   *   *   *

Another way of improving or protecting our traffic rights was by developing our Commonwealth airline partnerships.

At about this time Britain's colonies were being given their independence in fairly rapid succession. On independence they were no longer UK territory and became classed instead as foreign nations. BOAC thereby lost the right to carry all the traffic between Britain and her former colonies. At the same time they set up their own airlines to use their valuable new traffic rights. It therefore made good commercial sense for BOAC and the new airlines to exploit in partnership their third- and fourth-freedom traffic rights.

It is often alleged that colonies as they became independent set up airlines just for prestige. While not denying that prestige may well have motivated people such as President Nkrumah of Ghana, there is in fact a good financial case for an airline of one's own. It helps the national balance of payments, which the newly independent countries did not have to worry about while they were colonies. An airline required capital expenditure by the former colony, but thereafter it could retain in its own country a substantial part of the airline's earnings in air-fares.

I had already signed a partnership agreement with the new chairman of Central African Airways, Sir Albert Robinson, on 20 May 1957. Now in 1959 the time had come to start a partnership pool with East African Airways. I had some preparatory talks with their chairman, Sir Alfred Vincent, and the negotiations began in earnest – Derek Glover leading for BOAC and Colonel Mostert for EAA. Before the end of that year the discussions with EAA had been enlarged to include the SAA/CAA pool. Derek Glover succeeded in concluding a four-sided partnership, known as the quadripartite pool, covering all the routes from London to Nairobi, Salisbury and Johannesburg.

For years we had been trying to rationalise services between Britain and Canada, and to bring into existence a partnership with Trans-Canada Airlines, as Air Canada was then known. But anybody who has tried to establish joint transport arrangements with Canadians will know how reluctant they are to commit themselves. Possibly they fear getting entangled too much, a fear perhaps bred of old from the thinness of the line representing the 49th parallel.

I decided in 1959 to make yet one more attempt, as I sensed that BOAC might now prove more attractive because of our new aircraft. After two or three exploratory meetings I flew to Montreal in mid-November with Ross Stainton for further talks with Gordon McGregor, the TCA president. They proved successful. A partnership between us would come into effect at the beginning of April 1960, subject only to ratification by his board. The agreement was publicly announced on 26 November, by which time I was in Bombay having intricate discussions with Air-India and Qantas.

In 1959 Qantas and the Australian Government were in their turn having great difficulty with Air-India and the Indian Government. The trouble arose because, ever since the Kangaroo route from Britain to Australia started many years earlier, Qantas had been picking up a lot of fifth-freedom traffic out of India for destinations to the west. Air-India on the other hand carried no traffic eastward to

Australia and beyond. The balance of air traffic rights between the two countries was very one-sided, to India's disadvantage. With half the population of Fiji of Indian descent, India wanted traffic rights to operate not only to Australia but also on to Fiji. Australia would not agree. India threatened to abrogate the bilateral, which would have spelt death for Qantas's fifth-freedom uplift out of India – and indeed to all Qantas's traffic rights in India, not to mention their over-flying rights.

C O Turner and I had a good many talks about this in Sydney and London. I felt strongly that, with India sitting in the middle of our all-important Kangaroo route, the best answer was to bring Air-India into the partnership.

As the months went by, and the deadlock remained unbroken, CO came round to my point of view. I then had to sell the idea to J R D Tata, the renowned chairman and former owner of Air-India, and his general manager, B R Patel, of the old Indian Civil Service. We agreed that the three airlines would meet together in Bombay at the end of November 1959 to work out a tripartite agreement.

We duly met, and at the end of a week we had tied it all up. The tripartite agreement was signed on 4 December 1959 with appropriate ceremony – doubly significant because it coincided almost exactly with Qantas's fortieth birthday as an airline and with the 25th anniversary of the Kangaroo partnership between Qantas and Imperial Airways.

*   *   *   *   *

It remained to be seen whether there were any new areas of operation into which we could break out. The one part of the world in which BOAC had never flown before was the Pacific. Back in the mid-1950s Qantas had taken over the traffic rights of the former British Commonwealth Pacific Airlines (BCPA) and had started flying between Sydney and San Francisco. Then in 1957 Qantas extended their San Francisco service to New York and on across the Atlantic to London. This they called the Southern Cross route to Britain, to distinguish it from the Kangaroo route via India. We in BOAC started operating beyond New York to San Francisco at about the same time. Having worked together in partnership for many years on the Kangaroo route, we agreed to operate the San Francisco-London part of the Southern Cross route in partnership also.

But BOAC had no trans-Pacific service to parallel that of Qantas. In fact, in 1957, we simply had no aircraft with trans-Pacific range. But with the long-range Britannia 312s building up operations in

Prince Philip visits BOAC headquarters, 20 May 1959. In the Britannia hangar with Charles Abell, BS, Ted Chantler, Squadron Leader Severne and Harry Pearn. *(British Airways)*

A double event – Air India joins Qantas and BOAC in partnership, and Qantas celebrates its 40th birthday. With B R Patel and C O Turner in Bombay, 4 December 1959. *(Air India)*

With Kay at Buckingham Palace, 5 July 1961. *(Fox Photos)*

The management of BOAC in 1960. From left: Ken Bergin (Director of Personnel and Medical Services), Tommy Farnsworth (Deputy Chief of Flight Operations), Charles Abell (Chief Engineer), Ken Bevan (Financial Comptroller), Keith Granville (Deputy Managing Director), J B Scott (Chief Economics Officer), BS, Ken Staple (Secretary and Legal Adviser), Gilbert Lee (Commercial Director), Ross Stainton (GM Western Routes), Derek Glover (GM Southern Routes) and Basil Bampfylde (GM Eastern Routes) *(British Airways)*

1958 in addition to the DC-7Cs, we could begin to think about pushing across the Pacific in 1959.

When BCPA was wound up in the mid-1950s and Qantas started flying to San Francisco, the civil aviation side of the Ministry had allowed the British rights between America and Australia to lapse from the UK-US bilateral agreement. It was on these British rights, of course, that BCPA's operations had been based. Australia already had rights of their own to operate to America, in exchange for Pan American's rights to Australia.

That the civil servants allowed these southern Pacific rights to lapse seems to have happened through carelessness or oversight. It was to cost Britain dear. If and when we needed them we should have to give the United States more new rights to get them back. Until that happened, there was no question of our being able to fly with Qantas from London to Sydney via the US west coast.

We did have in the British bilateral agreement with America the right to operate from the US west coast through Honolulu to Hong Kong. This route was virtually an American monopoly at that time, though Japan Air Lines were on the point of starting up. It carried a lot of traffic, which would be increased still further when Japan lifted travel restrictions on its own nationals. It seemed a promising development, though heavily dependent on fifth-freedom traffic between United States territory and Japan. And it would link up with our London-Tokyo service via India and Hong Kong, providing us with a round-the-world route.

By March 1959 we were due to receive sufficient Comet 4s from de Havilland to put them on the London-Tokyo service via India. By that date, too, we should have sufficient Britannia 312 flying hours available to extend our London-San Francisco service across the Pacific to Tokyo and Hong Kong. With the necessary traffic rights to hand, we therefore planned to inaugurate on 3 April 1959 the first British trans-Pacific and round-the-world service. It would be operated with British-built aircraft – a Comet 4 coming from Britain across India and a Britannia 312 coming from Britain across America and the Pacific.

Aubrey Burke, managing director of de Havilland, flew out in the Comet 4 and Matthew Slattery, chairman of Bristol Aircraft, in the Britannia 312. They would meet in Tokyo. But alas – to my intense disappointment and annoyance – I learned, while waiting there for them to arrive, that the operation had been blocked by the American Government at the very last minute.

The Comet 4 and the pre-inaugural Britannia 312 did meet in Tokyo, but what had happened was this. The 1946 Bermuda

Agreement between Britain and America provided that both countries could operate between San Francisco on the American mainland and Hong Kong, a British colonial territory. In 1947 the United States added Tokyo to the American route as a transit stop to enable Pan American Airways to operate it, and Britain could do likewise when it needed to. So, early in 1957, two years before the possible start of our service, Britain did just that and added Tokyo as a transit stop on the British route to enable BOAC to match the Pan American operation.

Then in October 1958 BOAC formally applied, as required by American procedure, for a CAB (Civil Aeronautics Board) permit. This gave rise to a series of objections by various American carriers, all of which were rejected by the CAB. But as late as January 1959 Northwest Airlines suddenly objected on grounds alleging that the BOAC service would be contrary to the United States' public interest because American airlines would lose business to a foreign carrier.

In mid-March the CAB ruled out all Northwest's objections except this question of public interest, which it reserved for further consideration. We wondered whether we should have to postpone the start of our trans-Pacific service. But in view of the Bermuda Agreement, the Government in London assured us that it was inconceivable that the United States would withhold our permit. Accordingly, all arrangements went ahead for the start of the service at the beginning of April. But our diplomatic strength was not as great as had been thought. At the last moment, we didn't get our permit.

The CAB hearings dragged on and on. Once past the beginning of April the opportunities for delay were legion, and everyone seemed to think the Pacific was an American preserve. Some months later, in spite of the Washington lobbies, the CAB relented – as we felt they would have to. But not before their delaying had cost us a lot of money and exasperation. Even then, the CAB permit had to have President Eisenhower's signature before it was valid, and this could not be obtained without considerable efforts by the British Embassy in Washington. It had to be brought to the top of the paper mountain awaiting his signature before he went on holiday. By this time we had missed the best of the summer season. But we were at last able to start the first British trans-Pacific and round-the-world service on 22 August, 1959.

11 Government and Corporation

A change in the method of financing BOAC and other nationalised industries had been introduced by the Conservative Government in 1956. It gave to the Treasury and Ministry concerned with civil aviation far greater powers of influence over the corporation's affairs. Yet, profound though the effect was to be on BOAC's management in future, most people failed to appreciate its significance at the time.

What had been changed was the method of producing the corporation's capital. Until 2 August 1956, BOAC's capital requirements were met by the issue to the public of British Overseas Airways stock, as laid down in the Air Corporations Acts. But now these arrangements were to be discontinued. The only means left to BOAC for raising capital was to apply to the Minister of Transport and Civil Aviation for 'exchequer advances'.

The immediate effect was that all our capital requirements were subject to the exigencies of the country's annual Budget, which ranked them as current expenditure. Our capital expenditure was of course already subject to strict control by our board, who decided whether it would help to improve our profitability. But now, under the new system, the Treasury could impose capital cuts which would reduce our profitability for budget reasons quite unconnected with BOAC, or indeed with civil aviation.

We had such a cut in 1957. It was only a few hundred thousand pounds, and from the national point of view was not material in itself. But it was a sacrifice demanded of all the nationalised industries to achieve a better-looking surplus in the nation's budget then under consideration by Parliament. Our few hundred thousand pounds, however, were very important to BOAC; their elimination would hazard delivery dates of new aircraft. Pops d'Erlanger and I argued strongly with the Minister against the cut. The matter was settled only by the Minister telling a London Airport board meeting that we had damn well got to accept it.

Parliament had properly conferred on Ministers the power to give BOAC instructions, wisely adding that he should exercise that power only in the form of a written directive which should be published in our annual report. So we asked him for the necessary directive. He just laughed and said: 'Not bloody likely! What do you take me for?' In the fourteen years I worked in BOAC, there were several occasions when the chairman's or the board's arms were well and truly twisted by Ministers. But they all baulked at issuing a written directive. Their refusal to defend a policy in public can only be regarded as an admission of bad policy. Closed government is bad government.

The procedure which ensures that a publicly-owned industry must account to Parliament is wholly right and proper, ensuring that those who run nationalised industries are publicly accountable. But the Minister and his officials get away scot-free. They escape any form of public accountability – other than, in the Minister's case, a debate in the House of Commons, which is usually less effective than the searching cross-questioning of Select Committees.

This did not matter much before August 1956; but with each year of the new financial arrangements, Ministerial accountability became critical. After all, the Minister's Civil Servants were free to criticise BOAC and other industries to the Select Committee, but they were never themselves subject to criticism or held responsible for their influence on our affairs.

The degree to which the Ministry and the Treasury grip increased is illustrated by the fact that, while our shares issued to the public were reduced from £60 million in 1956 to £57 million in 1960, exchequer advances made to us by the Minister grew from zero in August 1956 to £72 million in 1960.

*   *   *   *   *

With his family background of banking, Pops d'Erlanger held strong views about the uncommercial manner in which Government forced us to deal with BOAC's finances. And he did not forbear to comment in our official annual report, though inevitably couched in restrained language.

One major financial problem stemmed from the fact that all our capital bore fixed interest. No provision was made in the Air Corporations Acts for us to raise any risk or equity capital; and this situation was not altered by the change from public shares to exchequer advances in 1956.

In any business there is financial risk. Risk is not eliminated by nationalisation, nor can Government safeguard itself against risk by issuing only fixed-interest capital. Inevitably there are ups and downs – good years and lean years. And that is doubtless why it was laid down in the nationalising Acts that one year should be taken with another over five-year periods.

Transport is more susceptible to swings in economic fortune than most other industries. You are producing seat-miles or capacity ton-miles; and if you cannot sell them when you produce them, they are lost for all time. You cannot, as in manufacturing industry, put them into stock on the shelf for sale later.

And international transport is very different from the monopoly-type domestic nationalised industries such as gas or electricity, in which charges to consumers can so easily be put up.

Airline operation is essentially a risk business. Someone has to carry that risk. That someone can only be the airline's owner, who in Britain has been the Government since BOAC was formed in 1939. Our capital structure, which permitted the owner to draw a fixed dividend even when there was no profit, was an economic absurdity.

Most airline costs are fixed once the operating plan is agreed. Financial results are therefore highly sensitive to the number of passengers it succeeds in carrying. In those days, 1957, five passengers more or less per flight affected annual profit by £3 million a year more or less. In such a business, a substantial proportion of risk or equity capital is essential.

So Pops d'Erlanger reported to the Minister in 1958: 'The Corporation bears a charge for interest on the whole of its capital whether or not a profit is earned. By contrast many of our overseas competitors normally have a material proportion of their capital in equity form which does not attract a dividend unless profits are available.'[1]

Australia's overseas airline, Qantas, was wholly owned by its Government; yet all its capital was in equity form and the Government were entitled to receive no greater dividend than the directors of Qantas, after consultation with their Minister, thought it right to distribute out of profits. No profits, no dividend.

Two years later, in 1960 – the last report before he retired – Pops returned to this theme again. 'In an industry,' he wrote, 'which is highly sensitive to the changing world situation, its ability to maintain a fixed rate of dividend on all its borrowed capital must necessarily remain somewhat precarious. . . . The financial risk involved properly belongs to the Government as the sole proprietor of the Corporation.'[2]

[1] BOAC Annual Report 1957-58, p 2. [2] BOAC Annual Report 1959-60, p 6.

*   *   *   *   *

Another major financial problem for us stemmed from the unreasonable and unfair way in which the Government left us to pay for the operational development of new British aircraft. We were expected to carry unaided the quite exceptional burden of expense – and responsibility – involved in introducing into service new types of British medium- or long-haul aircraft.

Since the Second World War, Pops reminded the Minister in 1958, BOAC had had 'to eliminate the teething troubles of successive types of long distance British transport aircraft. There is no other country in the world which expects its airlines to bear the additional expense entailed by this work of developing a new aircraft to make it fit for competitive service and for export. The Corporation considers that it should be afforded some form of financial assistance at least for its service to the wider national interests of the export markets' and by way of 'compensation for the additional costs it has to bear compared with its competitors'.[3]

The trouble was that the Government could not avoid having to make research and development grants to the private-enterprise aircraft industry, since such R&D work would otherwise not be done. But when part of the R&D work was done by BOAC, a nationalised industry, the Government could simply not bother to pay us.

So in 1959 Pops wrote: 'I make no apology for returning (to this subject). Before aircraft enter into regular service operations, they must go through a period of pre-operational development which involves considerable expenditure on aircraft modifications, associated flying and ground personnel.'

This, he said, 'had involved the Corporation in more expenditure for British types than for American types. This is due to the fact that the Corporation is the first operator of any British types it purchases, whereas an American type would be otherwise developed by the time the Corporation acquired it. It is the view of the Corporation that the expense attendant upon introducing an aircraft into service is part of its development which should be regarded as a proper charge against research and development moneys which are at the disposal of the Government.'[4]

*   *   *   *   *

But the additional expenditure Pops d'Erlanger referred to in the

[3]BOAC Annual Report 1957-58, p 2.   [4]BOAC Annual Report 1958-59, p 3.

passage I have just quoted was by no means the only handicap BOAC had been landed with in introducing British aircraft into airline service. Let us re-cap a little.

In the case of the Hermes, Handley Page submitted a redesign in late 1946. In April 1947 the Ministry of Supply ordered it – Ministry of Supply, be it noted, not BOAC – for delivery starting in June 1948. Deliveries did not in fact start until 1950, by which time it had been replaced – and outclassed – by the Canadair Argonauts. In November 1952 we had no use for it except as a tourist class aircraft. By October 1953, the Hermes were withdrawn from service and had to be coccooned pending disposal at knock-down prices because we were prevented by Government from tendering for trooping contracts. All losses on the Hermes were left for our account.

The story of the Comet disasters has already been related. But to the resultant financial losses have to be added the costs of buying short-period replacement piston-engined aircraft in a market that knew our predicament and understandably held us to ransom.

Then the Britannia 102, ordered in 1949 for delivery in 1954, had not been ready for service until 1957. The delay in itself was a serious matter at a stage in aviation history when aircraft became obsolete in only seven or eight years, being overtaken by improved and more economic types. It meant that BOAC lost nearly half the capital cost of the Britannia 102s before they entered service.

The long-range Britannia 312 was also years late, and we had to buy ten new piston-engined DC-7Cs from America to help bridge the gap until the 312 could be brought into service. We knew full well that when we came to sell the DC-7Cs in the jet age there would be few buyers, and we might well incur a further capital loss.

Then, on top of these capital losses, BOAC had to continue paying the Government the fixed rate of interest on our theoretical capital, most of which had been lost on behalf of the British aircraft industry. It was very convenient for the Government to be able to forget about the development costs of bringing British aircraft into service, leaving it to us to carry them, but it was really adding insult to injury to exact interest on the losses as well. Not only that – it was wholly unfair to those running BOAC, particularly as success is judged in Parliament and the press by financial results.

Let no one think that we in BOAC were anything but glad to be of service to the British aircraft industry, helping to develop new types up to reliable operating standards. Service delays experienced by the Britannia 102 along our eastern routes through the whole of its first year did much to undermine, temporarily, our reputation for reliable and punctual operation. But we were prepared to endure and overcome this in the general interest – as we have been glad and proud to put other new British aircraft into service. Our only complaint has been that the financial arrangements left us with an exorbitant and unjustifiable burden that was none of our making.

To start meeting this situation Pops d'Erlanger tried in 1959 to write a considerable sum off the values at which certain aircraft then stood in our balance sheet. But the Minister, Harold Watkinson, refused to allow us to do so on the grounds (it was stated later) that that would be tantamount to relieving the corporation of part of its capital debt!

So d'Erlanger tried to bring this matter home to the Select Committee on Nationalised Industries, which seemed to take the point. In 1960 d'Erlanger wrote in his report that 'the Corporation was gratified to note the view expressed by the Committee that the incidence of the cost of developing new British aircraft appears to fall too heavily on the Corporation and places them at a disadvantage compared with their foreign competitors who use American aircraft.'[5]

But it was all to no avail. Perhaps it was that, by nature, Pops d'Erlanger was too gentle a man.

*   *   *   *   *

Things had not been going well with our associated companies and their accumulating losses had naturally to be included in the overall results of BOAC. On these losses too we had to pay interest to the Government. They were destined to play a part in the politically inevitable financial clearing-up between Government and Corporation.

BOAC's investments in associated companies were held through a subsidiary company of which George Cribbett was chairman – BOAC Associated Companies Ltd, set up in September 1957. By March 1959 our involvement had increased to £12½ million – almost one-sixth of the capital we employed on our own operations.

BOAC Associated Companies turned in a loss of £3.1 million in the year to March 1959. Admittedly the largest single loss was that incurred by Middle East Airlines, amounting to £1.7 million; but this was the direct result of a political crisis in the Lebanon which caused America to land marines there and occupy Beirut airport. Even so, there were other losses of £1.4 million, and a further £1.2 million to come in 1959-60, bringing the accumulated losses up to

[5]BOAC Annual Report 1959-60, p 5.

over £7 million. This was many times more than the value of any feederline traffic these companies contributed.

So a drastic review had to be put in hand. Keith Granville had to devote more and more time to the affairs of BOAC Associated Companies in an attempt to pull them round, with the help of John Linstead as their general manager. The Minister appointed the Swash Committee to enquire into the running of these companies. And in April 1960 Keith was made chairman of BOAC-AC following George Cribbett's resignation through ill health.

★ ★ ★ ★ ★

Towards the end of 1959 there had been a major change in the organisation of Government responsibility for Civil Aviation. The Ministry of Transport and Civil Aviation was chopped up and civil aviation was removed from its scope. At the same time the old Ministry of Supply, through which we had to order British aircraft, was abolished as a Ministry on its own. Responsibility for civil aviation and aircraft supply (both civil and military) was then joined together in a new Ministry of Aviation. Thus we found ourselves being sponsored, as it was euphemistically called, by a Minister who was also acting on behalf of our suppliers – a situation of potential difficulty.

Harold Watkinson had been Minister of Transport and Civil Aviation for four years, since late 1955 – an unusually long time for a Minister to remain with us and a welcome change from having had to answer to seven different Ministers in succession during the ten years from 1945 to 1955. On the break-up of that Ministry he was moved across to be Minister of Defence.

At the same time Duncan Sandys was moved from the Ministry of Defence to the new Ministry of Aviation. On this occasion, however, the appointment of a new Minister did not seem to unsettle our chairman much. This was not what I had come to expect from my earlier experience of changes of Minister. I began to wonder what was afoot. I knew that Pops d'Erlanger was sadly disillusioned with the Government's treatment of BOAC.

★ ★ ★ ★ ★

Towards the end of January 1960 there was a feeling in the air of impending change. I got an inkling that Pops d'Erlanger might be on the point of leaving, though not yet 54. And so it proved to be.

At that time, we were at last able to resume services to the east coast of South America which we had had to abandon in 1954. Duncan Sandys went down to Buenos Aires on the 're-inaugural' service with Pops d'Erlanger. Because of increasing speculation about possible changes, the Minister issued a statement from South America. Soon after his appointment as Minister, it seemed, Pops had told him he wished to relinquish the chairmanship of BOAC, the official reason being 'the demands of his private business'. And shortly before Duncan had left England, George Cribbett had also warned him that for reasons of health he would not be able to continue for more than another three months. 'I have not yet taken any decisions about future appointments,' the Minister added.

I did not think there was any chance of my being appointed. Right up until the early 1970s, in fact, no one was ever promoted to be chairman of BOAC from within the Corporation.

In any case I did not yet wish to be regarded as a candidate for the chairmanship. To begin with, I thought it essential in a world-wide airline business that the offices of chairman and chief executive/ managing director should be held by different people. The task of managing the airline was big enough on its own without having to cope with Governments, public relations, and other airlines – not to mention the supervision of overall policy. This was the way Sholto Douglas and Tony Milward had worked together in BEA, and it had gone well.

Given that as a basis of working, I was not yet ready to give up being managing director and become non-executive. There was much more I wanted to do as chief executive before handing on that role to one of my colleagues. In any case, in 1960 I had not yet chosen him.

What concerned me greatly was the sort of person we might have imposed on us by the Ministry. It was vital that the next chairman and deputy chairman should be people with whom our top management, built up so well during the last four years, could work happily and productively. They should also be people who would give BOAC a good public image and improved industrial relations. I talked privately to a few friends about names. The difficulty was that the right of appointment belonged to the Minister; the board had no say in the matter and did not even have to be consulted – a situation unknown, and wholly unthinkable, in industry generally.

On the board, I discussed the matter chiefly with Francis Rennell. He had himself been deputy chairman in 1955-56. Together we worked out a short list of possibles and soon narrowed it down to one – Rear-Admiral Sir Matthew Slattery. He had been chief of naval air equipment at the Admiralty and since 1948 managing director and chairman of the Belfast aircraft manufacturers, Short Bros & Harland.

For him, a southern Irish catholic, to head up Shorts, a leading industry in protestant Ulster, might well have inflamed local passions. At the outset 'no pope here' slogans were painted on the walls of Short's guest house where he was staying. His response was typical. He promptly renamed the guest house 'Pope's Cottage'. After that, there was no more trouble.

To Francis Rennell and myself, Matthew Slattery seemed an ideal and opportune choice. He was nearly five years older than myself, which would leave me the chance to succeed him in time. I had seen a good deal of him since he became chairman in 1957 of Bristol Aircraft, our Britannia suppliers, and felt sure we could work together. Now that Bristol was being merged into the British Aircraft Corporation, he might well be available.

I had no doubt that the job would appeal to him. I felt, too, that his becoming chairman of BOAC might appeal to the Prime Minister, by whom appointments of nationalised-industry chairmen had to be approved – Matthew Slattery had been special adviser to Harold Macmillan on the transport of Middle East oil from 1957 to 1959.

So, in spite of the risk that the Ministry might react automatically against any internal proposal, I decided to put the suggestion forward. The Permanent Secretary of the Ministry thanked me, and told me that Slattery's name was already on the list. This may well have been true and not just a polite brush-off. At any rate the knowledge that Matthew Slattery would be more than acceptable to the board might help the Minister to decide. There was no more to be done but wait and see.

★　　★　　★　　★　　★

Soon after his appointment as Minister of Aviation at the end of 1959, Duncan Sandys set about the task of rationalising the British aircraft industry. There were to be two major firms only: de Havilland were to be merged into Hawker Siddeley; and Vickers-Armstrongs, Bristol Aeroplane, and the airframe side of English Electric were to be merged into a British Aircraft Corporation. To get these two mergers off the ground, the industry needed orders for new aircraft. But the proposed British Aircraft Corporation had few or none.

Accordingly BOAC was asked by the Minister if we could see our way clear to ordering a further ten VC10s, in a stretched and longer-range version to be known as the Super VC10, for delivery starting in 1965. We went into it carefully, but found it impossible to justify the need on top of our existing order for 35 standard VC10s, deliveries of which would start in 1964. We did suggest converting the last ten of these to ten Supers. This offer was unwelcome to Vickers, since it would reduce their order to 25 and they naturally wished to work out their order book rather than hand over part of it to BAC. Rumours circulated that Vickers might go into liquidation unless the British Aircraft Corporation merger was brought off. It was suggested that the absence of additional orders from BOAC would wreck the merger scheme.

Understandably, most of us on the BOAC board felt that the fate of the British aircraft industry was not one of our primary responsibilities. In any case we had not even been provided with design specifications – only minimum guarantees, so soft that they were useless for calculating aircraft economics.

In late spring I learned that Duncan Sandys had asked Matthew Slattery to take over the chairmanship from Pops d'Erlanger. Matthew and I had two or three private talks about the present state and future prospects of BOAC, and I was delighted when he told me he would join us. He knew about the Super VC10 proposal and, having agreed with the Minister to take on the chairmanship from the end of July, he wrote to Pops d'Erlanger asking him not to commit BOAC to ordering any further aircraft before handing over the chair.

Despite this, Pops d'Erlanger agreed with Duncan Sandys in June that BOAC would order ten Super VC10s on top of existing orders at an indicated price of £2½ million each, to make it possible for the Minister to go ahead with the Government plan for setting up the British Aircraft Corporation. When the board queried this, we were told that BOAC was committed in Cabinet.

Once again, we were clearly under Government instruction. The board could only do what it had been told to do. We were now saddled with another ten aircraft costing £25 million for which we had no foreseeable need. And such is politics that Duncan Sandys, in writing to thank Pops d'Erlanger for his action, said – and this was of course for publication – that he was glad to feel that the decision had been reached on commercial grounds!

One is left to wonder what possible motive could have made Pops d'Erlanger commit the corporation in this cynical way. He was about to leave BOAC, and he had been specifically asked by his successor not to commit us on this issue. Why had he let his arm be twisted to this extent? And had he really assured the Minister that his decision was commercial?

Be that as it may, on 20 June 1960 Duncan Sandys announced in the House of Commons that he had appointed Sir Matthew Slattery to be full-time chairman of BOAC with effect from 29 July. Sir

Wilfred Neden, already on our board, was to be part-time deputy chairman. Three days later, on 23 June, some five weeks before Pops d'Erlanger was due to leave us, BOAC signed the £25 million contract for the ten Super VC10s we did not need.

There was another change to come in that July of 1960. After only nine months in office as Minister of Aviation, Duncan Sandys was appointed Secretary of State for Commonwealth Relations. When the time came in the mid-1960s for BOAC to cope with its surplus VC10s he would be far removed from the world of civil aviation. But his letter to d'Erlanger would still be on the record.

12 A Phoenix from the Ashes

Matthew Slattery and I quickly found it easy to work together. For one thing, we both held similar views about the difference between our respective functions. As full-time chairman of the board, he would handle relations with Parliament and Government at home and overseas; and, because of their political implications, he would also take responsibility for overall policy in respect of aircraft types and route structure. It would be left to me to manage the whole of BOAC and our 19,000 staff, subject to the normal monitoring by the board of its executive management.

Matthew embarked on his new job with all his Admiral's aplomb and characteristic energy. He joined us on 29 July 1960 and started that day to go round all the different parts of our organisation at London Airport. I took him to Treforest in South Wales to see our engine overhaul factory. We went to St Mawgan near Newquay to see our flight crews being trained on the Boeing 707s, which were still being delivered. After that he went off to New York and Chicago to see our organisation over there – all this in his first month with us. He brought a welcome and enlivening breath of fresh air.

In August 1960, when Matthew Slattery had just become chairman of BOAC, we were full of confident optimism for the future.

★　★　★　★　★

In the four years since May 1956, when d'Erlanger had been appointed part-time chairman and I had been made managing director, BOAC had come a long way. We had made good much of the ground lost in 1954. And we had changed our fleet from 100 per cent piston-engined to 82 per cent turbine or jet.

With delivery of the Boeing 707s in 1960, we could begin to achieve our planned expansion across the North Atlantic. In fact, by August that year, we were able to operate as many as nine transatlantic services a day with a mixed fleet of Boeing 707s, Comet 4s and Britannia 312s. When all the 15 Boeing 707s had been delivered, the services we could offer the public over all our routes would be 51 per cent jet, 42 per cent turbo-prop and not more than 7 per cent piston.

In the four years since 1956 we had nearly doubled our annual output, from 250 million capacity ton-miles (ctm) to 450 million. Over the same period we had allowed total staff numbers to grow by only 700, to 19,000; we had improved our productivity per man from 14,500 ctm a year to over 25,000; we had brought our total costs per ctm down from the previous level of 16.7p to the much healthier level of 12.5p in the year we were then nearly half-way through, with a further planned reduction to as low as 10p by 1962 or 1963. All this meant that we now needed to fill only 55 out of every 100 seats in order to make a profit. But we could not forget that an operator of year-round scheduled services, as distinct from a charter operator, could never rely on selling much more than 60 per cent on average, even in a good year. Nonetheless, the bringing down of our break-even load factor to 55 per cent was a dramatic improvement.

By 1960, too, BOAC had climbed to second place in the league table of the world's international airlines, second only to Pan American Airways. Our traffic revenue in 1960 was running about 25 per cent up on the previous year, and we were pretty sure of repeating our 1959 achievement and turning in another record operating profit of some £4½ million.

★   ★   ★   ★   ★

All this had been achieved through a concerted management drive within BOAC. The rate of progress, though, was not entirely within our own control.

This was particularly so in the case of our engineering department. To push through all the changes in work procedures that were needed, we had to carry the different individual trade unions with us all the time. And when what we wanted to do involved (say) discontinuing inspection work being done by members of the Association of Supervisory Staffs and Executive Technicians (Asset) and having it done instead by members of the Electrical Trades Union (ETU), the situation was fraught with potential difficulty – not only at shop steward level, but also at national level.

Chief engineer Charles Abell and I had gone to some lengths to explain our ideas to the shop stewards. But in implementing radical changes in working methods, it was inevitable that susceptibilities would be trodden on from time to time. I told the shop stewards that, if anything like that arose, my office door was always open.

I was determined that this offer should not weaken the authority of middle management; but I felt it essential that a safety valve should be known to exist. It was used on only a few occasions, and the shop stewards had made very sure that they were on good ground before venturing to the highest level. There were still one or two unofficial stoppages but far fewer than without such a safety valve.

From the national officers of the trade unions concerned we received a welcome degree of co-operation. We used to have heated arguments, and sometimes could not make progress for weeks on end. But we all won through – even if too slowly for the Select Committee on Nationalised Industries, who were not used to dealing with trade unions. We won because, basically, all the union officials concerned wanted BOAC to succeed in its efforts to become more efficient. For instance, Asset, then led by the dreaded Ian Mikardo and Clive Jenkins, could have been one of the most obstructive unions because of the nature of the demarcation issues involved; in fact they proved in time to be one of the most co-operative.

★   ★   ★   ★   ★

Outside, we were grappling with a major change in our international traffic rights, a change which could have drastically reduced the air travel market open to BOAC. With the granting of independence to India and Pakistan in 1948, the process of dissolution of the British Empire had begun. The Empire became the Commonwealth, and throughout the 1950s and into the 1960s colony after colony was granted its independence. Fortunately from BOAC's point of view, some still remained colonies – such as Hong Kong. But every one that was given self-government became a separate nation for the purpose of traffic rights, even though it remained in the Commonwealth. Step by step, as each colony in turn acquired independence, BOAC was faced with the potential loss of significant traffic throughout the world.

Had we lost this traffic, on which much of BOAC's growth had been based, the financial future of BOAC – indeed the whole standing of the airline – might today be very different. KLM and Sabena changed materially after the Dutch East Indies became Indonesia and the Belgian Congo became Zaire.

Fortunately, most of air travel into and out of former colonies was Britain-oriented. This was due not only to the need for continuing contact on diplomatic and defence matters but also because, as a legacy of Empire, we share a common language. The Commonwealth remains a grouping of English-speaking peoples, and this greatly helped us to retain for British aviation the traffic we might otherwise have lost.

Our Kangaroo and Springbok partnerships with Qantas and South African Airways had shown that putting end-to-end third- and fourth-freedom traffic-rights together created virtual cabotage areas for through traffic between our respective countries. It seemed sensible, therefore, to try to do the same with colonial territories when they became independent and wanted to operate airlines of their own.

When Kenya, Tanganyika and Uganda became independent, the British Government proposed to set up an East African Federation – much as attempts were being made to form a Central African Federation of Southern and Northern Rhodesia with Nyasaland. East African Airways, which until then had been no more than a regional operator, asked for our help in starting up services to and from London. We were only too willing to help.

Across the Atlantic in the West Indies the move towards independence was also gaining momentum. The hopes of the British Government centred on a Federation of the British West Indies. We therefore developed even closer co-operation with the local airline, BWIA, which was based in Trinidad.

In South-East Asia federation was in the air, and the Singapore-based Malayan Airways was a ready-made airline for the short-lived Federation of Malaysia. The political objective of federation never survived there, nor in the West Indies, nor in Central or East Africa. But that did not weaken the connection of BOAC with the young local airlines. We had forged strong links between our respective managements. Twenty years later the Trinidad airline still keeps the B in BWIA.

The larger and wealthier colonies such as the Gold Coast (now Ghana) and Nigeria could justify an airline of their own in place of the West African Airways Corporation which BOAC had done so much to develop since the war. But through shareholdings or working co-operation we succeeded in retaining for many years a major share of the air traffic between us.

Had there been no British Empire with all its colonies, BOAC would never have been conceived on so broad a canvas. Had we not taken these steps to promote co-operation between Britain and her former colonies it is doubtful whether BOAC could have retained for so long its world-wide character and renown.

★ ★ ★ ★ ★

The evolution of the British Empire into the British Commonwealth had another facet that was of the greatest importance to BOAC in its coming of age in 1960 – twenty-one years after its establishment in 1939. Civil aviation had advanced to such an extent in the intervening years that it became feasible for the Queen and other members of the royal family to fly to any part of the Commonwealth. They were thus present on each occasion marking the independence of a former colony. This was in addition to visits the Queen wished to pay to her former Dominions.

In all of this BOAC was privileged to play a major role. 'Mouse' Fielden, Captain of the Queen's Flight to which we were the long-haul subcontractor, kept a close watch on the planning and performance of all these flights. Through the skill of our pilots, the help of air traffic controllers, the dedication of our engineers who prepared and serviced the aircraft, and the efforts of our ground staff seen and unseen, we established a punctuality record which has never been bettered.

In 1956 we flew the Queen and the Duke of Edinburgh to Lagos and back, and we carried the Duke to Mombasa. The next year we carried out five royal flights, to places as far afield as Accra, Salisbury, Kuala Lumpur, and Lagos. The highlight of that year was the flight of the Queen and the Duke of Edinburgh to Ottawa on 12 October, before their state visit to the United States. On their return nine days later, the royal couple left New York in the small hours of the morning; the distinguished persons seeing them off from Idlewild were all togged up, unusual for Americans, in white tie and tails.

In 1958 there were again five royal flights. By far the longest carried the Queen Mother to Auckland via Vancouver and Fiji. All the plans had been carefully made as usual. Even so, there are occasions when the best laid plans go awry; and this was one of them. The aircraft selected was one of our Douglas DC-7Cs; we needed its long range over the Pacific, and there would be ample spares available within easy reach of the Douglas base in California. It had been cleared for acceptance at all airports on its schedule.

The Queen Mother left London on 28 January, and all seemed set. But while the flight was in progress, we received news from New Zealand that the DC-7's clearance to land at Whenuepai airport, Auckland, was being withdrawn. The runway there was of abnormal constitution; it was made up of hexagonal concrete blocks and it seemed that the weather had caused some of the blocks to suffer some subsidence – not enough to prevent the runway being used by most aircraft but marginally too much for the hard tyre DC-7C wheels.

This presented us with quite a problem. Fortunately the Prime Minister, Mr Harold Macmillan, was in Australia and had chartered one of our Britannias for the whole of his tour. We were able to borrow the aircraft back from him for a couple of days and get it over to Fiji in time for the Queen Mother to arrive in Auckland on schedule.

The year 1959 was even busier for royal flights. There were seven – to places such as Rangoon, Nairobi, Santiago, Rio, Vancouver and Bangkok. Again the highlight was the six weeks' visit of the Queen and the Duke of Edinburgh to Canada, when we had the responsibility of carrying them from London to St John's, Newfoundland, on 18 June to start their tour.

Her Majesty was due to return to Britain in the Royal Yacht *Britannia*; but while she was in Canada came the news that she was pregnant, and we were asked to bring her and the Duke back by air from Halifax, Nova Scotia, on the day scheduled for embarkation in *Britannia*. A Comet 4 was immediately refurnished and flown to Halifax. The royal couple arrived back on 3 August to be greeted at London Airport by the Queen Mother and Princess Margaret with Prince Charles and Princess Anne. Prince Andrew was born on 19 February 1960.

Thus 1960 was a quiet year for royal flights. But over the past four years we had carried out as many as twenty, all over the world. The fact that it was BOAC that was regularly entrusted with this work somehow placed a hall-mark of quality on our operations, which was not lost on the travelling public – a feeling shared, I believe, by Matthew Slattery when he came to us as chairman at the end of July 1960.

★   ★   ★   ★   ★

Soon after that Sir Edward Fielden came to see me about the most comprehensive tour we had ever been asked to undertake. The Queen and Duke of Edinburgh were to pay a state visit to India, Pakistan, Nepal and Iran between 20 January and 6 March 1961. It would involve our aircraft flying them to no fewer than twenty-three different airports, with calls at Akrotiri in Cyprus on the way out and at Ankara on the way back.

Planning began at once. It was a most intricate itinerary. Two aircraft would be needed – a Britannia 312 for the Queen and the Duke, supported by a Britannia 102; the Queen's Flight would position two of their 10-seater Herons for local flights; and the Royal Air Force, Indian Air Force and Pakistan Air Force would each provide a couple of DC-3s or Sikorsky helicopters for the airfields at which the Britannias could not land. Capt A Meagher was selected to command the Britannia 312, and Capt C S Rowland the 102. Flight paths and aerodrome facilities had to be checked on the spot. Take-off times and flight times were all worked out in precise detail. Security arrangements were particularly intricate and within BOAC were handled by John Gorman.

The Queen's own party consisted of 35 people. In the countries being visited, they would be joined on most flights by local dignitaries and by UK Government representatives, the Foreign Secretary (Lord Home), and UK High Commissioners in India and Pakistan, the British Ambassadors in Nepal and Iran, and members of their staffs. All these people had to be moved around and brought to attend on the Queen when they were needed.

Throughout the whole six and a half weeks all flights were operated on schedule, without a hitch – a great tribute to all involved. Their work was recognised by awards and souvenirs from the Queen in the course of the tour.

Three months later, to my great delight – and complete surprise – I received a letter from the Keeper of the Privy Purse (Lord Tryon) saying that he was commanded by the Queen to tell me that it would 'give Her Majesty much pleasure to appoint you to be Knight Commander of the Royal Victorian Order in respect of your services to Her Majesty'. It was truly wonderful to be honoured with this appointment by the Sovereign herself – an honour I have treasured and enjoyed ever since.

★   ★   ★   ★   ★

So BOAC was riding high again as we approached the summer of 1961 much as it had been in the summer of 1953. With a record of service to the Queen and her family of which we could be proud, with the new Commonwealth partnerships building up, with our Comet and Boeing jets and our Britannia turbo-props flying hard and well, with our improved management, with the re-organising of our engineering department and our reduced operating costs.

In 1964 we would be celebrating BOAC's silver jubilee. To mark the occasion I felt we should have a history of BOAC's first 25 years written and published. The idea came into my mind through reading Dr Robin Higham's history of Imperial Airways, *Britain's Imperial Air Routes, 1918-1939*, first published by Foulis in 1960. That was a scholarly and well documented work and it seemed to me that Higham's style as an economic historian and his aviation knowledge could well produce a worthy and impartial account of BOAC's achievements in its first quarter-century.

Robin Higham came over from America to see me in the early part of March 1961 and we discussed the whole project. I told him he could have access to any of our records that he wished, including all board papers and minutes. He liked the idea very much, and I liked his approach to it. So the book was commissioned, to be ready by the end of 1963 for publication in 1964.

As time was to prove, and as Matthew Slattery wrote in his first annual report as chairman, our position was basically one of great strength.

13 Stormy Weather

But we were to undergo sore trials in the next couple of years before that basic strength could be demonstrated beyond doubt.

The first tentative indications that the world airline industry was on the brink of a slump became visible at the end of 1960.

Suddenly, as it were overnight, the impact of problems on management underwent dramatic change. Until then, management had been working in a period of unbroken growth. We took for granted that traffic would be there to be carried. The problems we had to concentrate on were relatively straightforward; to get our fleet right, to operate to the highest standards of safety, to get our costs down, to provide passenger service second to none, and to maintain a high-class reservation system and an efficient sales organisation. We tackled them all in a logical and purposeful order.

From the beginning of 1961 we entered an economic storm area in which we were subjected to repeated stresses and buffeting. It was no longer possible to work away steadily at our various problems according to plan. We had to react to outside pressures as they hit us.

★   ★   ★   ★   ★

After a decade of almost uninterrupted expansion at an average rate of just under 15 per cent a year, in December 1960 the trend of forward bookings began to fall off. The empty seats this foreshadowed became a reality in the third week of January 1961. For some time our passenger load factors fell 15 points below those of the corresponding weeks of 1960. This worried us greatly. In March sales picked up again, and we recovered the planned load factors. Things seemed to look normal again. But only for a while. After the end of March sales of seats (and consequently our load factors) slumped again. And it remained that way into the summer.

We naturally asked ourselves whether our sales department were falling down on their job. But then reports reached us from America that other airlines were doing just as badly. A couple of months later airline industry statistics confirmed that world air traffic had suddenly ceased to grow. The 15 per cent rate of growth we had been used to and which we had all been banking on was now down to nil.

An unforeseen trade recession had hit the United States in the late autumn of 1960 and by the spring of 1961 was beginning to threaten the financial viability of many American companies. In the past few years the practice of taking winter holidays abroad had grown enormously in North America. But at the first indications of financial stringency, holiday plans and travel were promptly cancelled. Whether on business or on pleasure bent, Americans were the greatest travellers in the world – the Japanese had not yet lifted their restrictions on overseas travel.

Then, as businesses throughout the United States tightened their belts, they slashed budgets for any items of cost that did not produce provable benefits; and business travel was one of them. Even Boeing, who needed to maintain continuous contact with customers all over the world, had had to cut their travel budget by as much as 50 per cent. Other industries would be cutting by even more.

To make matters worse for the airline industry, this American trade recession happened when airlines everywhere were bringing substantial numbers of the new jets into service. It came hard on the heels of the delivery of the last aircraft we had ordered in 1956, marking completion of our climb-back from the Comet 1 disasters to being the second largest international airline in the world. It could not have come at a more cruel moment.

★   ★   ★   ★   ★

On top of this, in a year when transatlantic traffic had simply stopped growing, when the US airlines were appealing to American travellers to 'fly American', and when the US Government was actively promoting a stay-at-home policy, the Cunard Steam-Ship Company decided to apply to the new Air Transport Licensing Board for a licence to operate air services between Britain and the United States in parallel with BOAC.

It was an understandable move on their part. The number of people crossing the Atlantic by ship had been declining rapidly. The airlines had first outcarried the ships in 1957. So, with a view to moving in on the growth industry of transatlantic air travel, they had recently acquired an independent airline – Eagle – and had set it up as a subsidiary company called Cunard Eagle under the management of its former owner, Harold Bamberg. They then ordered two Boeing 707s (for which they did not have to get, as we would, a Minister's approval) in expectation of getting the licence.

The timing could not have been worse from our point of view. If Cunard were allowed on to the North Atlantic with additional aircraft, it could only be at the cost of traffic that we badly needed in the recession then beginning.

It was therefore essential to resist this application. A hearing by the Air Transport Licensing Board was set for mid-May 1961. It was annoying to have to spend so much time defending our position when we really ought to have been devoting our energies to positive sales promotion. But there was no alternative. As our counsel we retained Mr H A P (now Sir Henry) Fisher. I was principal witness for BOAC and the hearing lasted three whole days. On 30 May we attended again to learn the unwelcome decision of the Licensing Board that Cunard Eagle were to be granted the licence.

We decided to appeal. The Minister appointed a retired judge, Sir Fred Pritchard, as the commissioner to hear the case at the end of September in the council chamber of the Holborn Town Hall. I was more than a little nervous at being cross-examined by so eminent a QC as Mr Gerald Gardiner (later Lord Gardiner and Lord Chancellor) who was retained by Cunard Eagle. Harry Fisher's presentation of our case was masterly. He argued that this was the worst possible moment to introduce another carrier on the London-New York route.

In his judgment, Sir Fred Pritchard concluded that the Air Transport Licensing Board, in granting the licence, had not exercised their proper function of furthering the development of British civil aviation. He recommended that the Cunard Eagle licence be revoked. On 21 November the Minister, Peter (now Lord) Thorneycroft, announced in the House of Commons his acceptance of that recommendation and duly revoked the licence.

The outcome was very gratifying. Though the time we had to spend in warding off this threat was wholly negative, it did serve to establish future guidelines for the Licensing Board. What we desperately needed in 1961 was not just to retain our business, but to increase it.

★   ★   ★   ★   ★

One problem that Matthew Slattery wanted to sort out was the VC10 order, and in particular the additional 10 Super VC10s which he had unsuccessfully asked Pops d'Erlanger to refrain from buying. The Standard VC10, of which 35 had been ordered in 1957, was designed to operate on the 'Empire routes' with a good performance out of hot and high airfields. In September 1960 we were still waiting for a full design specification from George Edwards for the Super VC10. When it came, we found it to be an aircraft with specialised application to long-haul temperate-zone routes.

We therefore asked George Edwards to modify the design to make it more usable on all our routes. He did so, and produced a design which Charles Abell, our Chief Engineer, regarded as every bit as good as the Boeing 707 – except, of course, for its extra weight and consequent higher operating cost. We were stuck with that as a result of Government policy to produce something different from the American-designed 707.

The improved economics of the Super VC10 reduced our need for Standard VC10s. Vickers told us they were committed to produce at least 15 Standard VC10s, but that we could take the rest of the 35 as Supers if we wished. Well, we did wish; and so the two orders for 45 aircraft were changed in early 1961 from 35 Standards and 10 Supers to 15 Standards and 30 Supers.

We really began to feel the bite of the recession in the summer of that year. We had to review yet again the whole question of how many aircraft we might expect to use with profit by 1966, when delivery of all VC10s was expected to be completed. Of course, it all depended on how long the recession would last.

We hoped it would last only a year. If traffic growth got back to its previous rate of nearly 15 per cent a year by 1963, and if, soon after, we retired all our other aircraft except the Boeing 707 – notwithstanding the capital loss we should have to take on the Comet 4 – we might possibly expect to find use for some 42 VC10s and Super VC10s. In getting at this figure, we were acknowledging that we were irrevocably committed by Cabinet to both VC10 orders; and we were assuming, too, that the Government would accept the financial consequences to BOAC of that Cabinet decision. We felt we had no alternative but to try to make the best of a bad job in the national interest.

We set out to persuade Vickers to cut the total order by at least three. In the end Vickers agreed – well aware by then of the predicament the recession had placed us in. We need not take more than 12 Standards (as against 15) but we would have to take 30 Supers. Even with that cut, the total order was worth £128 million, excluding spares, to Vickers and the new British Aircraft Corporation.

From then on production of the VC10s and their Rolls-Royce engines proceeded apace. The first aircraft was flown out of the airfield at Weybridge by BAC's Jock Bryce and Vickers' Brian Trubshaw on 29 June 1962. 'Flaps' Rendall and Frank Walton were the two captains BOAC appointed flight manager and his deputy of the VC10 flight that October.

The flight development programme revealed in its early stages some unexpected aerodynamic drag, which adversely affected performance in certain conditions. But George Edwards was able to introduce modifications which overcame this shortcoming satisfactorily by mid-1963; in terms of aerofoil design the aircraft was superb and its rear-engined layout certainly gave its passengers a quiet and comfortable ride. By March of that year, too, sufficient technical advances had been made for a decision to equip all VC10s with full automatic (or blind) landing.

Members of the board and management had their first flight in a VC10 out of Wisley airfield in June. Deliveries were expected to begin in February 1964, after the certificate of airworthiness – but this was some nine months late compared with the 1957 contract dates.

★   ★   ★   ★   ★

In the course of our continuing attack on maintenance costs, our industrial relations in the engineering department ran into difficulty. A bit of trouble arose in January 1961 because, so it seemed to me, BOAC had a new chairman and the shop stewards' committee wanted to flex their muscles to see how Matthew Slattery would react.

Sensing this, Matthew and I were anxious to get any trial of strength over as soon as possible. To the shop stewards there seemed to be an opportunity that January, while negotiations on a wage claim stood adjourned. The negotiations had not broken down, and to that extent the shop stewards were foot-faulted before they started. In any event, it was a weak issue to choose as a test case. And it was January, with the weather not good for open-air mass meetings. I felt management were on good ground and could not fail to win. This was the time for a showdown if it had to come.

In the two years or so since the unofficial strike of October 1958, I had been able to get the national officers of the trade unions to agree that mass meetings should not be held in the maintenance area or indeed anywhere on London Airport. There were two reasons: firstly, the publicity from resident press and television did much harm to BOAC; second, the national officers of our unions felt that at on-site mass meetings they were at a disadvantage in face of the support accorded to local shop stewards. We would continue to allow staff to attend mass meetings, but off the airport.

That January of 1961 the shop stewards decided to hold the

meeting on Feltham Green. The attendance was quite good – which was perhaps just as well, because the shop stewards failed to get the support of a majority of those present. Having tried their luck, and found it wanting, they let it go at that.

In early summer of 1961 we embarked on the next important phase of maintenance re-organisation. We had decided to introduce a new supervisory system which combined quality inspection with production supervision and required less staff for a given volume of work. Before that we had months of consultations, and had agreed to reduce staff numbers through wastage and non-recruitment rather than redundancy.

Regrettably, members of the Electrical Trades Union went on unofficial strike when we started to introduce the agreed new procedure. They were later joined in sympathy by other engineering staff. The National Joint Council was called together to resolve the matter, and full working was at length resumed on 20 July – but not before the strike had cost BOAC some £3 million in lost business in the high season of a year already made perilously difficult by the American recession.

Faced with our deteriorating financial position, I had been thinking how best to keep up morale when we had our backs to the wall.

At about this time I had several opportunities of talks with Lord Montgomery of Alamein. He journeyed around the world quite often in those days and was a convinced supporter of BOAC. He almost always sent a message ahead when he was about to pass through the airport, adding that he wanted no publicity. In fact he seemed always to welcome the attentions of the press as long as they were unsought. Whenever possible, I went over to the terminal to see the great man off or welcome him back. On these occasions, and with the need for better communication throughout the airline very much on my mind, I used to draw him out on the part communication plays in human leadership to see what I could learn.

'Monty' was fascinated with the problem and came several times to our headquarters at London Airport to talk to top management about it. He realised that the problem was very different in a scattered airline compared with a massing of troops. 'You may be right in working through your weekly news-sheet,' he said to me, 'but you must be seen about – the written word isn't personal enough. And you must talk to the troops and explain things to them.'

I told him I took the point, but I didn't see how I could get them all together because an airline is continuously 'in action' and our people spread all over the world. 'Yes, I realise that,' he replied. 'But you've got to find some way of overcoming it.' There was a pause. 'This is a very interesting question,' he went on. 'I have a friend with a factory in Lancashire who asks my advice about this. Of course, at a works he can call all his staff together and talk to them. In the Army, before an offensive, you have all your troops around you. I don't know what I would do in an airline, but I would have to get at the chaps personally, somehow. Before D day, you know, I made a point of that. There were too many of them, of course – but I managed to get as far down the line as Colonels, by taking seven hundred of them at a time.'

Seven hundred Colonels a time at a series of meetings! This seemed somewhat remote from getting at the chaps. A good deal would of course spread downwards to rank-and-file; in Monty's case it was his image that counted. I had somehow or other to explain to people on the shop floor, and in our aircraft, what we were doing and why. And apart from my meetings with pilots on stand-off duty and talking with whoever I met in hangars and offices or in aircraft, I had no alternative but to use the written word – video was not then available.

I decided to write to staff myself in a column in our weekly *BOAC News*. It would enable me to keep all staff continuously informed at first hand about the problems and progress of BOAC and about the reasons behind our actions and policies. I wrote my first weekly article on 30 October 1961, when I happened to be visiting our Hong Kong office.

Sad though it was to have had this unofficial stoppage that July, it is good to record, as I was able to tell Matthew Slattery, that in the year 1961 we were bringing down our aircraft engineering and maintenance costs at base to the new low level of 2.4p per ctm (compared with over 4.2p three years earlier). Our total operating costs would be down to 12p per ctm, and our break-even load factor down to no more than 52 per cent. That stoppage proved to have been the shop stewards' last fling of resistance to change.

Thereafter we made more rapid progress in completing the re-organisation of our engineering department and bringing our aircraft maintenance costs down still further.

★   ★   ★   ★   ★

Meanwhile, changes had been taking place at the top of the flight operations department. In 1959 Jim Weir suffered a severe attack of shingles. He had carried a heavy load of worry before we could accept the Britannias into service. He had a check flight that March, and passed successfully. But soon afterwards he asked to be relieved of his responsibilities as chief of flight operations. Fortunately our regional representative in Australia, Phillip Hood, was on the point of retiring. Jim Weir had been brought up in Australia and his wife Gwen was Australian. I posted him there to represent us throughout the South West Pacific.

Jim Weir's work as CFO had been carried on by his deputy, Capt Tommy Farnsworth. An able line pilot, and an even better development pilot, with a great care for detail, Tommy Farnsworth had been a first-class No 2. We now needed a new arrangement.

Wilfred Neden, Ken Bergin and I gave this a lot of thought. As a result of the 1955 pilot restlessness I had appointed practising pilots as head of the flight operations department and of each flight. But the extent of chairborne management in the job made it unrealistic to continue to combine the two qualities, as Jim Weir had been able to.

We decided to double-head the department by appointing as chief of flight operations a captain of long experience who had given up flying, and as chief pilot a captain current on the latest types of aircraft. The chief pilot would also attend management and board meetings when not flying on duty.

The two we appointed in October 1960 were respectively 54-year-old Denis Peacock and 45-year-old John Woodman, currently on Boeing 707s.

★ ★ ★ ★ ★

Important though human relations always are, the most pressing task facing us in 1961 was to win a greater share of the lesser numbers then wanting to travel. We could no longer be content with selling as hard as our competitors. Our selling had to be better and more effective than anyone else's.

Gilbert Lee, who had become commercial director a year before, brought together our sales managers, route by route, to concert plans for the coming months. In the first two months of 1961 Derek Glover and Basil Bampfylde held sales conferences for southern and for eastern routes, both in London; and Ross Stainton inaugurated a new sales drive in North America.

As we moved on through spring into early summer it began to look as though we were not going to fall far short of our traffic targets on eastern and southern routes. The number of passengers had not yet been significantly reduced by the travel hold-off in the United States. But in America the fall in passenger travel continued to be very severe. Not only the business recession was causing it. There was a 'Berlin situation' in 1961, and a French crisis in Algeria.

Americans felt that a holiday in Europe could be a risky venture.

Whatever the obvious or subtle influences at work, the fact was that, try as hard as we could, the number of our North Atlantic passengers remained 11 per cent below target through April, May and June. If things continued like that throughout the year, our revenue would end up some £10 million short.

This was very serious. It was no consolation that both the American international airlines, PanAm and TWA, were suffering in the same way; nor that US internal airlines such as American, Braniff, Delta, Eastern and the domestic side of TWA were in similar straits. So in the second half of June, Ross Stainton and I went to New York again in a further effort to improve their selling.

Justifying selling costs has fascinated me since my Hoover days of the 1930s, when more was spent on selling than on making the product. It is impossible ever to prove that selling expenditure is really worth it – impossible, because there is never any reliable and factual evidence. But management can try to ensure that you get your money's worth.

Ross and I determined to transform our sales department throughout the United States into a thoroughgoing marketing organisation. Without lessening the effectiveness of our current selling, we allocated people to carry out the necessary basic market research. We recruited our advertising agents in America to help in this work. I wanted our American organisation to be far more clear about what sort of people our passengers were; where they lived; why they travelled; what papers they read; how far ahead they decided to travel, whether for business or holiday; what influenced their choice of airline; and so on. By the careful use of sampling methods we soon acquired a deeper insight into our potential market, and the best ways of selling to it. Then we re-allocated the sales budgets to ensure that money was spent at the right point in the right way at the right time. There was to be no more hit-and-miss selling.

To achieve all this reasonably quickly, we naturally had to move a number of our managers around. Aware of the challenge, they set about it with great zest. To lead our selling Ross moved Leslie Hyland, his sales manager western routes, from London to New York. H O (Peter) Baker was also posted to New York from UK to be sales manager USA, with Bill Shepherd as his deputy. Soon after, in February 1962, Leslie Hyland was appointed manager USA to complete our American marketing revolution. That organisation was later acknowledged to be the most effective of any airline operating into and out of the United States.

To our great relief, traffic across the Atlantic had begun to pick up in July and August 1961. In fact, we succeeded in getting 2 per cent more than our target in those two months compared with 11 per cent less in the June quarter. But that proved to be no more than a temporary surge of demand which had been held back by the pervading financial stringency. The travel hold-off soon set in again and began spreading to other routes. To lessen its effects our American transatlantic competitors – PanAm and TWA – began to use their Boeing 707s to introduce nonstop services from New York to Paris, Frankfurt, Zurich and Rome, bypassing Britain.

Gilbert Lee was certainly having an uncomfortable run-in as our commercial director. We arranged to hold a world sales conference in London in December, the first we had held since the critical days of 1956.

Over the previous three or four years, while preparing for the jets and the competition they would bring, we had equipped ourselves with the necessary mechanics of selling. We had modernised sales shops and opened new ones in many of the key traffic-generating cities of the world. Since 1958 we had brought 62 new sales offices into use. By the end of 1961 we had a total of 142 throughout the world; and we had achieved this build-up while reducing the cost of selling per seat and developing an electronic seat–reservation system in the UK. Telephone and counter staff could now find out by pressing a button whether space was available on a flight or, if not, the best alternative flight. We had also methodically extended our worldwide communications system to the point that it was handling twenty thousand messages a day.

All this was done in the belief that, in conditions of keen competition, the airline that gave the quickest reliable answer would be likely to get and hold the business.

The mechanics of selling were dealt with. There remained the human side. At that time one extra passenger per flight would bring in £1½ million a year. So I told the world sales conference that December that all we needed to pay our way were six more passengers on every flight; and that it was on the sales department that the rest of BOAC relied to draw in those six missing passengers.

★　　★　　★　　★　　★

While all this was happening we had to review the whole forward policy of the airline against the background of lost revenue caused by the air travel recession.

By September 1961 we could see from current trends that we were heading for an operating loss of £5 million in the financial year to

March 1962, compared with an operating profit of more than £4 million in the year before. But though we were going to make a loss, the Government were still entitled to draw their fixed dividend of £6 million. Paying this out on top of a £5 million loss would make a deficit of £11 million.

That was in respect of our own operations. In addition, and because of the general slump in air traffic growth, it looked as though our Associated Companies would lose over £3 million. That would take our combined deficit up to £14 million.

We had to think hard. There could be no question of flying on blindly. Suppose traffic failed to grow for another year or two after that? What then? Had air travel reached saturation point? Had the air already taken from the sea all the traffic likely to change its mode of transport? These were the sort of fundamental questions we had to ask ourselves.

In the process of checking our basic assumptions about the future of our market, we were fortunate in having on the board two members of wide commercial and industrial experience – Sir Walter Worboys from ICI and J A Connel from Unilever. They helped us greatly in our critical reassessment of the long term. Whichever way we looked at it, we always came back with the same answer: the ease of air transport and its comparatively low cost were so attractive that there was no doubt that the air travel market would expand for many years to come. The present check to growth could only be temporary. Before long (yes, but before how long?) traffic would start growing again, and probably as fast as before if not faster. Then we should be profitable again – and more so than before, because of the substantial reduction in cost levels we had achieved.

*   *   *   *   *

We then had to ask ourselves what action, if any, we ought to take in the short term. Did we need the frequency of service we had planned on all our routes? Could we retire any aircraft from service earlier than planned? Should we cut out any of our routes, new or old? Would it improve matters if we reduced BOAC drastically in size and concentrated only on those routes with the heaviest traffic? These and other issues we considered at length.

To some extent, we were caught in a trap of our own making. We improved our efficiency and increased the productivity of our Boeing 707 and Comet 4 fleets to 4,000 flying hours a year, compared with 3,000 hours a year which we had thought in 1956 was all we could achieve. We had therefore already brought forward the retirement dates of all our propeller-driven aircraft, except for two

With Cunard Chairman Sir John Brocklebank and BOAC Chairman Sir
Matthew Slattery, after signing the BOAC-Cunard agreement, 6 June 1962.
(British Airways)

A BOAC-Cunard VC10 at London Heathrow Airport.   *(British Airways)*

The *Queen Mary* leaves the Solent for the last time 31 October 1967, bound
for Long Beach, California.   *(Daily Mirror)*

The *QE2's* hull design unveiled, 4 April 1967. From left: Dan Wallace, BS,
James Gardner, Lord Aberconway, and Tom Kameen.   *(Daily Mirror)*

DC-7C freighters. But the board considered that 'a radical cut-back in the scale of operations . . . was found to offer no immediate solution. The withdrawal of widely advertised, partly sold services at short notice would have served only to increase losses. The immediate and consequential sacrifice of revenue, competitive strength and goodwill could not be compensated for by the resulting savings in direct costs.'[1]

After a series of top-management meetings, the board decided to continue and even intensify our efforts to win more traffic, and not to allow overall policy to be governed by short-term considerations. In its wisdom Parliament had decreed, through the Air Corporations Acts, that one year should be taken with another for that very purpose. All of us on the board felt that it was of fundamental importance not to prejudice the corporation's future. In the meantime BOAC would have to ride out the turbulent weather.

★   ★   ★   ★   ★

That decision taken, we now had a settled and sensible policy. What more could we do? We were already tightly controlling costs, department by department. And we now had the help of our unions to avoid unofficial work stoppages. We mounted renewed drives in punctuality, and standards of service. That autumn I decided to impose yet another economy drive on all departments, and recruited specialist help in methods-study by bringing in Dr J E Faraday from ICI.

On the marketing side, Leslie Hyland had been doing so well in New York that in 1963 Gilbert Lee and I brought him back to London to apply his American experience to the rest of our sales organisation, and make our marketing more effective worldwide.

Marketing had become far more scientific than in the past and had taken on a new commericial meaning. As compared with the old concept of merely producing something and then trying to sell it, it now covered the whole field of research into what people wanted to buy before you even started to produce it. It was not possible to backtrack, of course, but in an airline marketing was seen to cover even such questions as aircraft type and cabin layout, routes to be operated, standards of service in the air and on the ground, fares to attract travellers, and the proper selling of our product to the public.

In fact, everyone in an airline is involved in selling. As I went round the corporation, in Britain as well as overseas, I told staff that selling BOAC was not only the responsibility of the sales

[1]BOAC Annual Report 1961-62, p 13.

department. It was something in which all of us had a part to play, whether we were flying aircraft or maintaining them; whether we were cabin crew or traffic staff in close contact with passengers; whether we were preparing aircraft meals or handling telephone calls from agents or the public; whether we were active members of trade unions or not; or whether we were engaged in any other of the hundred and one things that have to be done in the running of an airline. The way we all did our various jobs was vital in leading people to prefer BOAC. We all shared with the sales department the responsibility for selling BOAC to the public and meeting the great challenge facing us.

14 The Arguments go Round and Round

The chill wind did not abate nor did the sun shine in 1962. True, traffic began to pick up a bit on the North Atlantic but the revenue it brought increased hardly at all. For one thing, the continued 'Fly American' policy attracted traffic away from non-US airlines. For another, many airlines were still bringing new jets into service in large numbers, so that all aircraft flying the North Atlantic were far less than half-full. Why pay first-class when a passenger could generally get three economy seats to himself and spread himself out? In spite of this slight recovery in North Atlantic passenger numbers, there was no growth on eastern routes and there was an actual fall on southern routes.

But we had set our course. There was nothing for it but to beat to windward and weather the storm, as long as it lasted.

One of the storm's casualties that I felt most sad about was Eric Rylands' Skyways. Eric and his chairman Wavell Wakefield (later Lord Wakefield of Kendal) had always been convinced that the best policy for an independent airline was to supplement the work of BOAC as a genuine associate, and not to make things more difficult for us to compete internationally by taking our traffic away from us. They ferried our spare engines to and from UK and operated freight services for us on our eastern routes.

But in the early 1960s two things happened. As the proportion of our piston-engined aircraft fell from 70 per cent of our fleet to only 5 per cent, and as jet engines were proving so much more reliable in operation, our need for ferrying spare engines around the world fell right away. And with traffic standing still and the larger Boeings coming into service, we had so much empty space in our passenger aircraft that we could carry the cargo ourselves.

Matthew and I held a series of meetings with Wavell and Eric in the spring of 1962 to see if we could find a way round the problem. We could find none. To the sorrow of us all, we had to terminate the association and, with it, Skyways' chances of survival in the long-haul freighter field.

But Skyways were not the only independent to fall foul of the aviation malaise in the early 1960s. Quite a number were taken over or had to be merged in face of harsh economic facts and the increasing obsolescence of their aircraft. They also had to pay for the capricious way in which Government trooping contracts were distributed, making long-term planning difficult, if not impossible. Myles Wyatt's Airwork, Maurice Curtis's Hunting-Clan and Freddie Laker's Aviation Traders found independence difficult and came together to form British United Airways. For a time Eoin Mekie's Britavia became associated with the P&O shipping group, but disenchantment set in after the loss of trooping contracts. And Harold Bamberg had sold his Eagle Airways to Cunard.

★   ★   ★   ★   ★

Glad as I was that we had prevented Cunard Eagle from coming on the transatlantic route and taking much needed traffic away from us, it did seem to me that there was a good chance of strengthening British aviation on the North Atlantic if Cunard Eagle were prepared to enter into a genuine association with BOAC. In the first place, as Bamberg had appreciated, the Cunard name had a magic about it and could well bring additional traffic; Cunard had a dozen or two sales offices in strategic points throughout the United States which could become shop windows for air as well as sea travel.

Secondly, not only were the selling aspects attractive. Cunard Eagle had ordered two Boeing 707s. These could make a valuable addition to our fleet. For the present (early 1962) we had more capacity than we needed; but once traffic started to grow again, we could well find ourselves short of 707 aircraft on the North Atlantic.

Thirdly, I felt that if private capital had a significant stake in our enterprise, it would free us somewhat from the sort of pressures we had been under from previous Ministers to order British aircraft off the drawing board, contrary to our commercial instincts. A last point much in my mind, and which I thought would appeal greatly to our trade unions at a time when we were reducing staff numbers in our engineering department, was that BOAC could take on the maintenance of these two Cunard aircraft.

I tried out my ideas on Matthew Slattery one morning. He agreed immediately. He realised that, while Cunard had the two 707s, there was always the risk that they could persuade a Conservative Government to grant them another licence; and what I was suggesting would pre-empt that. He couldn't see why they should like the idea. Nor could I – except that it might just appeal to Cunard (as distinct from Eagle) in that it would bring their name into transatlantic aviation and give them a lasting interest in it. My idea was that we should set up a subsidiary company to hold some of our transatlantic Boeing 707s and Cunard would get their minority interest in this joint company in exchange for their two aircraft.

Here was a difficulty which we should have to get round in one way or another; the thought of a nationalised industry forming a joint company with a private-enterprise independent airline would be anathema to some of our trade unions. If they got the slightest scent of what was in the wind, they could block it on political grounds – regardless of whether it would bring additional work to our hangars and workshops. One way the unions often scented what was afoot was through management papers which, in the normal process of work, came into the hands of staff who happened to be members of ASSET, and who passed them on. There had, in fact, been occasions when it almost seemed that they had seen management minutes before management themselves. I instituted special security procedures during the Cunard negotiations. All copies of papers were numbered, circulation was strictly limited and recorded, and nothing was to be minuted until afterwards.

I then asked R F (Dick) Taylor of Cunard and Harold Bamberg of Eagle to talk about the situation resulting from the loss of their licence, now that the dust had settled a bit. They came to my office at BOAC headquarters at London Airport on 27 April 1962. Winnie Bray was with me and I outlined my tentative ideas. Harold Bamberg remained quiet throughout. But I had been right: and it became evident that Dick Taylor thought Cunard could well be interested in the possibility of promoting a company jointly with BOAC. We would have further talks after he had referred back to his chairman, Sir John Brocklebank. Meanwhile, I impressed on both the need for absolute secrecy.

It seemed that John Brocklebank and his board approved because matters went ahead fairly rapidly. The only contentious issue was the size of Cunard's minority interest. Matthew and I felt that we could not justify their having more than 25 per cent of the joint company and we reached agreement on this at a meeting on 16 May in Cunard's offices in Lower Regent Street. The proposal was now complete, and the time had arrived to seek Government approval – not that we expected anything but a warm welcome for it from Conservatives.

Matthew and I saw the Minister, Peter Thorneycroft, and duly received his blessing in principle. But a couple of days later Matthew was told that, for the proposed development to be politically acceptable to the Government, we should have to increase Cunard's share to 33⅓ per cent. We demurred at first but eventually compromised with the Minister (John Brocklebank did not appear to have taken any part in all this bargaining, which was obviously political). Cunard had 30 per cent and BOAC 70 per cent.

The BOAC-Cunard agreement was signed on 6 June 1962. Later that afternoon, Matthew, John Brocklebank and I announced it to the press at Londonderry House in Park Lane. At the same time we issued to staff a special edition of *BOAC News* which had been run off by outside printers who specialise in confidential documents such as company prospectuses.

Overnight, as I had half expected, all hell broke loose on the trade union front. Those who gave politics top priority were incensed that such a thing could have been arranged betwen a private company and a public industry. Worse still, Clive Jenkins seemed to be doubly incensed that his usual sources of information had not given him advance warning of what was afoot. After a good deal of steam had been let off in the next few days, the unions accepted that the agreement was good for their members in BOAC.

We decided to call the new joint company BOAC-Cunard Ltd, though it was some little time before the American authorities gave permission for aircraft to use that name on routes for which BOAC was the designated British airline. The new board met for the first time on 22 June 1962 at Airways Terminal in Buckingham Palace Road, and got quickly down to work. The following week we began to interchange staff between our various commercial offices.

★   ★   ★   ★   ★

Airlines all round the world were having a very difficult time. By July 1962 we learnt that Lufthansa, the West German airline, had lost nearly £11 million in 1961. KLM, the Royal Dutch airline, reported a loss of £4 million in the first quarter of 1962. American domestic airlines were said to have lost more than £7 million in the same period, despite some increase in traffic.

Pan American Airways and Trans World Airlines were also in temporary financial difficulty. PanAm had long resented their exclusion from US domestic markets enjoyed by TWA, and TWA's overseas routes mostly complemented those of PanAm. So Juan Trippe, PanAm's president, started talking about a merger of the two. But Howard Hughes, TWA's egotistic and autocratic owner, would have none of it; and the idea came to nothing. Indeed, it was not until the last days of 1979 that PanAm finally succeeded in taking over National Airlines and so realised its 30-year-old ambition to back up its worldwide international operations with a US domestic network.

Within our Commonwealth partnerships, too, there were severe strains – all brought on by the recession in one way or another. Traffic between Canada and Britain remained surprisingly good through 1961, in contrast to US/UK traffic, and this helped our newly formed partnership with Air Canada to take root. But Canadian traffic fell off badly in 1962, and sharing a diminished volume produced passing disenchantment, though no more than that.

Again, traffic between Africa and Europe virtually stagnated through both years, at a time when East African Airways were trying to build up its frequencies to London. EAA wanted to put on seven flights a week compared with eleven and four for BOAC and SAA respectively. The overcapacity was unwelcome to those of us who had run the long-haul services on those routes for the past twenty years or so.

Then there was Qantas, recently committed to operating both ways round the world from Australia to Britain (eastabout across America as well as westabout across India). The Australian airline was anxious to protect its eastabout route from the shortfall in American traffic by seeking a new route to Britain via Mexico, the Bahamas and Bermuda. The last two were still British territory for air-traffic rights purposes. We were still smarting from not having traffic rights between America and Australia in the UK/USA bilateral and we did not like the idea of granting these additional new rights to the Australians. The stage was set for a fierce and lengthy argument between BOAC and Qantas.

After several meetings stretching out over a couple of years, matters came to a head in May 1963. We held a joint meeting in San Francisco, mid-way between us. Cedric Turner and his team were ensconced in the Fairmont Hotel on Nob Hill and I and my team were in the Mark Hopkins nearby. Cedric was a tough negotiator, and had to be met with equal firmness. The remarkable thing about the BOAC-Qantas partnership has been that, however forthright and heated our arguments became, we always ended up with an acceptable *modus operandi* and remained the firm friends we had always been – the result no doubt of forty years in partnership and an awareness that both airlines owed much to each other.

*   *   *   *   *

In April 1961 the Government had issued a new White Paper

outlining the financial and economic obligations of the nationalised industries. Its purpose was to set profitability targets.

I for one have always believed that profitability is the only test by which people in a free society can say whether they value a business enough to warrant its continuation. If a business cannot earn for its goods or services more than it costs to produce them, then society does not rate those goods or services highly enough for them to go on being produced. Almost the best feature of this profit criterion – which is not the same thing as the profit motive – is that it is automatic and devoid of sentiment as a regulator of all forms of economic activity; its working is governed directly by the wishes of all the people in a free society as expressed in the way they spend their money.

I am not of course talking about social services. It is always possible for any society to subsidise particular activities for social or non-financial reasons.

The test of profitability should apply every bit as much to a nationalised industry as to any other. The only basic difference is that a nationalised industry does not go bankrupt or get wound up in the way that a private business does if it makes losses; it is kept in being by the Government. Indeed, the basic reason why certain industries have been nationalised is that the Government regards its products or services as of sufficient importance to the community for them to be kept going regardless of short-term financial considerations. But if they continue making losses indefinitely they can be kept only out of taxation.

In applying the profit criterion to the nationalised industries we have to remember that the working of this regulator depends on annual accounts and reporting. To that extent it is short-term and sometimes erratic in its effects. So, in the various nationalising Acts of Parliament, the Governments of the day have laid down that the industries concerned should be required to make profits 'taking one year with another', generally meaning a five-year period.

The April 1961 Government White Paper set out to discuss with the various nationalised industries the profit percentage that each must achieve, depending on its particular circumstances. It was a very sensible objective. But BOAC was well down the list and we did not enter into talks with Government until the early part of 1962.

When we were called without much notice to a meeting with the Minister, who was still Peter Thorneycroft, Matthew Slattery was away in Africa. Wilfred Neden and Ken Bevan went with me to the Ministry. Peter Thorneycroft was by then fully aware of our financial problems due to the traffic hold-off caused by the American recession. He was sympathetic and considerate. We acknowledged the purpose of the White Paper and indeed welcomed it – on the basis that, since the present circumstances were wholly exceptional, one year would be taken with another.

We tabled estimates of our financial recovery once traffic started growing again at 15 per cent a year. The Minister's civil servants wouldn't accept them, and trotted out target profits which we thought quite unrealistic. They knew we couldn't achieve them if – and here was the catch – we continued running BOAC on its existing lines. Whether this was a ploy to break up BOAC and parcel it out to private enterprise we were never to know.

We could see at a glance that the Ministry civil servants were not only using revenue estimates that were outdated and over-pessimistic even in current circumstances; they were also not crediting us with cost savings we were already achieving.

In any case, we said, target profit should not be just a figure expressed in millions of pounds but, according to the White Paper, a profit percentage related to capital employed. And the calculation of capital would give rise to important questions in the financial relations between Corporation and Government. These would need clearing first. We would come back for further talks with the Ministry when Matthew Slattery was back in England.

★　★　★　★　★

In doing our homework for those further talks, we naturally began by putting a value on all the matters raised by Pops d'Erlanger in successive Annual Reports. First of all, we had to make a tally of our total losses due to the late delivery, proving and introduction costs, short lives and low resale values of British aircraft introduced since the Second World War in accordance with Government policy. Back in 1959 Pops d'Erlanger had asked permission to write off some £6 million on this account, but had not been allowed by the Minister to do so.

But now, in 1962, with the knowledge of three more years, we could more accurately assess those costs. We now knew fairly definitely the dates for retiring British aircraft prematurely because they had been overtaken by more advanced American designs. And we now knew the effect of the new American jets on the prices we could expect to realise on second-hand aircraft.

The original Comet 1 had only 36 seats, all first class, when in 1952 it was the first jet airliner in the world to enter service. When the Comet was re-introduced as the Mk 4 in 1958, it had 20 first-class seats and 48 economy class, 68 in all. The Comet 4, proud as we were of it, had been far outstripped in design by the Boeing 707, which came into service only 22 days later. The Boeing 707 had 163 economy class seats at 34-inch pitch (more than double the Comet's) and a far greater range. The Comet 4 cost us 9p for every capacity ton-mile, whereas the Boeing 707 cost us less than 5½p.

The Standard VC10, which we had to order in 1957, would not be introduced until 1964, more than five years behind the Boeing. Even so, its capacity (conceived in 1957) would be no more than 127 economy class seats. The Super VC10 would have a 156-seat capacity, close to that of the Boeing 707; but it would be in service even later.

Faced with financial considerations of this sort, and the lag in British design compared with American, we were naturally forced to accelerate the withdrawal of our less attractive aircraft. The Britannias went after only four or five years in service. The Comet 4 would now have to go too, after working for no more than six years.

That was not all. Partly because air traffic had suddenly stopped growing just when many new jet aircraft were being delivered, but also because of the improved performance and economics of those new jets, the bottom fell right out of the market for second-hand airliners. We were confronted with a further serious loss of capital on this account.

The losses on British aircraft left unabsorbed in accounts then looked like this. First there was the loss of £1 million on the Avro Tudors inherited from British South American Airways in 1949. Next, the loss on the Handley Page Hermes disposed of because we were not allowed to use them for trooping, had cost us a further £3 million. The de Havilland Comet 1s cost us another £8 million – and that was only in respect of the capital invested in the aircraft themselves; it took no account of the consequential loss of business and the cost of getting aircraft to fill the gap. And then the Bristol Britannias accounted for £27 million – £22 million for themselves plus a further £5 million for the DC-7Cs to bridge the gap caused by the Britannias being delivered three years late. Altogether these losses came to £39 million.

That was not the only aspect of our financial relations with Government which needed sorting out before a sensible profitability target could be set. As Pops d'Erlanger had sought to point out, it had always been senseless to have to pay our stockholder, the Government, a fixed rate of interest or dividend whether there was sufficient profit or not. The rigidity of this fixed-dividend capital structure, and the total absence of risk-bearing capital so necessary to cushion the inevitable swings in any competitive market, was not only uncommercial – it was wholly unrealistic.

The risk had to fall somewhere; and it could fall only on the owners of BOAC. The Government might not like to think that it held equity (or the equivalent of a private-enterprise interest) in a nationalised industry. It was absurd for the Government to expect a fixed return on its money regardless of results. But that's what it did.

By 1962 we had handed over dividends worth £16 million more than the whole of our profits. What is more, we had to borrow that money back from the Government in order to pay it. From then on we would continue paying interest on the £16 million the Government itself had drawn.

Small wonder that Matthew Slattery, when asked at our 1961-62 Annual Report press conference what he thought of the way HMG arranged BOAC's finances, dubbed it 'bloody crazy'. Not perhaps the most tactful comment at that time, but it was a true assessment of the matter, and perhaps the only way to startle people into realising that the Government's method of dealing with BOAC's finances needed changing.

It was all very right and proper that we should have a profitability target. But, first of all, this overdrawing of previous profits by £16 million would have to be written off by the Government, together with the £39 million losses stemming from the Government's buy-British aircraft policy. At the same time we felt it was only common sense, in setting a profit target, for BOAC to eliminate the £15 million lost by Associated Companies under Cribbett's chairmanship. All this amounted to £70 million. Even this included no allowance for the inevitable future losses on the early retirement of Comet 4s and some VC10s, which it was then too early to calculate.

Secondly, since we did not operate in a closed domestic environment like coal or gas or electricity, but in intense international competition, we asked for a profit target referenced to actual airline-industry profitability rather than a hypothetical rate thought up by backroom boys at the Treasury or Ministry out of touch with the real world.

At the same time we asked for a substantial part of our Government-provided capital to be in the form of equity or ordinary stock, on which we should pay the Government no more than our profit would allow, less amounts necessary for us to retain for expansion and development.

★　　★　　★　　★　　★

As can be imagined, the Ministry did not like this a bit. We entered a period of very difficult relations with its officials. They were continually breathing down our necks and offering advice that was no doubt well meant but unfounded on experience of being accountable for results. An essential reason for nationalisation was that policy should be moulded with the long-term interest uppermost; yet the civil servants seemed more governed by short-term considerations. In politics the day-to-day view too often predominates. The thoughts of Ministers about numbers of votes in the constituencies, or the support they will get in the Cabinet, can be as short-term in effect as the unfettered profit criterion.

In trying to keep the Ministry mindful of long-term objectives, some of our top management worked under considerable strain, being urged one way and torn another.

The person who took most of the strain was undoubtedly Ken Bevan. As financial comptroller he was too often the nut in the crackers. His health began to fail; and the only sensible answer was to allow him to resign, which he did with effect from the end of September 1962.

Fortunately for continuity, Derek Glover was ready to hand, having added to his accounting experience a five-year spell in line management in charge of southern routes. I appointed him as financial comptroller from the beginning of October 1962.

The whole question of a profit target and what to do about our lost capital dragged on unresolved into 1963. We might have made progress if Peter Thorneycroft had not been moved across to be Minister of Defence in July 1962. A new mind – that of Julian Amery, Harold Macmillan's son-in-law – was brought in as the next Minister of Aviation.

It was obvious to us that the Government White Paper had presaged changes in the relationship between BOAC and HMG, whether we got what we asked for or not. For example, we had always understood that our main financial task as Britain's chosen instrument for long-haul air services was to earn foreign currency. We had in fact built up our foreign currency earnings so that 70 per cent of our total revenue was earned abroad compared with only 30 per cent in the UK; some 27 per cent was earned in the dollar area, 24 per cent in the sterling area, and 19 per cent elsewhere. We thus contributed substantial amounts to the national balance of payments.

When we reminded the Permanent Secretary of the Ministry, Sir Henry Hardman, of this he said: 'Well, yes, that was certainly necessary in the nineteen-fifties; but now that the country's balance of payments has improved so much, it is no longer so important to earn foreign currency.' We could hardly believe our ears.

Admittedly it was not the Treasury or the Board of Trade speaking: they might have said something very different. But it was, after all, the Ministry of Aviation, which was also sponsoring the British aircraft industry and urging it at that very moment to boost exports. The trouble was, I suppose, that our exports were 'invisible'. Or perhaps the Perm Sec just had to take that line if he was ever to put across the White Paper policy that domestic profits were what mattered now in nationalised industries, and the nation's balance of payments was left out of the reckoning. This policy obviously fitted the circumstances of domestic nationalised industries. But it was not adapted to our highly competitive international industry.

As we neared the end of 1962, information coming to us from the Vickers division of the new British Aircraft Corporation confirmed our worst fears about the higher operating costs of the VC10, both Standard and Super. In fact, Derek Glover, Winnie Bray and J B Scott calculated that we would save some £8 million a year and incur considerably less capital costs if we didn't take any VC10s at all but replaced them with more Rolls-Royce-powered Boeing 707s. Even if we had to incur a financial penalty for cancelling the VC10 contract, we should probably recover it through the first year's savings and thereafter be that much more profitable.

We told the Ministry all this. It was clear that, if we were going to be set a profit target by which we would be judged, we really ought not to take any VC10s at all. Wasn't that the logical outcome of applying the philosophy of the Government White Paper? The Ministry didn't know how to reply.

We had asked the question to make the point – that what would be in BOAC's financial interest under the new rules would not always be consistent with national policy. If the national interest required us to take all the VC10s on order, then we presumed our future profit target would be reduced by £8 million a year. That logic was most unwelcome to the Ministry: it would involve public acknowledgement of the fact that the VC10 was a high-cost aeroplane to operate, and this might seriously prejudice the British Aircraft Corporation's chances of selling it to foreign airlines and – dare I say it? – earning valuable foreign currency.

The arguments went round and round. They were still going round some 15 years later, in 1977, when I read about the problems of the Central Electricity Generating Board chairman. He was being pressed by the Government to order the Drax B coal-fired power station in Yorkshire. As reported, the chairman made it plain that he was opposed to nationalised industries undertaking without compensation unwanted capital projects deemed by Ministers to be in the national interest. It was of little value for the Minister concerned to claim some weeks later that Drax B would be an economic proposition as a coal-burning station. Ministers are never called to account for errors in their forecasting. When the day of reckoning arrives, they are almost always in some other department, or else they are in opposition. Unless there has been adequate compensation for the uncommercial elements in the Government's decision, the unfortunate head of the industry has to carry the can, and the industry has to suffer loss of public esteem.

★   ★   ★   ★   ★

But forewarned is forearmed.

For some time we had had before us George Edwards's outline ideas on the design of a Supersonic Transport (SST), destined to be known as Concord, later changed to Concorde in deference to the French company Sud-Aviation, who were going to make half of it at their factory near Toulouse.

We in BOAC were obviously alert to the probable development of supersonic travel at some stage. In 1959 I had appointed a supersonic transport committee to study the possibilities. It was led by Capt E C Miles, and included representatives from our engineering, operations planning, medical and commercial departments.

Soon after joining us in August 1960, Matthew Slattery had gone public on his SST views. He was convinced there would be supersonic transports 'provided we can overcome the noise'. BOAC would not be left behind in the race. He and I made it clear that BOAC was ready to assist in the design of an SST to come in eight or ten years' time.

But we also made it clear that, if we were going to be judged in future strictly on a financial basis, without receiving any credit or acknowledgment for our contribution to the national interest, we were determined not to order any SST until we were ready in our own commercial judgment. The price to BOAC must make economic sense; and the aircraft must be fully proved. We were not prepared to commit ourselves to a blank cheque.

The Ministry accepted that we should not be asked to make a premature commercial judgment as to its merits. Before the new Minister, Julian Amery, signed the joint agreement with the French Government in November 1962, he had put BOAC's views to the Cabinet: we preferred not to be fully committed at this stage to the Anglo-French SST – it was more important to have the best than the first. 'On the other hand,' Amery said, 'BOAC recognise that as a nationalised Corporation they have certain obligations and that, if the Government decide to go ahead with this project, they and they alone can provide the operating experience and advice which the builders will need. . . . They cannot afford to do this unless the Government agree to underwrite the risk until such time as a commercial judgment can be made.'

Well, HMG did agree to underwrite the risk. On that basis, we for our part were ready to be associated with the project 'until the early flight trials of the aircraft have taken place and an assessment of its suitability for service in the Corporation can reasonably be made'. BOAC was thus placed in the position it wanted, of being able to lend technical support to the Anglo-French SST without any commitment at that stage to operate it in commercial airline service.

In 1963 the technical and economic arguments continued in America and elsewhere as to the best SST. The size and range of the big subsonic jets had been largely determined by the defence requirements of the United States, with the broad oceans of the Atlantic and Pacific on either side of her; and in fact their development would not have taken place without US defence money. But supersonic transport was no longer regarded as necessary to US defence. No more defence money was made available. SST development cost would have to fall wholly on the civil version alone. At the same time, in a Government-funded civil competition, Boeing's swingwing project beat Lockheed's delta – and then was cancelled because of gross overweight. It was not long before America withdrew from the race to develop a supersonic airliner. This left the field clear for the Anglo-French Concorde, but at the same time ensured that its eventual lone arrival in airline service could only be uneconomic – wonderful technical achievement though it is.

15 The Un-reason of Politics

Some years later, when I was chairman of Cunard and negotiating the start of a partnership with the Australian National Line, I came to know and admire one of the greater statesmen of this century, the Rt Hon Sir John McEwen, Deputy Prime Minister of Australia from 1958 to 1971 and Prime Minister in 1967-68. In the course of time we became good friends. I remember talking to him at his home in Toorak during a visit to Australia in March 1976. It was about some development in British politics which I felt, doubtless in my ignorance, to be singularly stupid. 'I wouldn't know,' he said. 'You see, politics is governed much more by procedure than be reason.'

I found this observation so interesting that I noted it down at the time. And, in truth, it goes some way towards explaining the happenings of 1963.

I have not, and never have been, a political animal. Looking back on it now with hindsight, I can see that I made the mistake of simply getting on with my job and not guarding my political flanks. I had certainly not appreciated the dangers that would follow if our chairman were ever to fall foul of the Conservative Party's Civil Aviation Committee.

When Julian Amery took office as Minister of Aviation in July 1962, he found a number of problems on his plate – as any new Minister must do. But in his relations with BOAC, which it was his statutory duty to sponsor, there was a particularly knotty one. It stemmed from the arrival on his predecessor's desk of the Government White Paper on the Financial and Economic Obligations of the Nationalised Industries. Almost simultaneously there arrived reports of the slump in the growth of air travel and its effect on BOAC's finances.

For the second year running we were about to report an operating loss of some £5 million. We had, too, asked permission to clean up our balance sheet and write off £70 million of capital, most of it lost on Government account. We had also asked for a flexible capital structure in future, with substantial equity capital which would rank for dividend only when we made profits. We had also sought credit for the higher costs of introducing and operating British aircraft such as the VC10.

It was obvious from the case of the VC10 that there was now a built-in conflict between the new philosophy of the Government White Paper and the previously acknowledged role of BOAC as an instrument of national policy. This concept of BOAC's role had even been mentioned with approval by Julian Amery himself in his paper to the Cabinet about Concorde. As we said in our Annual Report of 18 September 1962 to Julian Amery, 'BOAC's present capital position is largely the result of policies that followed a concept of the Corporation's role that has now been changed.'

In view of the confusion created by the Government White Paper, Matthew Slattery submitted a paper to Julian Amery in August, and again in November 1962, seeking a new policy directive from the Minister spelling out our new role.

The problem before Julian Amery was how to deal with our request in face of this new conflict of policy. And this was where the procedure of politics began to take over. Whatever solution the Government wanted to reach – if indeed anyone had yet defined the solution – the Minister first summoned Wilfred Neden and myself (Matthew Slattery was again away at the time) to a meeting on 26 September 1962. There we were told by the Permanent Secretary, Sir Henry Hardman, that the Minister hoped we would facilitate an enquiry into our financial problems by an eminent City chartered account, John T Corbett, a senior partner in Peat, Marwick, Mitchell & Co. The purpose of the inquiry was to provide the Minister with an independent report on our financial situation, on the basis of which he could proceed to the next stage. We couldn't very well refuse, as we didn't want to make it difficult for the Minister to give us what we had asked. And if an inquiry would help, so much the better.

Two days later John Corbett came down to lunch at London Airport with another partner, G W Dunkerley, who was to work full time on the inquiry. I introduced them to all our top management – and in particular to Derek Glover, who was then taking over from Ken Bevan as financial comptroller – and left them free to see anybody and go anywhere they liked.

I didn't see much of Corbett or Dunkerley for the next four months or so, although they were around the place most of the time. It must be very difficult for someone who has never been involved in industrial decision-making to get a proper feel of how management has to work. I had been hoping for the help of a trained business mind to confirm our advice to the Minister, and to make positive recommendations. But as time passed the inquiry seemed to me more and more in the nature of an extra audit.

In mid-February 1963 the two consultants came to see me to check what they had written in their 'amortisation appendices'. These examined whether the annual amount we had provided had been adequate – despite the fact that our own auditors, Whinney Smth & Whinney, had already satisfied themselves about that. Anyone, not least myself, could take a different view with two or three years' extra hindsight.

I began to fear that nothing very positive or helpful would come of this inquiry. But it was approaching its end.

*   *   *   *   *

The setting up of the Corbett inquiry by the Minister had triggered off a good deal of speculation, which we had to counter. It was painfully obvious that we could not rely on our own Ministry for understanding and support. This was nothing to do with Julian Amery personally: it was the way the system worked. The Minister in charge of the department to which a nationalised industry was attached was described in the nationalising Act as that industry's sponsoring Minister. But never once in the fourteen years I served BOAC had any of the eight different Ministers who sponsored us done or said anything to encourage us – with the exception of Frank Pakenham (now Lord Longford) and Harold Watkinson, who asked for our 'shopping list' and got our Boeing 707 order through the Cabinet in 1956. These apart, they seemed far more intent on holding us to account than sponsoring us.

Matthew Slattery and I came to realise the stark fact that, when you were up against it in a nationalised industry, you had nobody at all to put your case across – least of all the Minister. When things went well, of course, the results spoke for themselves. But when things went awry, our sponsoring Ministry did little but criticise, thinking they knew better how to run the airline, of which they had no practical experience other than watching the game from the touchlines.

A Minister's most useful way of influencing a nationalised industry was through the appointment of board-members; and yet, having appointed men of the quality of Francis Rennell, Jack Connel and Walter Worboys, and placed them in a position to see the airline from the inside, successive Ministers never once consulted them or sought their advice.

Realising therefore that we had no-one to speak up for us

officially, and knowing something of the strength of the aircraft industry lobby in Parliament, Matthew and I made it our business to increase our informal contacts with those likely to speak on aviation matters when they came up for debate in the House of Commons. Labour were then in opposition and their two spokesmen on aviation were John Cronin and Fred Lee; both came down several times to BOAC headquarters. So did Neil Marten, Parliamentary Secretary to the Ministry of Aviation, as Basil de Ferranti had done before him. We never sought to provide them with a brief; we just gave then an opportunity to ask about anything they liked. They all seemed genuinely interested in trying to understand what was going on. But one influential group to which Matthew Slattery seemed *persona non grata* was the Conservative Civil Aviation Committee of backbenchers – and that was to have dire consequences before long.

Next Matthew Slattery and I intensified our meetings with all the regular air correspondents from early 1962 onwards. They were a diverse group of people dedicated to aviation and you couldn't pull wool over their eyes. Among the better known correspondents at that time were Arthur Narracott of *The Times*, Michael Donne of the *Financial Times*, David Fairhall of *The Guardian*, Angus McPherson of the *Daily Mail*, and of course Mike Ramsden of *Flight* and Thurstan James of *The Aeroplane*, both aviation weeklies. It was fortunate for BOAC's relations with the press at this time that we still had Freddy Gillman in charge of our press and information office – he was well liked and not due to retire until the middle of 1963.

I suppose we were expecting too much to receive sympathy and understanding all round. At this time I had the misfortune to fall foul of Mary Goldring, then writer on aviation and other matters at *The Economist*, and later to become its deputy editor. It was probably my fault, though I cannot recall anything I did or said that need have caused it. At any rate, from then on, nothing that I did in BOAC, or anywhere else for that matter, ever got a good chit from *The Economist*. This is just one of those things you have to live with.

Much as Matthew and I respected the air correspondents, we recognised that their field of interest was narrower than the issues at stake, once the Government White Paper on financial and economic obligations began to dominate the scene. We therefore held meetings with the industrial correspondents to help them appreciate the wider aspects of our current financial and management problems. These meetings included people such as Eric Wigham of *The Times*, Michael Shanks of the *Financial Times* and Trevor (later Sir Trevor) Evans of the *Daily Express*.

On top of that Matthew and I decided to go yet higher in our press relations. We held a series of private lunches for the editors themselves. We invited only two of them at a time so that the conversation could move freely along lines they themselves wanted to pursue. These talks were of great value – to us anyway, and I hope to them.

It was from these talks that something came to light which explained the curious reluctance of the Government to write off our £70 million of lost capital. Dick (later Lord) Beeching had been taken from ICI in 1961 and appointed chairman of the British Transport Commission to sort out its problems. It seemed that he was about to ask HMG to write off British Rail's lost capital too – and it was not just £70 million, but £900 million. If the Government had agreed to our request, it would have set a precedent they would not accept in the case of British Rail.

Our closer relations with the press were already producing a stirring of sympathy and understanding. In its issue of 25 April 1963 the weekly magazine *Flight*, which had by no means been uncritical of BOAC in the past, Roger Bacon (generally thought to be a pen-name used by Mike Ramsden) wrote: 'I think the time has come for somebody to say that BOAC are not – repeat not – inefficient. . . . One achievement, which has never received the praise it deserves, towers above all else. This is their breakeven load factor, which taking into account all costs is now probably less than 52 per cent. An airline with this sort of breakeven load factor cannot, I suggest, be represented as inefficient. . . . Compared with Pan American, BOAC now have a higher aircraft utilisation, a comparable total cost level, a lower cost per hour, and a higher output of flying hours per employee. BOAC are *not* grossly inefficient, or even mildly inefficient. They are now, after a real struggle, efficient by any standard except that of US domestic airlines. . . . BOAC's trouble is gross over-capacity, brought about partly by over-optimistic traffic-forecasting, and partly by their obligation to support the British aircraft industry.'

In March 1963, after two full years of the traffic-growth slump, we had made a further re-assessment of the number of aircraft we felt sure of being able to employ in four years' time. Caught in the net of our own greater efficiency, we were now getting about 11 hours a day out of our Boeings. Unless there was a rapid revival in air traffic, the foreseeable work-load in four years' time would now be less by ten large jet aircraft – the very same number of aircraft, it so happened, that we had been forced into ordering in 1960 so that the British Aircraft Corporation could be set up.

This meant, in turn, that we should now need fewer staff. We therefore started another round of frank discussions with all the unions and their shop stewards. Hourly-rated craftsmen would not be affected by the rundown, as normal wastage would operate. But in staff categories where wastage was normally low, we got down to working out with the unions ways and means of accelerating the wastage by early retirement and financial inducements.

News of this drastic re-assessment appeared in the press on 3 May 1963. I was thankful that Matthew and I had gone to the lengths we had to make the press aware of our position. They were able to assess the latest news in its proper context.

In a leading article, *The Times* wrote: 'The decision to revise downwards estimates of the size of fleet and number of staff needed in 1967 has at least been taken soon enough to prevent the Corporation being hopelessly over-loaded four years hence. In part the troubles that BOAC is suffering from are common to most of the world's international airlines. . . . BOAC has also been hit by difficulties peculiar at least in their weight to this one Corporation. As Sir Basil Smallpeice, the Managing Director, has pointed out, these have been the result of granting self-government to many Commonwealth territories. . . . One handicap facing BOAC . . . is that it has been charged with duties that are non-commercial. In the first place it has been instructed to give encouragement to the British aircraft industry. Secondly, it has been required to fly routes that may help Britain's trade and commerce in general, even though they involve the Corporation itself in losses. Most governments use their airlines as an instrument of wider economic policy. . . . In this kind of world it is not unreasonable that BOAC should have the non-commercial commitments with which it is charged. But if the Corporation is to act basically as a commercial operator it can fairly ask in return that these be clearly defined; that some allowance be made in its accounts for its prestige operations; and that there should be some recognised limit to the extent to which it must "buy British" to its commercial detriment. The shape of Britain's airline corporations must make sense, whatever the politics involved.'

The *Financial Times* of the following Monday, 6 May, also carried a leading article, applauding the downward revision of our fleet estimates as 'the proper course for the airline to take'. It ended: 'BOAC has been criticised enough. Now that it is seriously trying to put itself in order, it should be given every encouragement.'

Thank God, I thought, there are people about who have taken the trouble to understand our basic problems and appreciate what we are doing to overcome them.

★   ★   ★   ★   ★

The first signs that the two-year traffic standstill was ending were seen in June 1963. In the four-week period to 22 June passenger traffic grew by 8 per cent over the year before. The period to 20 July was not so good; but the period to 17 August was again up by 8 per cent with our aircraft 56 per cent full, something unknown for almost thirty months.

Meanwhile the 1962-63 financial year had ended, and a second loss of £5 million plus the Government 'dividend' of £6 million brought total lost capital to £80 million. We had heard little of Corbett's report on the inquiry he had conducted between October 1962 and April 1963. In mid-May Julian Amery had told the House of Commons that he expected the report to be in his hands by the end of the month. When asked about publication, he dodged the question and said: 'You will not get a frank exposition of ideas, which the Ministry needs, if there is to be publication at the end of the day. I will report to the House on the conclusions which I draw.'

He could, of course, have obtained a frank and confidential exposition of ideas on our affairs from his nominees on the board. But that would not have left him so free to disregard advice. Political procedure seemed to require a report by somebody outside the Corporation and therefore independent of it, even if not well-versed in it.

Shortly before the summer recess at the end of July, Julian Amery answered further questions in the Commons saying that he intended to make his views known to the House in due course in the form of a White Paper which would serve as a basis for debate. (Incidentally, this new White Paper was to be a Ministry White Paper, distinct from the Government White Paper referred to earlier.)

That promised debate could not now take place until well into the autumn. It might well be a long time before the process of politics could be brought to bear on the problem of getting our finances established on a new and satisfactory basis. Meanwhile Matthew Slattery had had no word in reply to the recommendations he had put to Julian Amery in 1962.

★   ★   ★   ★   ★

As we worked through the summer of 1963 and approached the autumn, it began to look as though the improvement in traffic was really going to hold. In the four-week period to 14 September traffic was up 13 per cent, with our aircraft as much as 60 per cent full once again. Gradually all of us in management began to exude a quiet confidence. If things continued as they were, we would produce an operating profit again in the financial year to March 1964.

It was with a feeling of relief and optimism that Matthew Slattery and I, with Gilbert Lee, attended the IATA Annual General Meeting, held that year in Rome from 7 to 11 October. I was pleased to know, too, that Robin Higham was making good progress with his history of BOAC for its first quarter-century, and it began to look as though we could hope to publish it on the Corporation's 25th birthday in a year of restored success.

The rest of October passed without any indication that the Government were doing anything about our requests for BOAC's capital reconstruction. On the twenty-first, we had the usual press conference on publication of our Annual Report for 1962-63 – the last of our two bad years. In it Matthew wrote: 'It is understood that Mr Corbett's report, which is confidential to the Minister, was completed in May 1963. On 29th July of this year, the Minister stated his intention of dealing with the recommendations of the Corbett Report by a White Paper, which he would be publishing when the House re-assembled after the summer recess. The White Paper is not ready for study at the time of writing this report.' Nor, indeed, was it yet available.

I was due to fly to Beirut on a VC10 training flight on Saturday 26 October for a three-day partnership meeting with C O Turner of Qantas and B R Patel of Air-India. On the Friday before I left Matthew and I had a talk in his office about the state of play with the Ministry. Neither of us had a clue when we would get an answer. Things must be being deliberately held up for some reason. The British Transport Commission had been dismantled and Dick Beeching had become chairman of a new British Railways Board, but there was still no write-off of capital. Neither of us liked the deathly hush that might well presage a storm.

★ ★ ★ ★ ★

After completing our tripartite partnership discussions in Beirut, I had to go to Abadan on the Thursday. On Saturday 2 November, while in Shiraz for the week-end, a cable arrived from Matthew. Matters were serious, it said. The Minister wanted to see me, so would I please return soonest.

I caught the first BOAC flight back from Teheran to London, reaching headquarters on the Monday. I went straight to see Matthew and learn what had happened.

Julian Amery had asked to see him on the Friday. Amery told him he had decided to reconstruct the board of BOAC. He had decided to appoint Sir Giles Guthrie to be the chairman of BOAC from the beginning of 1964.

Matthew and I looked at each other, recalling something we had noticed at the IATA meeting in Rome a month before. BOAC's seats had been just in front of BEA's. With Sholto Douglas and Tony Milward we saw Giles Guthrie, looking very pleased with himself. Giles had been a part-time non-executive director of BEA since 1959. Normally, non-executive directors of airlines never attended IATA meetings. So we jumped to the conclusion that, although the Minister had not yet announced it, Giles was to become chairman of BEA next March when Sholto Douglas, already 70, would retire on completion of his third five-year term of office.

How wrong we were! It was now obvious that Giles Guthrie knew before that IATA meeting in Rome at the beginning of October that he was to be the next chairman of BOAC, not BEA. Julian Amery must have arranged it some time previously. What is more, the BEA people there – Sholto Douglas and Tony Milward – must have known all about it, otherwise they would not have had Giles with them. The top civil servants with whom we dealt at the Ministry must have been aware of it too. And all along, the Ministry had been keeping Matthew and myself in the dark, until it might suit them politically to tell us and it would be too late to undo it.

How devious, two-faced and ignoble can politics become!

Amery had then asked Matthew to resign 'to facilitate the reconstruction of the board'. His successor having already been appointed, Matthew was in fact being sacked, however it was described for political purposes. There was nothing for it but for him to go. On what grounds? Matthew still did not know. He, the chairman of BOAC, had still not been allowed to see the Corbett Report, and there was still no Ministry White Paper to explain Amery's actions.

But Giles Guthrie was not only to be chairman; he was also to be chief executive. That was my job. It was an appointment reserved to the board under the Air Corporations Acts. Bearing in mind 1956, when the board had blocked the Minister's appointment of Cribbett as chief executive, Amery would reconstruct the entire board in order to get his way. He wanted to see me as soon as I could get back from overseas.

Obviously, I was to be sacked, too – whatever word Julian Amery used to describe it politically. But even if I had a choice, I would not have wished to stay on in face of Matthew's removal. The injustice of it all was monstrous.

Matthew and I and our predecessors had loyally supported the British aircraft industry. He and I had seen BOAC through the depression of the past two years, experienced by all other international and most domestic airlines. We had held down the operating loss in each year to as little, relative to our size, as £5 million. The recession of those past two years could now be seen as transitional only, and happily ending. In the current financial year 1963-64, now more than half way through, we expected to make not only an operating profit once more but a record one of £6 million.

As to BOAC's ability to trade profitably in future, we had brought down our break-even load factor (that is, the proportion of aircraft space we had to sell to start making a profit) from the traditional 60 per cent of the 1950s to 46 per cent in 1963 with a near-certainty of only 40 per cent in 1964.

Then, too, we had built up throughout BOAC an attitude of really working together amongst all our staff. Of course, misunderstandings arose here and there. But stoppages of work were negligible throughout 1962 and 1963, averaging no more than three minutes per employee. And in those two years there was no single interruption of BOAC services.

★   ★   ★   ★   ★

As arranged I went to see Julian Amery the next afternoon, Tuesday 5 November. The Minister seemed a little ill at ease and spoke in that rather fruity voice that may be a political affectation to cover uncertainty.

He asked me to resign. If not, he said, he would have to terminate my appointment. I still had about two and a half years to run. Would I sort that out with the Permanent Secretary – Sir Richard (Sam) Way?

I said I would think it over and let him know.

Was there anything else I would like to say?

Yes. First, we would like to see the Corbett report. Second, the two-year recession was now behind us, and we were in the process of making our biggest operating profit ever.

He seemed unmoved. It was not easy, he said, to get approval to write off Government capital; and he deemed it necessary for BOAC to have a new board.

It seemed, I thought to myself, that the procedures of politics required human sacrifices to propitiate the powers that be. There was nothing more I could do then but get up and go.

I am slow to anger. I do not claim it as a virtue; nature has blessed me with a low blood pressure, and I am not readily provoked to vent my spleen.

I needed legal advice, and political advice too – the latter because I wanted to know whether there was any chance of fighting the Minister's decision.

Legally, the issue was clearcut. I had an appointment running until mid-1966. The Minister could break that contract at any time provided he paid me for the unexpired portion. (I have always felt, since then, that to have a time-contract puts a man in a weak position; he can be bought out far more cheaply than if he was appointed *sine die*.)

For political advice I turned to Henry Brooke, whom I had come to know well in the 1940s when we served together on the Christian Frontier Council. He was Home Secretary in 1963 and let me see him at the Home Office the day after my meeting with Julian Amery. I told Henry what had happened. If matters like this rested in the hands of the Minister, I would fight it.

Henry Brooke said that he personally had no knowledge of the matter. But I could take it that Julian Amery would not be allowed to do such a thing on his own. There would be a committee of three within the Cabinet to hold his hand. Who they were in this case, he didn't know. But the action would certainly have had greater authority than that of the Minister himself, who was not a member of the Cabinet.

After that I realised that we had no chance at all of getting the decision reversed. We had no right of appeal. We could not even approach Mr Harold Macmillan himself, who had always regarded Matthew Slattery highly. The Prime Minister had been taken ill suddenly during a Cabinet meeting and had had to undergo an emergency prostate operation.

So I called on Sam Way next day, 7 November, to tell him I would 'resign'. It was agreed between us that nothing would be said until the Minister was ready to announce the changes in Parliament.

I had to go into University College Hospital on Monday 18 November for minor surgery on my lower lip. While there I was told that Julian Amery was to make his statement in the House on Wednesday the 20th; the Ministry White Paper would be published at the same time. I was not due to go home from UCH until the Friday, so when the news broke of the 'resignations' of Matthew Slattery and myself I was mercifully shielded by hospital procedures from the friendly, if on this occasion embarrassing, attentions of the press.

Matthew and I had still not been allowed to see the Corbett

Report. That annoyed Matthew greatly. I didn't worry too much; knowing it was being withheld I felt sure it would tell us nothing we didn't know already.

The Ministry White Paper, when we saw it, was in a different category altogether. It was not a carefully thought-out document, pointing to a reasoned decision. It contained a mixture of truths, half-truths and fallacies. It gave a wholly misleading impression of how BOAC's financial problems had arisen and of how the airline was being managed. It was obviously concocted without due regard for accuracy, for the political purpose of justifying the Minister's actions decided upon previously.

Robin Higham, whose professional competence and integrity as an aerospace historian is unquestioned, tells me he can only regard the White Paper as infamous.

Of the press comment following the Minister's statement in the House perhaps the most telling was the editorial in the next issue of *Flight*, published on 28 November. 'The Minister has spent six months reading Corbett and writing the White Paper. Then, without showing Sir Matthew and Sir Basil the White Paper, let alone the Corbett report, he devises their resignations, puts in a new man with no experience of airline management and tells him to produce yet another plan within 12 months. The BOAC leaders are cast aside on the basis of evidence which, since it is known to the Minister alone, they cannot answer. Some may feel that it is a most disagreeable political act.'

*   *   *   *   *

Now, why in Heaven's name had all this to happen?

Did Parliament really need to be assuaged with human sacrifice? Maybe. Certainly, it is true that within eighteen months Giles Guthrie was given everything we had asked for – the write-off of lost capital (with an extra £10 million thrown in for good measure), a substantial proportion of equity capital, and a clear directive as to the role of BOAC.

But Robin Higham believes, on the evidence available to him, that even before his appointment as Minister Julian Amery held the typically anti-nationalisation view that BOAC was an overmanned and inefficient airline. He refused to take action on the recommendations Matthew Slattery put forward in August and November 1962 – for the simple reason that he had already made up his mind that the people at the top would have to go. The procedural steps he took from July 1962 onwards were designed to bring this about, regardless of all other considerations.

It is difficult to think that Amery's view of BOAC was based on anything but pre-judgment. Let me recall that when I was appointed managing director in 1956 BOAC was at the nadir of its postwar existence. After the Comet 1 disasters of 1954 it was left with no front line aircraft, and morale was at its lowest ebb. In the seven years since then we had built BOAC up to three and a half times its previous size, so that it ranked as the world's second largest international airline. Across the North Atlantic the air was now carrying some 70 per cent of all passenger traffic compared with 30 per cent by sea. On the route to South Africa, where the sea lanes enjoyed good cruising weather, we had now got some 40 per cent travelling by air compared with only about 10 per cent in 1956. On the longer run to Australia, a route on which the shipping lines carried a substantial volume of subsidised emigrant traffic, the airlines had now increased their carryings to some 20 per cent of the end-to-end passenger trade compared with only 5 per cent a few years earlier.

Our own economic management had regularly controlled costs to within 1 per cent of budget. We had brought down our aircraft maintenance costs at base and overseas from 4.42 new pence per capacity ton-mile – a cost level that was demonstrably too high – to 1.47p, as low as any other comparable airline. We had brought down flying and passenger service costs from 5.07p to 3.09p, while still maintaining standards of operation and service equal to the best in the world, if not better. We had reduced traffic handling, sales and admin costs from 4.21p to 3.11p while at the same time improving our selling by making it even more market-conscious. In these and other ways the total all-inclusive costs of running the airline had been brought down from 16.7p to 9.5p in 1963 and was planned to come down still further to 8.5p in 1964.

As to the merits of that 'infamous' Ministry White Paper, for which Amery as Minister must take responsibility, let the words of my successor as chief executive, Giles Guthrie, speak for me. They are quite independent of my own views, and neither Matthew Slattery nor I had any opportunity ourselves to report on our last nine months in BOAC.

In his first annual report Giles said: 'BOAC found the criticisms in the White Paper particularly difficult to meet because they were expressed in such general terms. The experience available to BOAC was that its engineering costs were reducing at a faster rate than those of other airlines and that, by the end of the financial year 1963-64, there was every reason to expect that BOAC's engineering costs level would be comparable with the best achieved by other airlines –

and substantially better than most.'

'The allegations in the Corbett Report of weaknesses in financial control were not understood by BOAC.' There was 'nothing which would tend to confirm the allegations of mismanagement in the White Paper'.

'If BOAC were as inefficient as the White Paper implied, it could not have achieved the dramatic financial recovery which the figures for 1963-64 disclose.' (In fact the operating profit was even greater than the £6 million I had forecast in November; it was £8.7 million.)

'The new board takes no credit for this result. The foundation had been laid by its predecessor. . . . The arrangements made were sufficiently flexible to enable BOAC to take full advantage of the upsurge in traffic that occurred.'[1]

★　　★　　★　　★　　★

It was not just a matter of the two top people having to leave. The greater effect was the cutting of the leadership reins throughout the airline.

Politicians and civil servants who have never managed anything more complicated than their own offices seem unable to comprehend the part played by leadership in the management of industry.

The leadership function in top management is every bit as important as technical competence or financial ability. The making of profits and the development of modern technical processes and methods will not readily come about without a base of good human relations throughout an organisation.

Personal leadership in industry is even more important nowadays than it was in times past, when ownership or managerial skill carried its own arbitrary authority. Through the nationalising Acts that authority had been removed by Parliament in the mid-forties. Management of a nationalised industry had to win trade union approval or acceptance of what it wanted to do.

It is ironic that human relations throughout BOAC were indeed so good in 1962 and 1963 – a time when we were fighting our way out of economic recession under almost continuous political criticism. Relations had never been better before. There was a feeling that we were all in it together. As time was to show, staff relations were never to be so good again after this political upheaval.

All this had been achieved despite the need to cut back our aircraft orders and to run down staff numbers. But both needs were

[1]BOAC Annual Report, 1963-64.

understood and accepted by our trade unions at national level. At shop steward level my open-door policy had produced a new atmosphere of co-operation. I was also greatly helped in this by two people: Ken Bergin, director of personnel and medical services; and Billy Benson, who had become chairman of the shop stewards committee.

Perhaps the general feeling in BOAC is best summed up by a letter written to me in January 1963 by Capt Ian Jeffrey, chairman of the British Air Line Pilots Association: 'Although times have been hard for BOAC in 1962, I doubt if relationships, particularly at top level, have ever been better between BOAC and BALPA. We particularly value the real understanding between ourselves which exists at this level. This, I am sure, has gone a long way to promote a fine understanding between the executive management of BOAC and their pilots. BALPA looks forward to 1963 with confidence, certain that BOAC will surmount its present difficulties and go from strength to strength.'

★   ★   ★   ★   ★

I simply hated having to leave BOAC and all the fine people in it, and all that I had worked for in the past fourteen years. My last seven weeks as managing director of BOAC were a mixture of sadness and anger. At the same time they were very rewarding for the expressions of sympathy and affection they brought to me.

John Corbett wrote me a brief note which said, simply: 'Oh, no! this should not have happened'. I bear him no ill will for anything he may have said in his report – I realise he was merely being used. I have never seen it. In February 1964 Matthew was offered a censored sight of it, but he naturally declined the condescension.

Robin Higham came over from the United States specially to see me before I left BOAC at the end of 1963. He wanted to collect all available material as to what had been happening. His history of the first 25 years of BOAC was ready for publication in 1964, to mark the silver jubilee of the airline. But Giles Guthrie, I was told later, considered it contained matter that was controversial and decided to suppress it.

Higham's manuscript lay for many years in the archives. But, with Ross Stainton, I had it resurrected in 1975 after the merger of BOAC and BEA into British Airways. Robin Higham was then commissioned to extend it to cover the whole 35 years of BOAC's existence from 1939 to 1974. It is finished, but it is still being suppressed.

Why? The text is certainly not a public-relations document. But then good history does not set out to be that. Its aim is to provide an objective unbiassed and independent assessment of the facts. The Higham history may not present some facts as seen by all members of management at particular times. But people involved in events as they unfold are naturally biassed in their own favour. It is the task of a historian to form an independent judgment based on the records available. Robin Higham's competence and professional standing as an economic and aviation historian are such that his independence of judgment cannot be questioned.

The text of his book as I saw it in January 1977 is a social document of considerable importance. It is not only an interesting and independent record of the development of Britain's overseas airline throughout its 35 years of separate existence. It is also the only history yet written of the relations between a nationalised industry and the Government, based on full and unrestricted access to all records and board papers of the day. Now that so much of Britain's industrial activity is in the hands of Government through nationalised or semi-nationalised industries, Higham's book is relevant to some of the important problems with which the country is faced today.

Could the book's continued suppression be because what it might reveal would be unwelcome to Government and Civil Service? And because the rule under which Government papers may not be made public until 30 years later is being extended to cover the working papers of nationalised industries? If so, that would be an unwarranted and objectionable enlargement of the area of secret government which should not be tolerated.

But to return to 1963 – of the other members of the BOAC board Wilfred Neden decided to leave in sympathy with us at the end of the year. Walter Worboys left at the end of March 1964, and so did Kenneth Staple. As a gesture, Francis Rennell and John Tweedsmuir decided to delay Amery's reconstruction by staying until their terms of office ran out in mid-year.

I was not apprehensive about the fate of the management team. Keith Granville, the doyen of the prewar Imperial Airways trainees still leading the corporation, might have a problem with Giles Guthrie. Otherwise, they had nothing to fear. This team had carried all the departmental responsibilities of running BOAC in the last seven years, and would see it through to success in the future.

There were two occasions that touched me perhaps more deeply than others. One was an invitation to lunch with Douglas Tennant and some of his top people in the Merchant Navy and Airline

Officers Association in early January 1964. They had never done this before for a manager, still less a managing director.

In a brief speech Douglas said that his members in BOAC were so disgusted at what the Minister had done that they had wanted to stop work, and all services, for a day in token of their disapproval. He had, however, dissuaded them. A token strike would have achieved nothing and only harmed the airline. But as a different kind of token, they would present me with a pair of pens engraved with my initials.

The other touching farewell was during my last visit to our engine overhaul base at Treforest. In the morning our manager there, Charles McGibbon, warned me not to get alarmed if there was a lot of noise when I walked round the works for the last time that afternoon. 'Why?' I asked. 'Well,' he replied, 'they have a custom here in the valleys when one of their mates leaves or retires; to wish him well they drum him out by beating anything to hand with spanners. They want to wish you well, and they also want to show you that they think of you as one of their mates. This has never been done before for a boss.' At around half past four I was duly 'drummed out' to a most unholy din and a lot of smiles. I was so moved that all I could do was smile back; fortunately, as the din lasted until after I had left, there was no need of words.

Some two years previously, I had had the great honour of being created a Knight Commander of the Royal Victorian Order by the Queen. This was 'for services to Her Majesty', in the organisation of Royal flights. For the part I had played in rebuilding BOAC after the loss of our best aircraft in 1954, I received from my employers, the Government, not a word of thanks, only the chop.

Perhaps the last word was said by a detached American observer of the scene. John Meadows, the civil air attaché at the US Embassy in London at the time, who later became head of aviation in the State Department, was well informed on airline matters. We happened to meet again in Washington in May 1977. 'Well,' he said, 'you joined BOAC when, through no fault of its own, it wasn't all that much of an airline. But when you left it, it sure couldn't fail to be a great one.'

And with that verdict, from a source untrammelled by domestic politics in Britain, I rest content.

The *Queen Elizabeth*, 1968. *(Cunard)*

Queen Elizabeth the Queen Mother's farewell visit to the ship to which she gave her name. With Commodore Geoffrey Marr, 6 November 1968.

(Southern Evening Echo)

The Queen and Prince Philip visit the *QE2* on the eve of her maiden transatlantic voyage, 1 May 1969. On the starboard bridge wing, with (from left)
Capt Bil Warwick, Lord Mancroft and BS.   *(Cunard)*

The *Queen Elizabeth 2*, bound for New York, May 1969.   *(Beken of Cowes)*

16 After the Trauma

Thus, at the end of December 1963, exactly 14 years after I had started work in BOAC, I found myself out of a job, with no income, aged 57.

I have never worried very much about my own money. I had never inherited anything. But I didn't let the temporary loss of income bother me – and I was, after all, to receive compensation for the breaking of a contract which ran on into 1966.

Compensation for loss of office is far from being what is often thought. The salary payable for the remaining term has to be reduced by the salary you are thought able to command in another job, because you have a legal duty to alleviate the damages claimed for breach of contract. Then the remainder is further reduced by way of discount for immediate advance payment; and all compensation over £5,000 (at that time, now £10,000) is then taxed as income.

You receive a lump sum, but its value is much less than the published figures. In any case, nothing can compensate you for the break in continuity of your pension scheme.

The fact that I was 57 didn't worry me much. I have never been conscious of my age – although the upper fifties is not the easiest time of life to get a job. I was actually more bothered about having no secretary for the first time in 34 years, and having to write all my letters in long-hand.

In the last weeks of 1963 I had sought advice about what to do next. One of those I consulted was Lord Cobbold, Governor of the Bank of England when we used to raise capital by the issue of British Overseas Airways stock through the Bank. He had been appointed Lord Chamberlain of The Queen's Household in 1963; so when I went to see him it was to an office in St James's Palace.

Kim Cobbold advised me, in view of the traumatic experience I was going through, to go away for three to six months and try to forget all about it. When I came back he would see me again. Meanwhile he would see what sort of jobs were around.

Since coming home from Brazil in 1914 in the old *Andes* I had never made another voyage by ship. And the thought of blowing some of my compensation on a sea passage for my wife and myself rather appealed to me as the way to unwind. I went to Thomas Cook's to find out where we might expect to find fair weather at sea in February. They booked us a passage home on the P&O liner *Chusan*, leaving Hong Kong for London at the end of January.

That December, after our last meeting of the BOAC-Cunard board, John Brocklebank took me on one side. Would I consider joining the board of The Cunard Steam-Ship Company? I thanked him warmly and said I would certainly like to consider it; but I had decided to go away for three months and preferred not to make any decisions until I got back. Could we leave it that I would get in touch with him in March? He said that would be fine, and asked me not to commit myself to anyone else first.

I felt strongly that I did not want to fly BOAC so soon after giving up my job as its MD; so I arranged instead to fly to Bangkok by Qantas and then, after a short stop-over, to go on to Hong Kong by Air-India.

The *Chusan* sailed in the late afternoon of 30 January. The voyage home proceeded in a peaceful and leisurely way – two to four days at sea, then calls at ports, at all of which I had the warming experience of BOAC managers coming to welcome and look after us. By the time we got back home on a cold and grey day at the end of February, I felt thoroughly refreshed and re-invigorated.

Early in March I went back to see Kim Cobbold at St James's Palace. To my surprise he said it was just possible that there would be a job that I could do at Buckingham Palace; he couldn't be more explicit at that stage and there wouldn't be much in it financially, but if it came about, it was something that would be well worth doing. He asked me not to commit myself to other things just yet. I told him then of John Brocklebank's approach in the previous December and he said that a directorship of Cunard, resident in London, would not be inconsistent with what he had in mind.

We left it at that for the time being. Later that month I arranged to meet John Brocklebank again. Cunard had for long been represented in London by Ben Russell, whose name was a byword in the travel world. But he was on the point of retiring, and John felt the need to strengthen Cunard's position down south. It was not that I could ever be another Ben Russell, but John had in mind that I should be Cunard's London director – visiting Liverpool once a week for management and board meetings. That suited me well, I thought; and it would give me an office base in Lower Regent Street. I accepted his offer. I would be appointed to the main Cunard board in April.

Early in May, Kim Cobbold asked me to see him again. He wanted to introduce me to some senior members of the Royal Household; he had in mind offering me a job which included the introduction of modern budgeting and financial control. It was necessary that the Queen's private secretary, treasurer and others should feel that I was someone they could all work with.

Fortunately, I passed the test; and soon afterwards I was offered a new post with the title of Administrative Adviser in Her Majesty's Household. It was to start that October and Kim Cobbold estimated that it would be necessary for me to work in the Palace full time for the first month and thereafter a couple of days a week for a year or so. There was therefore no conflict with my commitments to Cunard, but he would prefer that I didn't take on other directorships in industry for the time being – at least not without reference to him.

This was a great, if awesome, opportunity – and it was so wholly unexpected. No one from industry had ever been appointed to the Royal Household before. I was naturally nervous whether I could do justice to the job – I would find Buckingham Palace very different from any business I had ever worked in.

The Queen's official expenditure as Sovereign is met by what is called the Civil List grant – an annual sum granted by Parliament as 'a reimbursement of the operating expenses of the official part of the Royal Household'.[1] The Civil List was in fact costing £517,000 in 1964 compared with Parliament's fixed annual grant of £475,000.

In those days inflation was only 4½ per cent a year. Even so, it was clear that it would be necessary before long to ask Parliament for more. When that time came Lord Cobbold would, as Lord Chamberlain, have the responsibility for presenting the case to Parliament through the Select Committee; he wanted to be able to assure MPs that Palace expenditure was controlled as effectively as in industry.

This was the initial purpose for which I was appointed. After I had completed my main task I was retained in a consultative capacity to give evidence to the Select Committee when the time came in 1971 for the House of Commons to review the Civil List grant.

In the Royal Household there is a strict and very sensible rule that those who work there are not allowed to write or talk about their experiences in it. But I like to think that the contribution I made was of some little help. And I have always counted it a privilege and an

---

[1] Report from the Select Committee on the Civil List 22 November 1971.

honour beyond measure to have been called upon to serve the Queen in this way.

★   ★   ★   ★   ★

Not long before I started work at the Palace Sir Nutcombe Hume and Sir Halford Reddish, whom I had come to know as regular BOAC travellers, asked me independently of one another to become a non-executive director of their companies – respectively the Charterhouse Group and Rugby Portland Cement. Because of my commitment at the Palace I had to turn down their offers at that stage; but I said I would be very glad to accept them in a year or so's time.

Around that time, too, Lord Baillieu was planning to give up the chairmanship of the English-Speaking Union of the Commonwealth (ESU). By then Clive Baillieu had been chairman for some twenty years as well as chairman of Dunlop. Nut Hume was a Governor of the ESU and set about trying to rope me in. Not that I was reluctant – I had long been fascinated by the invisible threads of the English language which seemed to me to hold so much of the free world together.

It was not only that the Pilgrims and the settlers in Virginia had taken the English language with them to America. Nor was it only that people of British stock had taken their mother tongue with them and planted it firmly in the former British dominions and colonies, so that English had become the official language of, for example, the whole of the Indian subcontinent. It had already established itself as the international language of such diverse activities as accountancy and civil aviation. All spoken international air traffic control communication in the free world has to be available in English. And it was on the way to becoming the language of international diplomacy.

The post of chairman of the English-Speaking Union was entirely honorary, but it would be of absorbing interest and one to which I might be able to make some useful cntribution. It was not a commercial appointment of the sort I had said I would not take on for the present. Although it didn't help me to build up my annual income, I was more than gratified when invited to join the Board of Governors of the ESU in January 1965, with a view to succeeding Clive Baillieu on his retirement as chairman the following November.

Following my appointment as London director of Cunard, Harold Watkinson asked me to join his Committee for Exports to the USA, sponsored by the Board of Trade – again, an appointment which was an honorary one and brought me no money but which helped to get me back into circulation and proved of great interest.

When you are down, you are very thankful for friends who help you to get on your feet again.

17 New Life in Old Bones

I started working with Cunard in April 1964. My 'sabbatical' had lasted only three months and I had not had time to get bored. I now had an office again, and a secretary.

Although I had been in transport for 16 years, I had no experience of shipping, except what I had learned from Roland Thornton about its economics. Being Cunard's London director did not involve me in managing anything; I was simply there in case of need. So I set about learning.

I went to Liverpool every Tuesday, sometimes staying until the Wednesday. Cunard's passenger business was still managed from Liverpool, although the big ships had been operating from Southampton for over 30 years. The management in New York was far stronger than that in Liverpool.

In Britain, Ben Russell in London had been the Cunard personality our passengers and sales agents knew; and Norman Hughes, our Southampton manager, had been the focal point of company loyalty for those working in the passenger ships. Top management in Liverpool hardly ever travelled on the ships, and when they did it was not to check how the ship was being run but merely to have time off.

Yet Liverpool was the ultimate power – what it did not grant the money for could not be done.

Cunard had been ruled for some 30 years by three Bates brothers, of the Liverpool merchant-bankers Edward Bates & Co. The eldest, who became chairman in 1930, was Sir Percy Bates – a great man. He saw that to provide an economic service between London and New York passenger liners had to be powered with engines that could get them across at 29 kt in five days, so that a regular weekly service could be provided by two ships only – not three as in the past. And it was he who, for this purpose, pushed through the development of the *Queen Mary* and the first *Queen Elizabeth*.

Tragically, Percy Bates died on the eve of starting peace-time transatlantic services with the *Queen Elizabeth* in 1946. He was succeeded by his brother Fred; and, in due course, Fred was succeeded by brother Denis.

Fred and Denis seem to have been by nature managers of money rather than managers of people. These two postwar Bates contributed little to Cunard management; they seldom visited our principal markets, the United States and Canada. I am told that they were not even provided with a secretary in Cunard Building and had to write all their Cunard letters by hand.

When I joined Cunard in April 1964, the board meetings in Liverpool were still conducted in a very bank-like manner. Board papers were not circulated in advance; we met in the next room a quarter of an hour before the meeting, supposedly to read through the papers that the management were going to put before us, but in reality to have a cup of coffee. And at the board meeting itself we would be told what the general managers wanted to tell us.

John Brocklebank had been reluctant ever to take on the chairmanship, but had to after Denis Bates died because no one else was available from the Merseyside Cunard families. He was one of the nicest people, and a great cricketer. He never pretended to be a high-powered businessman, and he continued to work the system he had inherited – except that he took his Brocklebank Line secretary with him from the first to the fourth floor of Cunard Building.

Ever since Sir Percy Bates died, power in the company had rested in the hands of the general managers. The last of the great ones had been Frank Dawson, but after him people seem to have been appointed on the basis that it was 'Buggins's turn next', to see them through to retirement.

There were other reasons for the weak state of Cunard's top management in the 1960s. Many great men are unconscious of the power they exercise, and the lead they give to an organisation. They see the business running nicely beneath them and give little thought to the need for fresh and stimulating talent to ensure success after they have left. Sir Percy Bates did little to recruit new talent throughout the 1930s when the name Cunard was at its highest, and when he could have taken his pick of the best young brains in the country.

This was in marked contrast to the practice of the other great Liverpool shipping group Alfred Holt, in which my friend and mentor Roland Thornton had been a partner. The Alfred Holt group, later Ocean Steamship and now Ocean Transport and Trading, had a deliberate policy of introducing young blood of the highest quality from Oxford or Cambridge. Although a family business, they were ruthless in refusing to employ members of the family who did not possess the qualifications required of outsiders. The effects of this difference between the two Liverpool shipping groups became apparent in their relative financial standing a generation later in the 1960s.

Moreover, the Cunard management had clung to Liverpool too long after the passenger ships had deserted the Mersey and moved their base to Southampton. Cunard's passenger business was mainly between London and New York, though some ships on the Canadian run continued to operate between the St Lawrence and the Mersey. The result was that the Liverpool management were substantially out of touch with their markets, operations and sea staff.

Cunard's transatlantic business seemed to be all that the Liverpool management was concerned about, but it was in fact only part of Cunard activity. The group also owned Port Line, based in London and operating cargo ships in the Australia and New Zealand trades; and it also owned Thos & Jno Brocklebank, based in Liverpool and running cargo ships to and from the east coast of India. But the Liverpool general managers had never sought to impose their authority on Port Line or Brocklebanks, even with the latter housed in the same Cunard Building at Pier Head in Liverpool. Both wholly-owned subsidiary companies were left severely alone. With Cunard's weak and inbred top management, this may have been better for the subsidiaries; but by not placing such responsibilities on the Liverpool managers, there was less challenge for them, and they became even less effective.

Top management did little more than manage ships trading under the Cunard name. Even then, they were far removed from the 'on the works' concept dear to Miles Thomas and myself. They were little more than office managers, working at a distance.

For all that, the business kept going – thanks to loyal staff in London, Southampton and New York; and the ships kept operating to very high standards thanks to the dedicated service of the ships' masters, engineers, pursers, stewards and other seagoing staff.

Dear old state-owned BOAC had been far, far better managed.

★   ★   ★   ★   ★

There was nothing I could do about the Cunard situation in 1964, for I was no more than a director based in London and effectively non-executive at that. But I assessed what was happening and that was to pay dividends later.

The passenger side of Cunard now earned revenue of only £24 million a year compared with £32 million in 1956, the last year in which more people crossed the Atlantic by sea than by air. In 1957 the number of North Atlantic air travellers topped the million mark, and outstripped the sea-goers. Since then the air had continued to draw traffic away from ships, so that the number crossing by sea had fallen to only 700,000 in 1964.

As well as attracting passengers away from the sea, the air had also opened up a very substantial new market thanks to much reduced journey times. By 1964 the number of people crossing the North Atlantic by air had grown to as many as 3½ million. The result was that Cunard's passenger ships were losing some £3 million a year. How long, I asked myself, before the sea-passenger market petered out? And how much might we lose in the process?

Yet Cunard's cargo trade had grown over the same period from 46 per cent of our business in 1956 to 60 per cent in 1964. Cargo revenue went up from £27 million to £36 million a year. Half of this was earned by Port Line in the Australia and New Zealand trades. Across the Atlantic, Cunard Line's cargo ships were now bringing in £10½ million a year and had overtaken Brocklebanks' £7½ million earned from Indian trades. But the total group's cargo profitability was marginal – no more than £2 million in 1964, not enough to offset passenger ship losses.

However marginal the current cargo profit, no one could doubt that there was a continuing future for seaborne cargo. Whatever claims might be made for air-freighting, it takes a lot of power and money to overcome the force of gravity. In passenger aircraft, this extra cost could be rendered unnoticeable, and air fares could be made competitive with sea fares, because a passenger needs only about 30 cubic feet in an aircraft compared with a hundred times that in a ship. Aeroplane passengers are more compressible because of the shorter journey times. But cargo is only marginally compressible, if at all. The carriage of most freight by sea would remain essential in an air age.

Thus the big question-mark then overhanging the shipping companies was the future of the passenger liners. And at that very moment, at the end of 1964, we in Cunard were on the point of placing an order for a new *Queen*.

The original proposal had been for a ship of tonnage equivalent to that of the first two *Queens*. It was known as the Q3. But it became apparent by 1963 that with modern materials a new *Queen* could have the capacity of the *Mary* and the *Elizabeth* but with a saving in gross tonnage of about 20,000 tons. At that time Cunard were blessed with a naval architect and a marine engineer of first-rate abilities – Dan Wallace and Tom Kameen respectively.

The designs for the new *Queen* were drastically revised, and the project renamed the Q4. Moreover, because of the new and stronger lightweight metals, we could design the ship either as a floating hotel for cruising or as an A to B passenger liner. All we had to do was to negotiate a Government loan, since Cunard did not possess anything like enough capital.

I decided to experience for myself what it was like to cross the Atlantic by sea, never having done so before. Well, to begin with, the Atlantic in summer is by no means a fair-weather ocean and sitting out on deck in Cunard's famous deck-chairs was not all that I had been led to expect. I soon realised why those deck-chairs had to be so heavy – they would have been blown overboard otherwise. And to one used to crossing the Atlantic by air in half a day or less, five days seemed tedious.

But it was exceedingly comfortable, the Cunard staff were first-class, and the chance to relax was very welcome if one could spare the time (which I could, then). The *Queen Mary* left Southampton on Thursday, 30 July, wearing Captain Divers' blue ensign, and reached New York on Tuesday, 4 August, having passed the *Queen Elizabeth* homeward bound on the Saturday. After spending the rest of the week looking at our New York organisation, I went on to Montreal and three days later boarded the 22,000-ton *Franconia* in Quebec for England.

It began to dawn on me that one economic factor against the conventional passenger ship was their hold space, which was becoming more and more difficult to fill with money-earning cargo. Passengers and cargo shippers didn't always need the same ports; and, in the new and competitive air age, passengers did not relish waiting for cargo to be loaded or unloaded.

For these reasons Cunard had brought half-a-dozen small cargo ships of up to 7,000 tons into North Atlantic service. This decision undoubtedly provided a better cargo service to shippers, but it removed essential revenue from the passenger ships, and in due course would hasten their withdrawal from service. Thank goodness, I thought, the cargo space in the *Queens* and in the Q4 was minimal.

For most of October and November 1964 I was pre-occupied with my Palace work. In any case, I was not personally involved in the executive direction of Cunard, nor in the negotiations for the building and financing of Q4. Agreement on the Q4 was finally reached and the contract signed by John Brocklebank on 30 December, 1964. John Brown's tender of £25,427,000 plus escalation was the lowest and gave the earliest delivery date. The

Board of Trade had agreed to provide a loan of £17.6 million at 4½ per cent on delivery of the ship, which would be covered by a consortium of clearing banks during building. To get the full benefit of £5 million investment allowances, we arranged to pay for the ship in full on signing the contract.

The Q4's keel was duly laid in John Brown's yard at Clydebank in June 1965, where it was labelled Yard No 736. Thereafter the board's interest in the new *Queen* shifted to questions of interior design and decoration. Not surprisingly, in view of Liverpool's dearth of management experience in this field, Lady Brocklebank had taken upon herself the responsibility for these matters. Although the chairman's wife, she had no official position in the company, and it was an untenable arrangement. All the same, she brought in Dennis Lennon – an association destined to prove very fruitful.

As we moved through 1965 it became obvious that John Brocklebank was far from well. Perhaps the worry of Cunard's financial commitment to the Q4, or even of the company's decision to go ahead with the ship, weighed on him much more heavily than any of us realised. He was off duty for six of the first nine months of the year. The general manager would reach retirement age in April 1966; and the board were unwilling to promote the assistant general manager to fill the vacancy, with the result that he resigned with effect from the end of 1965. The Cunard ship had no-one at its helm.

As if this were not enough, Australia's overseas trade to Britain and Europe suddenly began to fall off. Port Line, our largest but still very modest profit-earner, began reporting much reduced profits. Clearly, something had to be done. Our deputy chairman, Bill Donald, a notable shipping personality and for many years chairman of Port Line, had retired from the Cunard board after the AGM in June of 1965 and I had been appointed deputy chairman in his place. It therefore fell to me, with Ronnie Senior (who had succeeded Bill Donald as chairman of Port Line in 1961), Donald Forrester (our largest private shareholder, who had joined the board in 1964) and Philip Bates (then managing Brocklebanks) to sort matters out.

Not long afterwards, on 8 November, 1965, John Brocklebank decided to resign on health grounds; and on that day my colleagues on the board appointed me chairman and I assumed the role of chief executive of the Cunard group.

★   ★   ★   ★   ★

This was the kind of challenge I needed. Having been an airline man for 14 years, it was intriguing to find myself the head of one of the most renowned groups in British shipping, and in the company of the 'shipping knights' – Sir Donald and Sir Colin Anderson, Sir Nicholas Cayzer, Sir John Nicholson, Sir Errington Keville and others known to Master Mariners as the 'blood royal' of their industry.

A daunting prospect lay ahead. Cunard's total volume of business had remained completely static for the last ten years at least, with revenue of no more than £60 million a year throughout the period. From 1961 to 1964 the passenger business had lost as much as £16 million. Cunard had been living off its capital – no less. Its cash position had been kept liquid only by income tax repayments of £12 million and by selling off assets to a like amount; these sources of 'blood transfusion' were no longer available, and the company was heading for bankruptcy. It was a life-or-death situation for Cunard and its subsidiaries.

I had no doubt what we must do. We must try to save Cunard, not only for its stockholders but even more for the sake of those who worked in it.

The trouble was that I could see little if any prospect of growth anywhere in our existing trades. The air was taking most of our passengers away from the sea, except for those wanting to have a break on board ship. And even though the volume of seaborne international trade was increasing generally, Britain's entry into the European Common Market would force Australia and New Zealand to develop outlets other than Britain for their products. Their trade with the United Kingdom would not grow as in the past.

The outlook was bleak indeed. Without growth there can be only decay. So the effort must be made. As a start I could see plenty of room for improving the efficiency and reducing the costs of our current operations. And if by that means I could get Cunard back into profit again, the group would not only survive but it would also have time to diversify into industries with opportunities for expansion.

My immediate problem was to re-organise the management. The general manager and his deputy would be leaving us soon. It was essential to have someone at the head with plenty of drive and energy to carry through the necessary reforms.

In the weeks leading up to John Brocklebank's decision to retire I had had frequent talks about this with Philip Bates, who had been on the group board since 1958 and was the son of Denis Bates. He certainly had the qualities and I knew that he would give up his job as managing director of Brocklebanks to take on the task of remoulding Cunard Line. So I promptly appointed him managing director of Cunard Line; and together we appointed Nick Anderson to head up its commercial side, with Tom Kameen and Captain Letty in charge of operations, John Whitworth in charge of personnel and David Hughes as chief accountant. Regrettably, we had no-one at that date to take charge of the hotel side of ship operations.

I started the practice in that November of 1965 of writing to staff about changes and developments as they arose. On the first occasion, I felt I must warn them of a possible rundown in Liverpool – a matter of great importance to six hundred staff employed there.

As most Cunard Line passenger ships had operated for many years from Southampton, the management of Cunard Line (as distinct from the headquarters of the group) was wrongly placed in Liverpool and would have to be based in Southampton. We could no longer avoid this necessity. I realised the difficulties of this long-deferred decision for many staff. We undertook financial assistance for those who would move south and compensation for those who would not go. We also set up an internal employment agency to help them find other jobs in the Liverpool area. Philip Bates must have found it hard to pull up his family roots from Cheshire and plant them again down in Hampshire, but he did.

★   ★   ★   ★   ★

So far so good. That at least was a start. But it would take two or three years to turn Cunard Line round financially. And I had yet to look at the operations of Port Line and Brocklebanks, of which I had so far seen little. Until then, members of the Cunard group board had not been vouchsafed much information about either. Admittedly, I had been asked along to lunch with the Port Line board in Cunard House, Leadenhall Street; but that had been all. Fortunately, Philip Bates had got together a good team in Brocklebanks. When he moved across to Cunard Line that November there was Tommy Telford ready to step into his shoes, with Bill Slater as an able No 2. I felt sufficiently confident of them not to interfere for the time being, apart from putting myself on their board and becoming their chairman. But with Port Line's profits fast ebbing away, I felt I had to look much more closely into their operations; so I joined that line's board too, glad to know that Ronnie Senior would continue there in the chair.

This was my first look at the operation of a cargo shipping line, and I didn't like what I saw. Port Line had some 30 conventional cargo ships. A typical round voyage to Australia and New Zealand took 162 days, of which only 66 were spent at sea; the ship was tied up in UK ports for as many as 37 days, and at other ports for 59 days in all. I had learnt from my 14 years in aviation (and two in the railways) that no transport vehicle – whether aeroplane, wagon or ship – could possibly operate economically with all that immobilised time. A ship only earns money when it moves cargo, not when it is tied up.

Then I found an unacceptably high proportion of empty space in our ships, aggravated by the imbalance of northbound and southbound cargoes. We obviously had too many ships. In addition, there was little standardisation in ship design so that we were forced to carry extra spares; our overhaul planning was expensive; we were over-officered by comparison with other lines; and we had rather a high proportion of twin-screw ships.

No wonder that Port Line, which was then the only remaining financial prop of the Cunard group, was at best only marginally profitable. In fact, even that overvalues the situation. The profit was marginal and unacceptably low. Port Line employed £20 millions of capital (calculated on a written-down historical cost basis) and had succeeded only twice in the past ten years in making profits of £1.3 million – not even 7 per cent on capital. Over the ten years, the profits made by Port Line averaged less than 5 per cent. No business could survive indefinitely on that. What worried me was that its management seemed satisfied with things as they were.

I would obviously have to think very hard. Fortunately Ronnie Senior decided to ask Sir Geoffrey Gibbs to join the board, and he came to us in June 1966. Gibbs Bright were Port Line's agents in Australia and Geoffrey brought a wealth of knowledge of conditions there. He also had the experience that went with being a senior partner in Antony Gibbs, the London bankers. I was thankful that I could talk matters over with someone so wise and understanding.

I next turned my attention to Brocklebanks, who employed some £10 million of the group's capital. Their problems were fundamental and apparently unchangeable. Since 1958, India and Pakistan had been claiming 50 per cent of all the Bay of Bengal/United Kingdom traffic for their own national merchant fleets. As a result there was by 1965 a chronic excess of British ship capacity in those trades. P&O, British India, British & Commonwealth, Ellerman City Liners and Anchor Line were all affected too. Brocklebanks had to adjust to the loss of half their business; and in the circumstances they had done well. They had stopped their losses, even if they had not yet got back into profit. And faced with a contracting business Philip Bates, while still Brocklebanks managing director, persuaded the group board to take over Moss Tankers, including brokers H E Moss. He ordered two more products-carriers to improve their financial position, and to ensure that the sea and shore staffs of Brocklebanks and Moss

Tankers together would have an expanding business. In 1965 they made a tiny profit again, for the first time since 1958.

★ ★ ★ ★ ★

Looking at the Cunard group as a whole, I came to feel very early on that only major changes would enable it to survive. But what changes? And how to implement the changes when we had decided on them? Apart from the small team Philip Bates had collected round him in Brocklebanks, there was little if any dynamic management anywhere else.

It seemed to me that the chief hope of a successful future for Cunard and its staff lay in a merger with another large British shipping group, to bring to us the management we so badly needed. John Brocklebank had had an understanding with Sir John Nicholson, the head of Ocean Steamship, that if Cunard wanted to go in with another shipping line, it would be offered to Ocean first. I was in honour bound to see John Nicholson; and in any case Ocean Steamship fitted in with my own views.

John Nicholson surprised me by asking if I would mind him bringing P&O into the picture. I shouldn't have been surprised, I suppose, because Ocean knew little about passenger ships. I agreed. Soon afterwards Donald Anderson, P&O's chairman, and John Nicholson arranged for their two finance chiefs to make a strictly confidential study of merging Cunard in with their own operations.

This inevitably took time, and not until May 1966 did I receive their answer. They had concluded that Cunard was nothing better than a break-up situation. Accordingly neither saw any benefit in any part of Cunard's business.

This was a shattering judgment. While I was rather relieved that P&O didn't want to gobble us up, I was sorry that nothing had come of a merger with Ocean Steamship, shipowners whom I had long admired and whose cargo trades were complementary to ours. I suspect that John Nicholson might have seen advantages in integrating our cargo operations with theirs; but he would have realised that there was no future for passenger liners on the North Atlantic. I imagine that, as between two Liverpool shipping companies, he would not like Ocean to bear the reproach for taking Cunard's passenger ships out of service.

As if being rejected by our shipping colleagues was not enough, we suffered a severe body blow through a National Union of Seamen's strike. This disrupted the whole shipping industry from 16 May to 1 July, 1966, and cost the Cunard Group at least £3¾ million. We were now heading for a loss of over £6 million that year. The strike sapped much of what little financial muscle we had, and it could not possibly have come at a worse moment, if it had to come at all.

I have seldom felt so powerless as I did throughout that strike. In BOAC the management would have been in frequent communication with union officials and shop stewards. But management in a shipping company could not treat with its sea-going staff at all when an industry-wide strike was in progress. Responsibility for dealing with the National Union of Seamen rested with the Shipping Federation on behalf of all shipowners. Individual managements were unable to influence matters in any way. Even if there had not been so much at stake for us financially at that particular moment, I found the lack of personal contact and communication with my staff very hard to bear.

I was simply not prepared to see Cunard go under. From the point of view of our shareholders, the position when I became chairman in November 1965 was that the shares had stood at about 70p; if we were forced into liquidation, I did not think they would realise more. I felt confident, despite what others had said, that the Cunard group's position could be improved so that shares might rise to 150 or even 200.

But however confident I felt, I wanted to come clean with our shareholders and the financial press. Shipping companies had never disclosed much information of value in their annual accounts, claiming that to do so would help their competitors. How wrong, I thought. Shareholders must be given enough information to enable them to form a proper judgment about their company and its prospects. So in my first annual report written during the 1966 seamen's strike, I provided a full analysis of where our profits and losses came from and how each subsidiary company had performed. I was far more frank than many another chairman would have been.

*   *   *   *   *

Patrick Sergeant, the *Daily Mail* city editor, was not alone in welcoming my uninhibited disclosures as unprecedented and fascinating. 'Sir Basil's report,' he said, 'paints a complete background to the problems . . . It may well be rated as the finest clinical appraisal of the shipping industry yet undertaken and put on record.'

Perhaps because of the frankness of my report, I was paid the compliment of being invited to address more than 4,000 members of the Institute of Directors at the Albert Hall on 8 November 1966. It was invigorating to find myself sandwiched between such eminent speakers as Cardinal Heenan, then Archbishop of Westminster, and the Rt Hon Quintin Hogg, both earlier and later Lord Hailsham.

Being in the van of technical progress, as I had been in BOAC, had been tremendously exciting. But, as I surveyed our problems in Cunard, I had come to feel them just as exhilarating. It was no less important for an old-established industry to survive and succeed in changed circumstances.

One of the basic features of Darwin's theory of natural selection is adaptability. Animals that don't adapt become extinct. The same goes for human institutions. The higher the development of the institution, the greater the need to modify it.

Britain's circumstances had changed dramatically since World War II. We had withdrawn from Empire in the late 1940s and 1950s. In the 1960s we were living beyond our means as though we still owned it. We seemed to lack the resource and the courage to adapt ourselves to the modern world. So I took this as the theme for my talk at the Albert Hall.

Cunard, founded in 1840, had been an early child of the first industrial revolution. In the dawn of new experience, and in the sunshine of spectacular success, Cunard's management had come to believe that its 19th century attitude and methods were valid for all time. But the arrival of transatlantic flight changed all that. This was Cunard's day of reckoning. We must adapt or go under.

★   ★   ★   ★   ★

I was as much concerned for our staff as for our shareholders. I believed that we could provide a majority of those working in Cunard with an interesting and continuing career – and many of our sea staff had no other means of livelihood. I wanted them to know that we at head office believed there was a future for them, and were determined to do all we could to save the company.

I sent a shortened version of my report to all Cunard employees. I particularly wanted to put the sea-going staff in the picture and explain our plans to fight for survival. So I started visiting our ships away from home as often as I could, not just for the ride but to inspect the ships and meet the staff so that they would recognise me by sight and know me a little.

Most of our sea staff worked in the passenger ships and I would join them at one port and get off at the next. I always made a point of attending liaison committee meetings between the staff captain and the staff representatives, so that I could explain what the company was doing and learn of their problems.

The cargo ships were more difficult to get at, except in port. But I believe that those who worked in the ships and provided the service to our customers came to feel that I and the board bore their interests very much in mind.

That I was getting my message across was confirmed a year or so later by a presentation from the master of the *Carmania*, Capt J C Woolfenden, on leaving his ship. The device presented had been made by the ship's carpenter, and looked like an antique morse-code tapper. It was in fact a revolving toy grinder with a long arm, so designed that it couldn't grind anything; and on its base there was this message:

GENUINE
CUNARD BULL GRINDER
EXECUTIVE MODEL

———————

For cutting red tape
For breaking conversation ice
For relieving nervous tension
For advanced stages of thumb twiddling
A reducing gear for big wheels
The world's most useless necessity
For those going nowhere

———————

The newest Cunard Status Symbol.

I was amused and delighted. If a ship's company could take the mickey out of their chairman in this sort of way, then he must be well on the way to bridging the communications gap.

18 Queen Elizabeth 2

As it happened, the seamen's strike was partly responsible for forcing Cunard to sell back to BOAC our 30 per cent interest in BOAC-Cunard. When that joint venture began in 1962 Cunard invested £8½ million in it, and bore its share of initial losses. By the autumn of 1963 it had started to yield profits – slowly at first, and building up through 1964 and 1965. But the damage which the 1966 seamen's strike caused made us look for assets to sell to make good the cash loss.

We would almost certainly have had to give up our aviation interest in any case. In mid-1966 BOAC warned us of orders for more and bigger North Atlantic aircraft, and asked us for 30 per cent of the additional capital. Well, if any of us on the Cunard board had any doubt, this finally settled it. The additional capital would be in tens of millions – quite beyond our capacity, committed as we were to the Q4. BOAC must buy us out.

I was now sitting on the opposite side of the table. I had not been able to see in 1962 what benefit the joint venture would bring to Cunard; and now that I was on Cunard's side, I still could not see it. BOAC-Cunard was an investment, yes. But it had already tied up a lot of capital, and carried a liability to contribute considerably more as air travel expanded. Moreover, the whole operation was run by BOAC, so that it brought us no jobs, nor the chance to acquire new skills.

Accordingly, in September 1966, we concluded a satisfactory financial deal with BOAC, who paid us £11½ million. We recovered our investment of £8½ million in full and also drew out a profit of £3 million. It was sad to think we should no longer see aircraft bearing the insignia BOAC-CUNARD, but we just had to bale out for the sake of the rest of our business.

★　　★　　★　　★　　★

In fighting for our lives in the short term, it was essential to be clear about our longer-term aim.

None of us believed in a continuing and profitable future for a year-round North Atlantic passssenger liner. The only commercial future for Cunard passenger ships was for leisure. This offered the prospect of an expanding market. How many ships we could afford, and operate profitably, would be a matter of nice judgment later.

Meanwhile we had the Q4 coming along. We were committed to her size, which was larger than ideal for cruising. Our urgent first task was to confirm that she was usable in the leisure role, however we might want to employ her in the year or two after her introduction. It was not only a question of interior design. It would be essential for her to pass through the Panama Canal. *Queen Mary* and *Queen Elizabeth* had beams of 118 ft, and could not do so. But the Q4, with a beam of only 105 ft, could just manage it with 18 inches to spare. And with a draught of 32½ ft, 7 ft less than her predecessors, she could enter most ports that cruise passengers would want to visit.

On the cargo side, there were two principal areas of policy. One was the whole question of cargo-ship management and operation – how to improve loading and unloading, and how to increase the proportion of their time spent at sea earning their keep. The other problem, arising from Britain's entry into the Common Market, was to move our Australian and New Zealand operations into growth trades.

In both passenger and cargo business we needed an early and sustained drive by Cunard Line, Port Line and Brocklebanks to reduce costs and increase profits from zero or 5 per cent to 15 per cent before tax. Without such a profit there could be neither security of employment nor replacement of ships. I left the management in no doubt about the importance of achieving this target profit.

★   ★   ★   ★   ★

Having clarified our policy objectives, I must next strengthen our board. I had decided to move board meetings from Liverpool to London. I needed London-based directors to replace those who had served in Liverpool. And because we were losing so much money on our passenger ships, and were intending to change the whole character of that side of our business, I looked first for people to help us in that sphere.

I needed the help of someone with experience of marketing in the leisure and travel industry, and secured the full-time services of Lord Mancroft to work on Cunard Line's passenger operations, alongside Philip Bates. After giving up politics, Stormont Mancroft had joined the board of Great Universal Stores in 1958 to head up their travel subsidiary, Global Tours, and had been president of the Institute of Marketing from 1959-63.

Because half our customers would be women, I persuaded Lady Tweedsmuir to join us as a part-time non-executive director. She brought to our meetings not only a woman's mind but also a wide knowledge of the United States and Canada, our principal passenger markets.

In addition I wanted to bring on to the board someone experienced in modern management. John Wall (later Lord Wall) had been EMI managing director before being seconded to the Post Office, and was willing to find the time. In talking to each of them, I did not conceal the seriousness of Cunard's position. But they all thought it was a cause worth fighting for, and joined us in September 1966.

I still needed someone with experience of hotel direction. That was a side of our passenger business in which Cunard Line's management was notably amateur. I talked matters over with Maxwell Joseph, the founder and chairman of Grand Metropolitan Hotels, and I was delighted when he said he would join our board at the end of the year.

We began to gather strength for the tasks ahead.

Philip Bates was getting on well establishing the management of Cunard Line at Southampton instead of Liverpool. Our staff who moved south took kindly to their new environment; and the organisation, reduced in scale and cost, began to settle down well in July 1966 after the disruption of the seamen's strike.

In London one of my top priorities, which Ronnie Senior willingly shared, had been the Q4's design and decor, to supplement the naval architect's work already done by Dan Wallace. I turned for advice to Sir Colin Anderson, a director of Orient Line and of P&O, but also a member (and later chairman) of the Royal Fine Art Commission. I consulted also Sir Duncan Oppenheim, then chairman of the Council of Industrial Design.

Both recommended James Gardner to tackle the exterior design. Dennis Lennon had already been commissioned to do the interior design and decor, and they told me he was in fact the best. The only problem was whether Gardner and Lennon would be able to work together.

Both welcomed the joint arrangement. The volume of interior work was far more than Dennis Lennon could cope with. He would do a substantial part and co-ordinate the work of other designers (who eventually included such stars as Michael Inchbald, Jon Bannenberg, David Hicks, Stefan Buzas, Jo Pattrick and Gaby Schreiber).

From time to time James Gardner and Dennis Lennon would submit their ideas for us to consider; our design committee at that time consisted of Ronnie Senior, Dan Wallace and myself, now augmented by Stormont Mancroft and Priscilla Tweedsmuir.

Altogether, I think I can fairly claim that, along with Dan Wallace's and Tom Kameen's departments in Cunard, the group led by Gardner and Lennon proved to be the best ship design team that there has ever been. I can say this because it was they, not I, who produced the results.

★   ★   ★   ★   ★

Our programme for replacing the pre-war generation of passenger ships was to keep the *Queen Mary* in service until October 1968, when her crew would be available for transfer to the Q4. But to add to the setback of the seamen's strike we ran into a 20 per cent recession in passenger business in the summer of 1967.

This was not just a problem for us: most other parts of the leisure industry suffered a similar recession that year. But to us who were trying to stage a comeback and to make a profit by 1968, it was very cruel. We were forced to advance the *Queen Mary's* retirement by a year, to October 1967 – and this would have to be followed by the withdrawal of the *Queen Elizabeth* in October 1968. Half of the two ships' companies could be held for the Q4 but, sadly, the rest would become redundant.

These decisions were difficult and painful, involving the jobs of so many people as well as the premature rundown of our passenger fleet. But there was no evading the issue. To help maintain morale I got Colin Norton-Smith to start a news-sheet called *New Cunard* to keep them better informed about our plans for the future.

This was a difficult time for our staff, sea and shore. But it was more than that. The retirement of the two *Queens* would mark the end of an era – the end, almost, of a way of life, for travellers and for those in many trades ashore who supplied the ships.

The City of Long Beach, California, wanted the *Queen Mary* for use as a static maritime museum and tourist complex. By the end of July 1967 we exchanged contracts, under which the City would pay us £1¼ million. And on 31 October 1967 the *Queen Mary*, after 31 years' proud service and flying her long paying-off penant, left the Solent for the last time, bound for California round Cape Horn.

★   ★   ★   ★   ★

Meanwhile, Philip Bates had warned us that, as a result of the recession, he now forecast another £3½ million loss on the passenger ships in 1967. And in July John Brown's, the Q4's builders, had given us a revised cost – it would probably be £28½ million, compared with the contract price of under £25½ million.

Even if Q4's cost was not further increased, that £3 million on top of further passenger ship losses meant that the Government's financing aid would prove inadequate. We were quite unable to make up the shortfall ourselves. We had to warn the Board of Trade that we might have to abandon the project unless the Government would agree to increase their loan.

There would be obvious political repercussions if the building of the ship were stopped. A decision would be needed soon, as the Queen was due to launch the Q4 on 20 September 1967.

Intensive discussions with Government took place in August and into September. We had a board meeting scheduled for 14 September, and felt that this was the very last date for a decision. If it were to come to the worst, we must be able to give the Queen at least five days' notice of the cancellation.

We had no indication of what the Government were prepared to do by the afternoon of the 13th. Geoffrey Seligman (of S G Warburg, our merchant bankers) and I asked to see Harold Lever, the Financial Secretary to the Treasury, that evening. We met him in his flat in Eaton Square. This gave us the opportunity to present our case to him in a simple and straightforward manner, not through officials. Without a larger loan from Government, we should almost certainly have to stop building the ship; her new cost was much higher than quoted in 1964 and we could not meet it in full. He listened with evident sympathy and asked questions to fill gaps in his knowledge. He promised to let me have a written answer before or during our board meeting next morning. And with that, which was all we could have expected, Geoffrey and I retired to our respective homes and Harold Lever left – late – for a dinner engagement.

While waiting for the Financial Secretary's letter, we had time at our board meeting to consider what we would do if the Government's response proved negative. Geoffrey Seligman was with us, and so were Sir Henry Benson and Anthony Pinkney, our auditors. It was a grim prospect. We might even have to put Cunard into liquidation. At last the long-awaited letter arrived. To our great and undisguised relief, we found that our basic requirements had been substantially met.

Harold Lever had arranged for our loan facility from the Government to be increased from £17.6 million to £24 million. Interest would remain unchanged at 4½ per cent.

I was more than grateful for the help and encouragement that

Harold Lever and Anthony Crosland, the President of the Board of Trade, had given us. It was a great relief to have got over that frightening hurdle, to know that the Q4 could be launched by the Queen as planned, fitted out and put into service, and to feel that we could after all get Cunard back into profitable operation.

★   ★   ★   ★   ★

The names of Cunard ships have in the main ended with the letters '-ia' ever since the company's first ship, built with a wooden hull in 1840, was named *Britannia*. The only royal names had so far been the *British Queen*, our first iron ship, and the two *Queens* of the 1930s.

The story goes, though I cannot personally vouch for it, that when Sir Percy Bates saw King George V about the name of the 80,000-ton ship which the Queen was going to launch at Clydebank in 1936, he asked if the ship could be named after 'our most illustrious Queen' – meaning Queen Victoria. To his consternation, the King replied: 'My wife will be absolutely delighted. How kind of you.'

There could be no going back on that. Sir Percy couldn't say that he had wanted to name the ship *Victoria*. But the King's instinct was sure. No two names could have caught the imagination of the world better than those of Queen Mary and Queen Elizabeth, the Queen Consorts of George V and George VI.

In thinking about the name for Q4, I could not ask the Queen to give it her own name, because only battleships had ever been allowed to take the name of a reigning monarch. On the other hand, it was to be a successor *Queen* ship, as the cypher Q4 indicated. I talked the matter over with the Queen's Private Secretary, Sir Michael (now Lord) Adeane. In the end we decided to recommend that it should simply be named *Queen Elizabeth* – just as, for example, we had had two *Mauretanias* and two *Caronias*. After all, the new ship would be coming into service almost immediately after the first *Queen Elizabeth* was withdrawn, and the two *Queen Elizabeths* would not be in service on the high seas at the same time.

Her Majesty had the same sure instinct about a name as her grandfather had had. As was customary at all launching ceremonies, John Brown's managing director, John Rannie, had handed the Queen a slip of paper with the name written on it – *Queen Elizabeth*. But those of us standing near noticed that she never looked at it. I could hardly contain my delight when, in launching the ship, the Queen announced without a moment's hesitation: 'I name this ship *Queen Elizabeth the Second*.'

It was what I had wanted but had not dared to ask for. No name could have assured the ship of more worldwide renown. It remained only to decide how to write the name. I did not feel we should use 'Queen Elizabeth II', which is the official designation of the Queen as sovereign; it would be wrong to use that style in all our advertising and publicity. I thought the use of an Arabic 2 instead of the Roman II might make a sufficient distinction, and I was pleased to hear from Michael Adeane that the Queen had approved the styling of the ship as *Queen Elizabeth 2*.

★   ★   ★   ★   ★

Thus the *QE2* was duly launched and securely moored in John Brown's fitting-out basin at Clydebank. The *Queen Mary* had been retired after a 31-year working life and was on her way to a permanent home on the coast of California. And an adequate Government loan ensured that we could pay for the *QE2* when delivered at the end of 1968. It now became urgently necessary to plan 1968 operations to maintain the 1969 passenger market we should need to make a success of the new ship's first year in service.

In the spring of 1966, when we started selling Mediterranean and Canary Island cruises outside the peak transatlantic season, I had been to see the *Queen Mary* in Cannes harbour. Next morning the *France* arrived too and dropped anchor a few hundred yards away. I had never been aboard the *France*, so I asked the *QM's* captain to signal the *France's* captain to present my compliments, and to ask if I could visit his ship. After a slight delay, he replied that the president of the Compagnie Generale Transatlantique (CGT) was on board and would like to meet me. Would I come across for lunch? I said I would gladly. It was good to meet Edmond Lanier, and after lunch he took me all round his fine ship.

I have been told that no Cunard chairman had ever before met a president of the French Line CGT. Whether that is true or not, the fact is that the top echelons in the rival shipping lines had remained very much aloof from each other. Edmond Lanier and I took to each other from the start. We obviously had common problems in the changing pattern of Atlantic shipping, and we agreed to meet again as occasion demanded.

And soon one of those occasions arrived. With Cunard reduced to one large ship only, the *Queen Elizabeth*, and with the *France* also operating on her own, it was good sense to arrange our timetables so that we sailed into New York in alternate weeks and maintained a weekly joint service throughout the summer season. Assuming that proved satisfactory, we could repeat the arrangement in 1969 with the *QE2* in place of the *Queen Elizabeth*. Edmond Lanier and I discussed the idea in London in November 1967, and agreement was quickly reached.

Following the transfer of board meetings from Liverpool to London, I decided in December 1967 it was time to move Cunard's registered office and official headquarters to London also. Apart from Brocklebanks' diminishing cargo services, our other cargo operations and our passenger business were based in London or Southampton.

I now needed to bring someone on to the board as finance director to take off my own shoulders the top-level responsibility for financial control. And I felt confident enough of Cunard's survival to attract a person of ability. It happened that at that time Philip Shirley was wanting to change his job. An Australian by birth, he had been chief accountant of Lever Bros for a number of years and had latterly been deputy to Lord Beeching, the chairman of British Rail. He had been actively concerned with the promotion of 'freightliner' trains for the inland distribution of containers, but on Beeching's retirement from British Rail he also decided to leave. He joined us at the beginning of 1968.

With Philip Shirley's help, the selling of our passenger ships proceeded apace. *Carinthia* and *Sylvania* realised £2½ million, the *Queen Elizabeth* was contracted to be sold for £3¼ million, and the *Caronia* for £1¼ million. In fact our success in disposing of these ships enabled us to advise the Board of Trade in August 1968 that we would not need to draw £4 million of the Government's £24 million loan facility. On delivery of the QE2 we should not require a loan more than £20 million.

*   *   *   *   *

In the summer of 1968 the arrangements we had made for the *France* and the *Queen Elizabeth* to operate a joint service began to produce the benefits we hoped for. This, together with the retirement of *Carinthia* and *Sylvania* and the general slimming down of our passenger ship organisation carried through by Philip Bates, enabled us virtually to eliminate all loses on our remaining passenger ships. This was a tremendous relief after the £25 million losses made by our passenger ships from 1961 to 1967.

In November the *Queen Elizabeth* had to be retired. This was another sad moment for all in Cunard. But she had served us and the country well in war and peace throughout the 27½ years of her life.

Queen Elizabeth was the largest and finest passenger liner ever built. With an overall length of 1,031 ft, she had a gross tonnage of 83,673 and a passenger capacity of 2,082. Launched in September

1938, she was still unfinished when World War II broke out. A large target for bombers, she left the Clyde 'secretly' for New York in March 1940 for completion. Converted in Singapore to carrying 15,000 troops each voyage, she started her war service in April 1941, from Australia to the Middle East, and worked across the Atlantic after America entered the war. In the five years to March 1946 she and her sister ship *Queen Mary* each moved over 800,000 troops.

Sir Winston Churchill said of them: 'Built for the arts of peace and to link the Old World with the New, the *Queens* challenged the fury of Hitlerism in the Battle of the Atlantic. At a speed never before realised in war, they carried over a million men to defend the liberties of civilisation.

'Often whole divisions at a time were moved by each ship. Vital decisions depended upon their ability continuously to elude the enemy, and without their aid the day of final victory must unquestionably have been postponed. To the men who contributed to the success of our operations in the years of peril, and to those who brought these two great ships into existence, the world owes a debt that it will not be easy to measure.'

After re-conversion, *Queen Elizabeth* made her maiden trans-atlantic passenger voyage in October 1946 and, with *Queen Mary*, established a reputation for reliability and quality of service that will never be surpassed.

The day after her withdrawal from service – 6 November 1968 – Queen Elizabeth the Queen Mother visited Southampton to say a fond farewell to the ship she had given her name to and to lunch with the Cunard board in the famed Verandah Grill.

★   ★   ★   ★   ★

By the end of 1968 the *Caronia* was also retired, and we had only two passenger ships left in service – *Carmania* and *Franconia*. *Queen Elizabeth 2* was due to join them in January 1969, and a specially selected crew was ready and eager to man her.

But work on the QE2 was behind schedule in John Brown's fitting-out basin (now part of Upper Clyde Shipbuilders). However, Royal engagements provide a powerful incentive to keep things up to scratch. Prince Charles had agreed to visit the ship on 19 November, when she was due to sail down the Clyde to begin her sea-trials. So sail down the river on that day she did. The Prince of Wales toured the ship, but he was steered away from most of the incomplete work.

The QE2's acceptance trials were due to start on 4 December 1968.

But the ship was nowhere near ready. Eventually, Upper Clyde Shipbuilders told us she would be able to start them on 23 December. In Cunard we hastily assembled numbers of staff to travel on the ship over the Christmas holiday to give the cabin staff practice in serving passengers in the new environment. I would have gone too, but Kay was due out of hospital; so I decided to stay at home and leave matters to my deputy Stormont Mancroft. I went to the Clyde to see the *QE2* off to the Canary Islands, but flew back from Glasgow that night.

The Cunard staff on board found a shambles of unfinished work in the crew quarters and the passenger cabins on the lower decks. They spent the first three days helping to clean up the ship, washing and scrubbing everything in sight. Over a hundred of the world's pressmen were to come on board at Las Palmas.

On Boxing Day, on her way south to Las Palmas, the engines broke down. Upper Clyde Shipbuilders' chairman Anthony Hepper and I flew out to Las Palmas on 28 December to assess the position on the spot.

When we arrived on board about 8 pm we went straight into a meeting in the Card Room. It lasted until after four next morning. Tom Kameen, our marine engineer, reported that the builders of the turbines (John Brown Engineering) did not yet know what had caused their failure, nor how to prevent a recurrence.

Disappointing and unpleasant though it was, Cunard would have to refuse to accept delivery of the ship until the turbine faults had been corrected; and until that was done, we would make no further payments to Upper Clyde Shipbuilders (which was now John Brown's parent). The press had joined the ship on her arrival at Las Palmas, and oh! what a story. It went right round the world. After a couple of hour's sleep I had a press conference at 9.30 am to brief them on what had happened. And I used the *QE2's* public address system to keep the ship's company informed of what was going on.

I didn't like the situation any more than Tony Hepper did, though our reasons were different. There was bound to be a delay of several months before we could get the ship into service and profits. Expecting that the *QE2* would start commercial service with a maiden cruise on 10 January 1969, we had mounted an expensive advertising and marketing programme. That was now a dead loss. We had to cancel all advertised sailings until further notice. In addition, the crew – trained and in readiness – had now to be retrained on standby with full pay. The high cost of that, too, would have to be written off. And if we missed the start of the summer transatlantic travel season, we might well find that many of our passengers had decided to go by air. Yet no-one but Cunard seemed anxious to do much about it.

The press and media were very sympathetic. By their attitude they undoubtedly brought pressure to bear on the Ministry of Technology, and on John Brown Engineering (JBE) which gave the matter top priority.

With the help of Sir Arnold Lindley and Dr Frankel and the efforts of JBE's own experts, the cause of the turbine damage was soon diagnosed. It was the effect of steam excitation on the blades in stages 7 and 8. These were unexpectedly found to remain permanently in the high vibration band when the ship was operating at normal cruise power.

This didn't speak well for JBE. Such an elementary fault should have been found on the test bed in the first hour. Shades of the BOAC Britannia turbine problems!

We were assured that, after modifications had been made, the ship could operate at full power without risk of breakdown. Upper Clyde Shipbuilders were then able to plan the acceptance trials over Easter and, assuming they were successful, to hand the ship over to us on 18 April 1969. It was touch and go – this was about the latest date for catching summer traffic.

JBE's modifications proved successful, and UCS delivered the ship to us on that date. Nine months later her cost was finally agreed at £29,091,000.

QE2 was now in our hands at last. She entered commercial service on 22 April, with a short shakedown cruise to the Canary Islands. This gave her officers and crew the necessary experience in handling her at sea; and after returning to Southampton she was ready for her maiden transatlantic voyage on 2 May 1969.

★   ★   ★   ★   ★

The Queen visited Southampton on the eve of that maiden voyage to inspect the ship which she had named. Officers and crew were all on board. It was a memorable and moving occasion for everyone. The Queen was in splendid form, talking freely to the officers in the Ward Room and to seamen around the ship.

At lunch in the Grill Room we sat at tables of four. I had the honour of being placed on the Queen's right, with Captain Warwick on her left and the Vice-Lieutenant of Hampshire, Lord Malmesbury, opposite her. The conversation got on to aeroplanes and at one stage the Queen wondered whether the pace of life wasn't getting too hot – 'no wonder people get coronaries'. I confessed that I had just been out to Australia and back in eight days. 'If you don't mind my saying so,' she said, 'I think you must be mad.'

'As a matter of interest,' interjected Lord Malmesbury, 'how long did it take you to recover from so long a flight?'

'He hasn't yet,' said the Queen, looking at me with that wonderful twinkle.

A year or two later the Queen herself made a flying visit to Australia – out and back in eight days!

After lunch we were passing through the Queen's Room, as the principal lounge was named. Stormont Mancroft pointed out to the Queen the Oscar Nemon bust of herself. 'You are putting it here, are you?' she said. 'How did he manage to finish it so soon?' 'Oh, it's not finished yet, Ma'am,' Stormont said. 'This is only a plaster cast, painted over.' The Queen continued: 'He is a great perfectionist, isn't he? I have now sat seven times for this bust, and each time he finds something wrong with it. "That's no good," he says, and wrenches my head off' – using her hands as she spoke to demonstrate his wringing her neck.

Others will treasure their own memories of the Queen's visit. Nothing could possibly have done more for the morale of the whole ship's company, nor have given the ship a better send-off.

★   ★   ★   ★   ★

The even flow of selling our withdrawn ships had been interrupted by one or two nasty hiccups from the buyers. The *Caronia* was first sold to Constantinides, then to Star Line of Panama, and finally to Universal Line SA under contract dated 24 May 1968, having been renamed *Columbia* and *Caribia* in the process. The *Queen Elizabeth* was sold on 5 April 1968 to Stanton Miller of Philadelphia for berthing at Port Everglades, Florida, on 8 December that year. But on 10 December The Elizabeth Corporation defaulted. She was eventually sold to C Y Tung of Hong Kong to convert into a floating university. In the process of conversion there, she caught fire, burnt out and sank – a sad end for a ship that had played so significant a part in World War II and was the largest passenger liner ever built.

But her successor, *Queen Elizabeth 2*, had had a triumphant maiden voyage. She was now, through the summer of 1969, proudly showing off her paces and realising all that we had hoped of her. In the course of 11 round voyages across the Atlantic, between 2 May and 30 September, she made a profit of £1,674,000. The winter was still to come and we were not yet certain how well she would be received as a cruise ship in the American market, which was so vital to her future. But to have stopped that persistent annual drain of £3½ million by the passenger ships was quite an achievement, and to be making a real profit at last was even better. Indeed, we were doing well enough to reduce the Government loan by another £3 million, bringing it down to £17 million. And we had rescued Cunard from almost certain bankruptcy.

19 Containerships: Another Revolution

In an age of air travel for passengers, the cargo side of our business was bound to become the more important, if less spectacular.

Before becoming chairman of Cunard in November 1965 I had heard of the new type of cargo vessels called containerships. These were being introduced by Sealand between New York and Puerto Rico. On the way back from Australia in the spring of 1966 I stopped off in New York and asked if I could see the new container terminal (or dock, as we would probably have called it) at Port Newark across the Hudson River in New Jersey.

Malcolm McLean was a highly successful trucker in the United States. An important part of his business consisted of bringing cargo by truck into New York for onward carriage by sea to Puerto Rico. He was horrified at the unscientific way shipping companies loaded and unloaded their ships, wasting much time and money. He reckoned that, by applying the ideas he had developed in his trucking business, he could do much better than the shipowners and undercut their costs.

So he bought and converted some tankers to make them capable of rapidly loading and unloading his 35-foot containers. These would move unopened from point of despatch in the United States to point of destination in Puerto Rico, and *vice versa*. He then designed a completely different sort of terminal on which all the cargo could be moved about on wheels. He realised that the old style of dock, with a conventional cargo ship berthed on each side of a narrow pier allowing no room to assemble the cargo properly, had been the root cause of slow cargo-handling.

I was told that he calculated on 15 to 17 acres of flat land to back up each berth, so that containers for despatch overseas could be laid out on chassis ready for quick loading. There was also vacant space to permit rapid handling of inward-bound containers. He acquired Port Newark land ideal for the purpose. His ship-operating

The Queen in the Queen's Room of the *QE2* demonstrating how Oscar Nemon, when he was dissatisfied with his work, would wring her head off the bust he was creating for the ship. *(Cunard)*

The *QE2* enters the King George V dry dock at Southampton after a year in service, 7 April 1970. *(Daily Telegraph)*

With Jim Payne, unveiling the design of the first ACT containership, 23 January 1968.

company he named Sealand; and with good planning, he could get one of his ships on the berth, completely unload it and reload it, and get a turn-round of 16 hours compared with many days using the old-style piers on Manhattan's Hudson River.

I was fascinated. It was the answer to the wasted time and money that I had deplored when I studied our conventional cargo-ship operations. Methods of loading and unloading ships had remained unchanged for centuries. We were now on the brink of a technological revolution in shipping – as great as the replacement of sail by steam. And the change would result from a trucker, not a shipowner, bringing his mind to bear on the problems of ship operation.

Shipowners had been thinking for some time about the possible use of containers to cut down manual dock labour, with all its deep-seated troubles, and to eliminate or reduce pilferage. In concentrating on that, they overlooked the main economic benefit to be got from containership operation – to reduce ship turn-round time in port. For this, the key requirement was to have extensive flat land backing up each berth. This mistake was exemplified by their 1968 decision (only now being corrected) to build containership terminals inside Sydney Harbour (which has little or no flat land) instead of in nearby Botany Bay. Consequently, in the limited space available, they had to pile up their containers five high. To get a container from the bottom of the stack cost time and money to move aside those above, even if there was anywhere to put them. Ships were kept waiting outside the terminal for days for others to clear the berths, cancelling much of the economic benefit of containerships.

I wasn't the only one to grasp the logic, and to learn much from Malcolm McLean. Other companies knew that the transport of containers by sea must be applied worldwide. Four major British shipping lines – P&O, Ocean Steamship, British & Commonwealth, and Furness Withy – had got together to form OCL (Overseas Containers Limited) in 1965. The plan was the gradual introduction of containerships in the 1970s, beginning with the UK and Europe-Australia trade.

This was a trade in which Cunard's Port Line and Ronald Vestey's Blue Star Line had substantial interests.

W T (Bill) Rae for Blue Star Line suggested to OCL that their new development should be extended to include all lines in the trade. He was given no encouragement. Because the Australian trade was being led by P&O at that time, Ronnie Senior and I approached them privately to see if Port Line could join OCL. We too, as I half expected, received a polite brush-off from Donald Anderson.

It seemed that the four OCL lines thought that they could sweep the cargo board and leave the rest of us to fade into obscurity. This provoked Ronnie Senior into arranging a meeting with Bill Rae and Alexander (Alec) Hull, the chairman of Ellerman Lines, the other deep-sea cargo line with some interest in the Australian trade. The question was how to counter the OCL move. It was decided to invite Ben Line (of Edinburgh) and Harrison Line (of Liverpool) to join us in setting up a rival British containership group. We called it Associated Container Transportation (ACT) and its first chairman was Alec Hull. Sadly, Alec died in April 1967; and I was then asked to become ACT chairman in his place.

Others watching the development of container shipping were the Swedish Transatlantic Line headed by Per Carlsson, Swedish American, Wallenius and Holland America. They had their eyes fixed on the trade routes between the US and Canada on the one hand and the UK and northwest Europe on the other.

Also watching these developments, we in Cunard kept our transatlantic cargo interests out of ACT. Individual shipping lines built up on conventional cargo were too small to operate containerships alone. So we had to join up with another line. Cunard had only two partnership options on the North Atlantic: United States Lines, or Swedish Transatlantic. American anti-trust legislation made it impossible to promote a joint company with US Lines. So Philip Bates and I started talks with Per Carlsson, who was then also talking to the French Line.

The two Swedish lines already had four ships on order, though their design was not yet finalised. A plan soon developed for the consortium, to be called Atlantic Container Line (ACL), to have a fleet of ten 23 kt ships. These would provide a weekly year-round service between Europe and North America. Two of the additional six ships would be provided by Cunard, two by the French Line, one by Holland America and one by Wallenius. Each containership does the work of about half-a-dozen conventional cargo ships, so we were in effect contributing the capacity of about a dozen ordinary vessels.

Cunard's application to join ACL was welcomed at a meeting in Paris on 17 December, 1966, and from then on we had the benefit of all the planning and ship design work done in advance by our new partners.

Thus we were planning to containerise our Australia and New Zealand trades in partnership with Blue Star Line and Ellerman Lines (Ben Line and Harrison Line having no rights in those trades), and we were joining the Swedes, the French and the Dutch to containerise our transatlantic cargo business. I was now more than glad that P&O and Ocean Steamship – who had thought we were fit only for breaking up – had spurned my original merger offer. With the Cunard group about to stop losing money on passenger ships, and the whole business back in profit, the long-term prospects were exhilarating.

★   ★   ★   ★   ★

In the meantime we had more to do than containerise. We must improve the efficiency of conventional cargo ships, and search for areas of expansion and growth.

The total volume of world trade in dry cargoes had increased from 375 million tonnes in 1937 to 730 million tonnes in 1965 (of which about half was in bulkers). Business still appeared to be increasing. But Britain's trade with Australia and New Zealand was a special case, adversely affected by our entry into the Common Market. But Australia's total trade would certainly grow, with her vast mineral resources and expanding population.

Australia had only coastal shipping. It seemed to me that such a large island continent was bound to need an overseas shipping line of its own one day, just as Qantas was its overseas airline. The economic reason was simple: to avoid paying foreign lines to carry its trade. It occurred to me that the Australian Government might buy a substantial interest in Port Line as a start; that might allow Port Line to expand into other Australian trades, and it would benefit the Cunard group as a whole.

So I went to Australia in February 1967 to explore. The Deputy High Commissioner in London, John (later Sir John) Knott, gave me an introduction to Sir Alan Westerman, head of the Department of Trade and Industry in Canberra; and the High Commissioner, Sir Alexander Downer, arranged for me to meet the Prime Minister, Harold Holt. Both introductions proved invaluable and put my mission on the right level of approach from the start. As if that were not enough, Lord Casey, the Governor General, whom I had come to know well as Australian Minister for External Affairs when I was managing BOAC, asked me to dine with him on the evening before my meetings in Canberra. This gave me a good opportunity to let him know privately what was in my mind.

Francis Graham, the head of Gibbs Bright in Sydney, Port Line's agents in Australia, warned me that Alan Westerman was no friend of British shipping. But Francis did not know what I had in mind. There was a vast difference between British shipowners who wanted to keep Australia out of deep-sea trades and those like me who wanted them in. In fact, Alan Westerman appeared considerably interested in my ideas when I met him for the first time on 28 February, 1967. The prospect of a Cunard partnership evidently appealed; and he asked me to explain my ideas to John McEwen, who was not only Minister for Trade and Industry but also Deputy Prime Minister.

We took the matter further when Alan came to London in the spring and when I visited Australia again later in the year. He hoped to give me the Australian Government's views by the end of November. But sterling was devalued on 18 November, 1967, and this deferred the decision. And then in December Prime Minister Harold Holt was tragically drowned. In April 1968, John McEwen and Shipping Minister Ian Sinclair obtained the new Prime Minister John Gorton's agreement to examine my proposal constructively and with all speed.

★   ★   ★   ★   ★

Things were not standing still back home in England throughout this 15-month period. Uncertain how my Australian approaches would turn out, I felt we must improve Port Line's management. Ronnie Senior was due to retire at the end of 1967 and I was to become the next chairman. Geoffrey Gibbs and I talked the problem over, and concluded that we must work with another shipping line. But which?

The competing line was Blue Star Line. I put the idea to their chairman, Ronald Vestey. I don't think he took me seriously at first, because Blue Star had been regarded by the British shipping establishment as interlopers, having forced their way into the club only in this century. But as meetings progressed, understanding grew. In August 1967 we commissioned Jim Payne and Derek Hollebone (managing directors of Blue Star Line and Port Line respectively) to work out a basis for jointly managed services. On 16 March, 1968, we set up Blue Star Port Line. Ronald Vestey was appointed the joint company's first chairman. This became the vehicle for managing all the conventional cargo ships of both lines after the containerships came into service.

While this move was being conceived, the three ACT lines operating the Australian trades – Cunard's Port Line, Blue Star and Ellerman – had decided in March 1967 to order three refrigerated containerships for delivery early in 1969. British yards could not match that date, which was vital because our OCL competitors would be starting operations then. So the order went to the German yard Bremer-Vulkan.

These three containerships would be equivalent to replacing 18 conventional ships. It was the first order placed by any of the five ACT lines; and as Ben Line and Harrison had no Europe-Australia rights, we set up a separate operating company, ACT (Australia), with Jim Payne of Blue Star as managing director. This joint company would carry all our Australian traffic capable of being containerised.

★   ★   ★   ★   ★

I was also determined to improve the management of our Cunard cargo ships on the North Atlantic and of Brocklebank ships working to and from the Bay of Bengal. We had talks with all the other British lines in the Indian trade. Each for its own reasons feared rationalisation and no progress was made. There was nothing we could do with Brocklebanks but sell off half their ships, leaving us two small cargo units, Brocklebanks and Cunard, with separate managements and therefore too much overhead. So we put them together as Cunard-Brocklebank under one management, headed by Tommy Telford and Bill Slater.

In the ordinary course of events I would have wanted Philip Bates to head this management team, and indeed he did become its first deputy chairman. But following our entry into ACL, Per Carlsson had pressed me to release Philip Bates to become ACL's chief executive. Chairman of ACL – which hadn't started operating yet – was Count Bernadotte, who wanted the head office in Stockholm. Per Carlsson agreed with us that the head office should not be at the end of the line in the Baltic, but on one side or other of the English Channel. He favoured Southampton.

Atlantic Container Line was going to be important for Cunard. As Philip Bates would be based in Southampton and could continue to serve on Cunard's board, I agreed to second him as ACL's executive vice-chairman for two years from mid-1968, to get its operations properly established. I didn't like parting with him, but Cunard's conventional cargo ships were now in Cunard-Brocklebank and the work of moving Cunard Line's passenger ship management down to Southampton had been completed.

Our order for two ACL containerships was placed in 1967 with Swan Hunter and Tyne Shipbuilders. Time was not so important in this case; their tender was originally high but had been reduced with help from the Minister of Technology to match foreign bids. They were due to come into service in late 1969, augmenting the Swedish and Dutch ships. Philip Bates proved himself of such value that I and my Cunard colleagues were pressed by Per Carlsson and our other partners to let them appoint him full-time executive chairman for five years from April 1969. We agreed, with some reluctance; but the commercial logic of the change from old-style cargo ships to containership consortia was compelling. It was essential to ensure that the consortia were expertly managed. With Philip Bates and Jim Payne managing ACL and ACT(A) respectively, we felt confident of the outcome.

★   ★   ★   ★   ★

Staff morale remained high throughout these re-arrangements of Port Line and Cunard-Brocklebank. It is largely due to the loyal support I received all along that these joint ventures have worked out so successfully.

The reshaping of our cargo operations meant that my Australian proposals now broadened out. The Australians could take a share in a Port Line operating only conventional cargo ships and managed jointly with Blue Star. They could take a share in the ACT(A) containership company, if our partners agreed. Or they could nominate an Australian company to operate one of our containerships in partnership with ACT(A).

By August of 1968 I learned that any lingering Australian Cabinet opposition to overseas shipping had been overruled. I was to expect a visit from the Deputy Prime Minister, John McEwen, the following month. We all met in John McEwen's room at the Savoy Hotel; Ronald and Edmund Vestey and Jim Payne for Blue Star, Dennis Martin-Jenkins for Ellermans, and myself and Philip Shirley. We learnt from him and Alan Westerman what the Australian Government were prepared to do.

They would not take a share in Port Line or ACT(A) because they could not own ships that did not sail under the Australian flag. But, subject to Cabinet approval, they would be willing to take over one of our three ACT(A) containerships, to enter the Conference, to claim a share of the trade from *all* its members and not just from us, and to enter into a partnership with ACT(A) on a basis that reflected the number of ships we each owned.

All three ACT(A) lines warmly welcomed this proposal. Later that month, John McEwen's wife Mary launched the first of the three containerships at Bremen-Vegesack.

By the time the Australian Prime Minister submitted this partnership for Cabinet approval at the end of November 1968, we had agreed to enlarge its scope to include the trade from Australia and New Zealand to the east coast of North America. This was a significant development. For in that market we British lines were third-flag carriers or cross-traders – the equivalent of fifth freedom operators in airline parlance – and I regarded our share as liable to be eroded as the national-flag carriers developed. But a partnership with an Australian-flag carrier could well strengthen our position. So the ACT(A) lines decided in September to call for tenders for four more containerships for delivery in 1970-71. The Australians could have one if they wished.

We still did not know who our Australian partners were to be. The Liberal/Country Party ministers handling this project in Canberra held their cards very close to their chests. But soon we were told that our partners were to be the Australian National Line, wholly owned by the Government through the Australian Coastal Shipping Commission. I was delighted. I had a great respect for ANL chairman, Captain Sir John Williams. The grand old man of Australian shipping, he had started his career sailing before the mast round Cape Horn and, at 73, was now embarking on yet another new venture.

Early in 1969 lengthy and intensive discussions took place in Canberra to hammer out the details of a partnership agreement. We signed the Canberra Agreement, as it came to be called, on 22 April in the presence of John McEwen and Ian Sinclair. Two years and two months had passed since my first tentative approach to Alan Westerman in February 1967. That is not altogether surprising. The move by Australia into trade conferences, and into overseas shipping in partnership with British lines, was a major break from previous Australian policy. It might have been accomplished more quickly; but we had worked out a joint operation which would be of benefit to all for many years to come.

We held the first meeting of the partnership's co-ordinating board in Canberra soon after the signing. I was asked to be its chairman – a post which I held for the first ten years of the partnership. The first containership in service, *ACT 1*, completed her maiden round voyage at the end of May 1969.

Four ships were ordered for the east coast North America operation, which we decided to call Pace (Pacific America Container Express) Line. Bremer-Vulkan were anxious to become leading containership builders, and the price they quoted in January 1969 was still under £5 million each. When the partnership decided in March 1970 that a fifth ship was needed, the price had risen to over £7 million. This additional ship would bring our total combined fleet up to eight, of which two would be operated by ANL. The Australians thus had in overseas shipping the carrying capacity of a dozen conventional cargo ships.

All this represented a quite remarkable development for British and Australian cargo shipping. John Williams said it well in a speech at the Australian Club in Melbourne in February 1979, when I handed over the chair of our partnership to Neville Jenner, by then chairman of ANL. 'There was a time,' he said, 'when it seemed highly likely that the entry of the Australian National Line into the European trade would become bogged in a morass of argument and recrimination. . . . In his quiet fashion Sir Basil entered the fray, convinced the contending parties that in their own interests and in those of Australia they should work in harmony. From his intervention at that time emerged the ACTA/ANL partnership, and incidentally the first vessel wearing the Australian flag to participate in an overseas trade for forty years.

'In my book, therefore, not only has his been the guiding hand which has brought the partnership to its pre-eminence in the sea transport world of today, but to him also is the credit for the ANL being in that partnership at all.

'Sir Basil brought to us strong, farseeing, unobtrusive leadership during those formative years; an uncanny ability in pouring oil on the troubled waters of human relationships; a standard of integrity of the highest order; and far from least, abiding common sense.'

What greater reward could anyone have than such a tribute from such a man?

20 Ripe for Predators

The financial result of our efforts was that Cunard made profits of £2 million in 1968 and £3 million in 1969 – the best results we had reported for more than twelve years. The value of our shares rose to over £2.50 compared with 70p in November 1965.

But how had our staff fared?

To save the company from bankruptcy, we had had to reduce staff numbers substantially. Over three years we had to reduce the number of sea staff from 7,344 to 4,867 – one in three. And the number of shore staff had been cut by almost half, from 2,332 to 1,311.

Remarkably this scaling-down had been achieved without a single strike – the seamen's strike of 1966 having been an industry-wide action ahead of Cunard's action.

I had made a point of keeping our two unions – the Merchant Navy Officers and the Seamen's – fully in the picture. They knew how close we had been to going under. They realised that there was no alternative to reducing our passenger services and containerising cargo. Even so they might have taken protest action, but they didn't. I had been keeping their members fully informed by letter and by visiting ships and they, too, understood the inevitability of change.

It hadn't been easy, but we were greatly helped by external factors. The loss of our passenger market to the airlines was obvious to all our sea staff. Many were already looking round for other jobs. Another factor was that holiday resorts all round Britain were booming at that time, and there was no shortage of land jobs for the hotel staff in our ships.

For the two-thirds of our sea staff we were able to keep on, we improved their contracts of service and pensions. And at the end of 1966 I encouraged the setting up of 'liaison committees' in all our passenger ships so that staff and management could keep each other informed of their plans and worries.

On the cargo side we needed smaller crews to handle the new-style carriers. Modern navigational aids had made the handling of ships at sea more automatic. Moreover, marine engineers had applied to the ship's engine room the aircraft-style remote control which put all engine controls in the 'cockpit'. The work required in a modern ship's engine room was now virtually limited to control and inspection. For these and other reasons our containerships needed only 30 officers and men, compared with 50 to 70. We needed not only fewer staff per ship; we needed only one new-style containership to carry the cargo previously carried by five or six conventional ships. So where we replaced conventionals by containerships we needed only 10 or 12 per cent of the staff for a given amount of cargo traffic. The fact that we accomplished this industrial revolution without a serious dispute is a great tribute to managers and unions.

Here again, external factors helped us to accept the inevitable. The container revolution was bringing a marked change in the nature of a seaman's employment. A round voyage to Australia took only about 70 days compared with 160 or more for a conventional cargo ship. With only 16 hours scheduled for each turn-round, seagoing staff had to spend virtually all their time overseas on board ship – 'a wife in every port' was a thing of the past, and there was little time for friends ashore. Again, there were fewer ports of call and therefore fewer opportunities to roam more widely.

These changes in the nature of the work at sea coincided with great social changes in life ashore. With television and modern heating in nearly every home, fewer people wanted to go to sea to earn their living, separated from wives, families and friends – even though separation was now only two or three months compared with five or six in the past. In fact, we were actually finding it difficult to recruit sea staff. So for those we needed to retain we started to improve the terms of employment and conditions of service, as we had done in the passenger ships. For instance, we (and other shipowners) allowed officers to take their wives to sea with them on occasions, according to rank; and on new ships seamen were provided with separate cabins.

Thus we had succeeded in adjusting Cunard to the two new technologies bearing upon us; the coming of mass air travel, which had taken away most of the market for which our passenger liners had been built; and the introduction of containerships for transporting general and refrigerated cargo, which required far fewer people.

There were not only changes in the nature of a seaman's work. Dock work changed too. The coming of containers, with trans-porter cranes and straddle carriers in new-style terminals, meant that port employers no longer needed muscle-power in quantity but just a few skilled and specialised drivers.

No shipping line employs dockers because operational frequency does not warrant it. A major airline, on the other hand, will have the frequency to justify its own loaders. An airline can discuss with its own staff the effect of impending changes, but a shipping company has no such links of human communication. All the docker knows is that the whole character of his working life is being changed by shipowners with whom he is completely out of contact. Small wonder if he feels stunned and at the mercy of an unkind and inconsiderate fate.

Enforced change is never welcome at the time. But, because our staff in Cunard had been led to understand the need for it, we could carry it through without being blocked by industrial action. Admittedly we had been helped by the external factors I have described. But management can claim some of the credit, not least for having had the sense to use these factors to advantage.

★   ★   ★   ★   ★

The result was worthwhile jobs for almost two-thirds of our staff. But not only staff are at risk under the impact of new technology: executive directors and top management are at almost greater risk.

Certainly the board knew that, having brought Cunard to record profits from the brink of break-up in 1966, we were now exposed to the risk of take-over. We had slimmed ourselves down and were more commercially healthy than ever. But we had only the travel market and the deep-sea liner business to rely on. If they and our profits were to slump again, causing our share price to tumble, we would be a sitting duck to the take-over sportsmen.

We could see that, to protect ourselves, we needed to diversify into growth industries complementing our own activities. But first we needed to provide ourselves with the cash to do this. We took advantage of the rising property market in December 1969 to sell Cunard Building in Liverpool to the Prudential for £2¾ million. Not long after we sold Cunard House in Leadenhall Street, London, to a subsidiary of the Crown Agents for £8¼ million.

We had already begun diversifying in 1968 by buying Offshore Marine for £2½ million from Hay's Wharf. This was an interesting little business run by Brigadier Teddy Parker, operating a fleet of eight vessels from Great Yarmouth to North Sea oil rigs – clearly a growth business, as we all know.

Moreover, we now felt confidence in our concept of cruising, another growing market. We issued specifications for a couple of new cruiseships for delivery at the end of 1971, to replace *Carmania* and *Franconia* – now only marginally profitable. And we could get Shipbuilding Industry Board finance up to 80 per cent for new ships.

We were also encouraged by the success of our Australian containership operations, and extended them to include the New Zealand trade. For this ACT(A) and OCL ordered four additional ships – one each for Cunard's Port Line, Blue Star, P&O and Shaw Savill & Albion (part of Furness Withy). Swan Hunter's yard gave us the most practical bid, but the cost of the ships (admittedly larger than our others) had gone up to £11 million each.

In March 1970 we decided to move into bulkers for dry cargoes, as distinct from the specialised vessels of Moss Tankers. The lowest British bid we received was too high at £2.9 million a ship, so we authorised management to enter negotiations with a Spanish yard for delivery of six small bulkers from the end of 1972 at only £2¼ million each.

Having brought the company thus far along the road to re-establishment and profit, I needed now to secure my eventual succession. I aranged to transfer John Whitworth from Southampton to be group administration director at company headquarters in St James's Square. I brought in Norman S Thompson from Swan Hunter's at the beginning of 1970 to be over-all manager of our various cargo enterprises. I should be 65 in September 1971, so the board now had a good two years to decide who should succeed me as chief executive. As to the chairmanship, I was prepared to carry on until 1974 at least, by which time Philip Bates would be back with us from ACL and a likely contender for that post.

★   ★   ★   ★   ★

The budget for 1970 that Philip Shirley presented the previous December forecast profits even higher than the £3 million achieved in 1969. But clouds began to move across the summer sky at the end of July 1970. Our accountants revised their profit forecast to a million down on the previous year's figure, not up.

As the anxious months passed, things grew worse. By the end of November it was clear that we would not make an operating profit at all but run into loss once more, perhaps as much as £2 million – £5 million down on 1969, but this fall in operating profit would be more than offset by our one-off profit on property sales.

On the cargo side, our Australian and New Zealand trades were down by £2½ million compared with the previous year; our Indian trades were also a million down; and the gloomy picture was relieved only by the Atlantic – half a million up. The passenger side, too, was falling off by a million and a half; the United States cruising public had not yet fully accepted the *QE2*, which would need more promotion and time.

Then Donald Forrester, our largest private shareholder, resigned from the board. This worried me because of the possible effect of his departure on share prices. Sir Siegmund Warburg advised that the board, when next meeting their shareholders, should be armed with a report on company prospects from outside consultants of world standing such as McKinsey.

We were not alone in suffering unexpected major setbacks in 1970. The whole shipping industry was affected. A drop of five million in P&O or Ocean Steamship profits would be regarded as just another cyclical downturn that shipping encounters from time to time; they were regularly making large enough profits to absorb such shocks. But we in Cunard had painfully worked our way back into profit only in the past two years. We had as yet no margin to absorb a shock of this magnitude; and going into operating loss again would affect the price of our shares on the Stock Exchange, which is what anyone intent on taking us over would be watching.

The downturn in the New Zealand trades had the most serious repercussions. Even P&O had liquidity problems as a result of this, and decided to withdraw a subsidiary from the New Zealand/east coast of North America trade. When the four lines which had ordered ships for the Europe/New Zealand trade met again in October 1970, John MacConochie warned us that Shaw Savill might have to withdraw. The capital we should each have to find was now nearer twenty million pounds than eleven. New Zealand could not finance containership ports so we British shipowners would have to provide them.

In our straitened circumstances I had to say, in January 1971, that Cunard also could not proceed. Two of us having withdrawn, P&O and Blue Star had to follow – though P&O's ship was well advanced in building and had to be completed.

It would be another six years before adequate containership ports would allow the UK and Europe/New Zealand service to be built up as it should have been.

I am sure that Siegmund Warburg's advice to bring in McKinsey was good. Their report certainly proved a useful defence at the AGM. But such reports can be a distinct liability in resisting a take-over bid. With outside consultants in a business you have to publish their forecasts in support of your case. This need for publication forces them to play safe and to under-estimate your prospects. That is no help at all when trying to fend off a bid or to negotiate a higher price for the company shares. It seems to me that in this respect the Take-Over Code is heavily loaded in favour of the bidder: the defender must justify all his claims, but the predator need justify nothing.

The McKinsey report proved to be our Achilles' heel. We had been on tenterhooks since we first foresaw disappearing profits. Then on 29 June, 1971, a bid seemed imminent, for there was an untoward upsurge in our share price on the Stock Exchange. During our board meeting next day I received a message from Nigel Broackes, the chairman of Trafalgar House Investments (in whose building we happened to have our head office) to the effect that he and Victor Matthews would like to see me that afternoon.

I knew what to expect.

Their bid valued Cunard shares at around £1.85. Warburgs advised that, to oppose the bid, we must be absolutely confident of the future. Philip Shirley was now budgeting for a 1971 return to profit – only a small profit, but a marked improvement on 1970. But Cunard was balanced on a knife edge, and Philip's forecast profit could be wiped out, as in 1970. If we were to reject the bid, Warburgs confirmed that McKinsey and our auditors, Coopers, would prepare forecasts for publication; these were bound to be ultra-cautious and perhaps unduly sceptical of Shirley's projections.

In the circumstances, Warburgs could not advise us to reject the bid; nor could we justify a higher price on such estimates. I delayed accepting the bid for a while, and by the end of July Nigel Broackes increased Trafalgar's offer to £2.10 per share.

Why should a group like Trafalgar House want to go into shipping? They were basically a diverse property and construction group. They doubtless wanted to expand and diversify their activities into other industries. Cunard were on their way up, despite the 1970 setback, and had an effective management. But I believe what led them particularly to shipping was our value for tax purposes.

Free depreciation allowances had been granted to shipping companies, deferring their liability to tax and encouraging them to order new ships. These allowances did not particularly help British shipbuilding, their apparent purpose; they were granted to shipowners whether they placed their orders at home or abroad. Nor were they of much benefit to shipping itself because the industry did not make sufficient profit for the tax allowances to be significant. In 1971 Cunard had over £50 million of accumulated free depreciation allowances; but we could not use them as we had no profits to set them against. A conglomerate making profits in other industries could turn them to good account, because shipping depreciation allowances could be set off against profits made anywhere within a group.

Free depreciation allowances had done little to help shipping, but had whetted the appetites of others. They fostered the formation of diversified groups through Trafalgar's take-over of Cunard and P&O's eventual merger with Bovis. The benefit of these allowances was in fact being used elsewhere – a good example of how the best of political intentions can produce a completely different effect.

Well, that was it. We couldn't fight off Trafalgar's approach. Considering the downturn in profits in 1970 I think we got our shareholders a reasonable price; and Trafalgar got a bargain, with profits which I felt sure would come but couldn't prove and which were to make Cunard the most profitable of their take-overs until shipping went into recession again in 1978. With the aid of our accumulated tax allowances, which they were in a position to turn to advantage, they were able to defer payment of corporation tax for several years after the take-over.

It was simply maddening to think that once again others were going to enjoy the benefit of all our efforts in the last six years. As always in such cases, the people at or near the top are liable to suffer most. A number of senior management fell by the wayside. Inevitably, all members of the group board (save Norman Thompson, who stayed on as managing director for a while) lost their jobs in Cunard.

We held the last meeting of the board of Cunard as an independent company of 93 years standing on 25 August, 1971. I stayed on as a member of the Trafalgar House board for another five months, but there was little or nothing I could do there to help the Cunard ship; and then, with sadness in my heart, I let myself quietly over the side and went ashore.

21 One Face of Capitalism

This was the second time in my business career that I had been robbed of the harvest from seed I had sown. I had learnt long before that there is no sense in pining over matters that do not turn out as hoped. You simply have to come to terms with the situation as it is, and take it from there.

During the five months after the take-over that I stayed on the Trafalgar House board, I wondered what to do next. I was now 65. The three members of the ACT(A) containership consortium – Vestey's Blue Star Line, Ellerman Lines and Trafalgar's Cunard – asked me to stay on as its independent non-executive chairman. The Australian Government and the Australian National Line asked me to continue as chairman of the co-ordinating board of the ACT(A)/ ANL partnership. But those two chairmanships could not take up more than half my time, if that.

In March 1972 I was in Australia for a meeting of the ACT(A)/ ANL co-ordinating board. The day before I was due to return to England I had a phone call from Kay at Esher to say that a despatch rider had called at our home the previous evening, with a message from the chairman of Barclays Bank, Sir John Thomson. He had tried unsuccessfully to get hold of me at my office and wanted to see me urgently.

I wondered why. I was a member of Barclay's London Local Board, but didn't think it could be anything to do with that. Anyway, I went to see John Thomson in his Lombard Street office the day after getting back to London. He told me that Duncan Sandys was about to become chairman of Lonrho and had asked him as a friend to enquire whether I would consider joining its board.

All I knew about Lonrho was that it was a company based in London and originally operating in Rhodesia. In recent years it had expanded rapidly throughout black Africa and had run into a liquidity crisis. Its merchant bankers, Warburgs, had resigned some six months earlier. Peat Marwick Mitchell & Co, a leading firm of chartered accountants, had been appointed to investigate the company's financial affairs and management.

John Thomson told me that Peats had completed their investigation. Sir Ronald Leach, Peats' senior partner, who had been in charge of the investigation, now considered that all would be well if Lonrho could raise another £10 million in cash by issuing new shares to the public. For this to be successful, Lonrho needed additional directors of repute acceptable to 'the City'. John Thomson said that Sir Leslie O'Brien, Governor of the Bank of England, hoped I would seriously consider Duncan Sandys's approach.

I saw Duncan Sandys on 22 March at his home in Vincent Square. This was very different from having to attend upon him as Minister of Aviation, nine years previously. He asked me to support him by accepting a part-time appointment on the board of Lonrho when his own appointment as chairman was announced. If I wanted to know more, would I see Ronnie Leach and Leslie O'Brien?

So I went to see Ronnie Leach, whom I had known of old on the Council of the Institute of Chartered Accountants. In their investigation of Lonrho, Peats had found many short-comings in financial reporting and company procedure; but 'Tiny' Rowland, Lonrho's managing director (who is not as large a man as his nickname implies), had undertaken to introduce all Peats' suggested improvements, including the appointment of a new finance director. Assuming all that was done, and a proper industrial system of financial reporting and control was introduced by the newly-recruited chief accountant, Roger Moss, he considered the company would be clean.

I then went to see Leslie O'Brien at the Bank. Duncan Sandys's appointment as non-executive chairman was to be announced on 4 April. Sandys was a politician and not a businessman. O'Brien therefore regarded it as essential for there to be people on the board such as myself to reassure 'the City', and the public providing Lonrho with the ten millions it needed, that the company would in future be run on orthodox financial lines. The good name of the City of London was at stake. So that I was not alone in doing this, he would also nominate to the board another person respected in financial circles.

Lonrho's then chairman, Alan Ball, was to become executive deputy chairman when Duncan Sandys became chairman on 4 April. To discharge effectively my responsibilities to 'the City' and the shareholders, I felt I too must have the rank of deputy chairman, but non-executive. I saw Duncan again on 28 March and told him I would accept the appointment on that basis. This was quickly agreed with Tiny Rowland; and I was appointed to the board of Lonrho along with Duncan Sandys and Edward du Cann.

The way was now clear for us to start work on the issue of new shares to raise the needed £10 million. The offer document or prospectus for the rights issue was prepared by the company's lawyers, Linklaters & Paines, with the help of Peats, Keyser Ullman and some of us on the board. It listed some eight specific undertakings as to the way the company was to be conducted in future. The City gave the new board and its professional advisers a handsome vote of confidence by fully underwriting the rights issue. When the offer document was issued to shareholders on 25 May, 1972, it was fully subscribed; and Lonrho received the £10 million it needed.

★   ★   ★   ★   ★

So Lonrho's immediate cash shortage was dealt with. That was a good start, viewed from outside. But viewed from inside things were not so good. During June and July I had become increasingly concerned about a number of things.

The Governor of the Bank had not after all arranged for a second 'City name' to join me on the board.

Peats had selected a number of possible candidates for appointment as Lonrho's new finance director in place of Butcher. The appointment of the man chosen by a committee of the board was vetoed.

At the board's meeting on 11 May, an undertaking had been given to merchant bankers Keyser Ullman, and to auditors Peats, specifying work to ensure the liquidity of the company. Without this the rights issue to raise the £10 million could not have been made. But nothing was being done to fulfil this undertaking.

In the offer document approved by the board on 24 May and issued to shareholders next day, eight separate undertakings had been given about the way the company would be managed in future. The offer document was a prospectus, and the company could be regarded as contractually bound to implement those undertakings. But, again, nothing was being done.

As an example of the way the board was treated, Rowland had talked at length at that meeting on 24 May about his ideas for growing and refining sugar in the Sudan, giving no indication of any financial effect on Lonrho. He might have been just airing his thoughts. But I learnt early in June that on 10 May he had settled in Khartoum a draft agreement under which Lonrho would provide the capital required for the scheme (£80 to £100 million, less any amounts he could persuade the Governments of sugar-consuming countries to contribute).

Here he was, a fortnight before floating a rights issue to raise £10 million essential to Lonrho's future, initialling a draft indicating that the company might invest several times that amount in a new development in the Sudan. However worthwhile the business might one day become, he had not consulted the board – intentionally or unintentionally. Nor was the board aware of a document that should certainly have been disclosed in the prospectus.

Some of us were able to discuss the matter informally in Tiny Rowland's office on 7 June. In its revised form the agreement was confined to the carrying out of a feasibility study only, without further financial commitment by Lonrho. On that basis it was acceptable.

Matters dragged on in this unsatisfactory way through the autumn and winter. Lonrho's financial year ended on 30 September each year. The audited accounts and draft annual report to shareholders for the year 1971-72 were circulated for consideration at a board meeting on 15 February, 1973. There were one or two queries, so they were not then formally approved.

Four days later I was asked by Ronnie Leach if I could see him at his office in Ironmonger Lane at 9.45 am next morning, 20 February. He apologised for the short notice. He couldn't say more on the phone, but it was important. On arrival I found his No 2 on the Lonrho audit, Jim Butler, with him. What they told me was shattering.

Peats had been trying for some weeks to get an explanation from finance director Fred Butcher of a loan made by a company called Anglo-Ceylon and General Estates. It was not until 14 February, the day before the annual accounts were due for approval by the board, that Butcher gave them an oral explanation.

The loan had been made to a Lonrho subsidiary in the Cayman Islands, Consultancy and Development Services. Until that moment Peats had not been aware that Lonrho had a subsidiary in the Caymans. Out of that loan, the sum of £44,000 had been paid in March 1972 through yet another Cayman company, London Overseas Services, to Duncan Sandys 'by way of compensation'.

What was I expected to do about it? I asked Ronnie. He replied that Peats as auditors could not sign Lonrho's accounts without qualification, unless the payment was ratified by the board. They handed me the draft of a resolution which they wanted passed by the board at its next meeting. I didn't like it, but there it was.

In the end, the resolution was not needed. To Duncan's credit, he decided that he would tell the board that, as he had no knowledge until very recently that the compensation arrangement had not been approved by the board, he declared it to be null and void. He undertook to refund in full the amount he had so far received.

★   ★   ★   ★   ★

There was much else to worry us, too. Much more could be told, were it not for the uncertainties of the law. It must therefore suffice to say that the revelation of the compensation arrangement having been concealed from the majority of the board for close on twelve months released the pent-up feelings of many of us. We could no longer go on working in a company being run this way.

My own inclination was to resign from the board immediately. I consulted Nicholas Wilson, a partner in Slaughter & May, the City solicitors who had advised me when chairman of Cunard. Nick took me to a leading Queen's Counsel.

Counsel advised that, if I were to resign, I might have to defend myself against a possible legal action for dereliction of duty. In his opinion my only course was to take the matter up with the Department of Trade and Industry (DTI) and ask for an inspection under the Companies Acts. This would discharge my duty fully.

What was good legal advice for me was also good legal advice for the other directors who felt as I did. We were caught in a trap. We couldn't resign. We couldn't remain and do nothing without being guilty of failing in our duty.

During the next fortnight, Gerald Percy, William Wilkinson and I met to discuss what to do, together with Major Colin Mackenzie and S S W (Peter) Dalgliesh, both non-executive directors. It was agreed that I should find out how to proceed with a DTI inspection as recommended by Counsel. I should also tell Duncan Sandys what we were doing, as well as Ronnie Leach and Leslie O'Brien.

After visiting the DTI office in Bunhill Row, I couldn't believe that a DTI inspection could ever be private. Their inspectors would have to work in Lonrho's offices in Cheapside, and their presence would be bound to get known. But I saw no alternative.

On 15 March, I was asked to see Leslie O'Brien. The Governor of the Bank of England was sympathetic to my problems in straightening out Lonrho affairs, but pressed me strongly not to take the matter further with the DTI.

By this time, eight of us on the board now felt we could no longer serve as directors of a company with Tiny Rowland as chief executive and managing director. The four I have already mentioned, and myself, were joined by Nicholas Elliott, General Sir Edward Louis Spears and Dr A Gerber (of Wankel).

Tiny Rowland had joined Lonrho in 1961 and was largely responsible for its growth in the 1960s, mainly by acquisitions. As a result, profits increased from a mere £½ million in 1962 to £14½ million in 1969. In that year the share price reached a peak of around £3.00. But much of the profit arose in Africa and could not be remitted home to UK shareholders. From 1970 onwards, Lonrho's performance had been unimpressive.

On Monday, 19 March, 1973, after much thought and discussion, all eight of us signed a document stating our belief that it would be in the best interests of the company for Rowland to cease to be chief executive and managing director, and to give up all executive appointments on the board of subsidiary companies as well. We suggested that he should remain a non-executive director of Lonrho because he was a substantial shareholder and because his knowledge and experience of Africa was valuable.

We then called on Duncan to conclude arrangements with Rowland along these lines. Failing that, we would jointly propose a resolution to that effect at the next board meeting – a resolution we knew we could carry, because there were eight of us and under Lonrho's Articles of Association Rowland could not vote on this issue.

When the full board met on 18 April, Duncan Sandys reported that he had been unable to make any progress. Thereupon Colin Mackenzie and Louis Spears put to the board the eight's resolution for the removal of Rowland from all executive offices in the company.

We were then told that Rowland had that day applied to the High Court for an injunction to restrain the board from passing that proposed resolution. Discussion continued in a desultory, if awkward manner. We wondered how things were going at the Law Courts.

It was the Wednesday before Good Friday and the courts would be under pressure to clear a lot of business before the Easter recess. Or they might hold it over until afterwards. About 5 o'clock a message came that Mr Justice Foster had granted Rowland an interlocutory injunction restraining the board from taking any action until after the recess. That delay proved fatal.

After Easter we learnt that Tiny Rowland was taking all eight of us to court to prevent us removing him from the board.

Each of us had to prepare affidavits in defence of our actions and there was little time left. We spent the whole of Sunday afternoon and evening, 29 April, with Nick Wilson and others at Slaughter and May's offices in Basinghall Street. My pocket diary reminds me I arrived home at 01.00 next morning. So, too, on the Monday and Tuesday following.

At one of these late night sessions at Slaughter and May's Nicholas Elliott remarked that the information we should have to reveal in our affidavits to the Court would create an unholy public row in the press. Wouldn't it be better, in the public interest, if all eight of us simply resigned? Nick Wilson reminded us that we had a legal duty we were obliged to pursue; to resign might expose us to a charge of dereliction of that duty; we could not opt out.

Tiny Rowland's case in the High Court to prevent his removal by the board was heard by Mr Justice Plowman. The hearing began on Tuesday, 8 May, and continued until the Friday. We were called back on Monday, 14 May, to hear his judgment.

Mr Justice Plowman dismissed Rowland's motion. He did not regard it as the duty of the court to interfere in what was primarily a matter for the board of the company. But he added that it was for the defendant directors to decide whether it was wise or desirable for them to take action, now they were free to do so, in advance of a decision by the shareholders at the general meeting fixed for 31 May.

Tiny Rowland had taken us to court to stop us removing him from the board – and had lost. But we had lost, too, in another sense. With all the postponements and the law's delays, the shareholders' meeting was now only 17 days away. At that meeting Rowland would seek to remove all eight of us from the board. We discussed with counsel the judge's point as to whether it was sensible and right for us at this late stage to remove Rowland from executive office. We all agreed it would be irresponsible to act now. The shareholders must decide.

The outcome of the shareholders' meeting was a foregone conclusion. Tiny Rowland's 20 per cent shareholding was virtually unbeatable, and his supporters worked hard to get many more proxy votes to keep him in office. One by one, the eight of us were removed from the board at that meeting on 31 May, 1973.

*   *   *   *   *

What had been achieved by the stand taken by the 'straight eight', as we had been nicely dubbed by the press?

We all lost our jobs with Lonrho, from which the three executive directors among us suffered most. But we had done our duty, however unpleasant it had been, and our consciences were clear.

Tiny Rowland calls himself 'a revolutionary capitalist' (*The Times,* October 1977) scornful of 'paper merchants' – meaning, no doubt, myself and others of a similar outlook. Well, if being a paper merchant infers that people should justify in writing how they intend to use other people's money, and honour pledges given in writing, I am content to accept that label.

I don't mind anybody being a revolutionary capitalist with his own money. But I do mind if he is revolutionary with the money of others I represent. That is what Prime Minister Edward Heath called at that time 'the unacceptable face of capitalism'.

Perhaps, in consequence of the stand we took and without admitting it, Tiny has become more amenable to the disciplines essential in a public company. I was succeeded as deputy chairman of Lonrho by Sir George Bolton, a past executive director of the Bank of England and chairman of the Bank of London and South America. George Bolton is still with Lonrho, so one can but assume that both Tiny and the company have undergone some transformation as a result of our action.

The Department of Trade and Industry appointed two inspectors – one a Queen's counsel and the other a leading City accountant – to review the Lonrho happenings. It was not until the summer of 1976 that their work was completed and their report running to 660 pages was published.

Throughout those three years from 1973 to 1976 I could get little or no work to replace the income I had lost. In the private sector of industry, I had to live down the unwelcome publicity of the court case without people really knowing why I had to do what I did. That would take time; and by 1976 I was 70.

In the sphere of public work, the Civil Service have a list of 'the great and the good', so called, from which people are chosen for Government appointments. On enquiry, I was told that my name had been removed from that list because I had been a director of a company still under investigation.

I couldn't even get back some income tax I was reclaiming throughout those three years. Even at Somerset House it seemed I was *sub judice*. It was not until December 1976, well after publication of the DTI Inspectors' report, that the Inland Revenue paid a claim dating back to 1971-72.

That's life. Justice herself remains unmoved by it all.

22 Reflections

Soon after joining the Lonrho board in April 1972 there began the worst year of my life.

It was not only the difficult and unpleasant time that I had there, trying to discharge the responsibilities I had accepted on appointment – though that was bad enough.

I had cataract in both eyes, and had to have one eye operated on in April and the other in July. During the four months between the two, I had only limited sight. After July I had to wear thick post-cataract pebble-lens spectacles; they have restricted 'tunnel' vision, and among other things you have to learn not to walk into things or people outside your tunnel of sight.

This could not have come at a worse time. I was in my last year as chairman of the British Institute of Management and it made the conduct of council meetings far from easy. Pebble-lens spectacles are not available in bifocal form. I had to change repeatedly from nearsight spectacles for reading the papers in front of me to longsight ones for seeing people across the room. I had to do the same at board meetings, which didn't help me to impress Tiny Rowland. Moreover, I couldn't blame Lonrho shareholders if they regarded me unfavourably – my press image in thick pebble-lens spectacles was awful.

Then my wife Kay became critically ill at the end of 1972. For four years she had had a blood disease for which there was no known cure. After its first flare-up in December 1968, it had appeared again in 1970. Now it flared up again. I was warned that, if it settled in the kidneys as it worked its way round her body, it would be terminal. And, indeed, it was; Kay passed away in the early hours of 2 February, 1973, and more than 41 years of life together came to an end.

★   ★   ★   ★   ★

But it was not long before I emerged into smooth air again. I soon learnt to wear post-cataract contact lenses in my eyes, which gave me back as good sight as I had ever had. I could see to drive a car and to play golf again.

Then one evening in New York, an American friend wondered what I would do now. 'Over here,' he said, 'it is an understood thing that widowers are left alone for three months. But after that, watch out! If you were living in America you would find well-intentioned friends asking you to meet unattached ladies.'

I was amused and thankful that I lived in England. I continued to live in the same house in Esher, and was fortunate to retain as housekeeper a widow who had helped us during Kay's illness. As the summer passed, I sensed that she might have ambitions. She certainly tried to become more possessive. But I kept her on; I couldn't run the house without her.

That September some kind friends asked me to stay for a weekend in the country. I drove down to Kent in the lovely Rolls-Royce Silver Cloud that I had been lucky enough to buy from my friend Nut Hume's widow. I felt full of well-being and was looking forward to a couple of days' complete relaxation. But staying in the house, having arrived ahead of me, was an attractive divorcee. I am probably flattering myself, but at 67 I suppose I was still fair game. And I had the impression that we were being paired off.

At any rate, I took fright.

Thinking about things on the way home after the weekend I decided that I must soon marry again. I hoped I could take as my wife someone I already knew and could trust – if she would have me.

Rita Burns had been my secretary at Cunard since 1966, and I had great respect for her character and admiration for her personality. I prayed it might be mutual.

Thankfully, it was; and she accepted me. The age difference did not worry her – she was 25 years younger, but her father had been 40 years older than her mother. A Roman Catholic, she saw no problem in marrying a Protestant. Having decided to marry we saw no point in a long engagement, in the course of which everyone would gradually get in on the secret. So we were married very quietly, with only half a dozen of our closest friends present, on Friday 2 November 1973.

That started something wonderful. We came to share a community of thought, a richness of understanding, and a depth of love I had not thought it possible to regain. I have never ceased to thank God for having blessed us so.

$$\star \quad \star \quad \star \quad \star \quad \star$$

I continued as chairman of ACT(A) and of the ACT(A)/Australian

National Line co-ordinating board until 1979, when we celebrated the tenth anniversary of the partnership. Jim Payne had given up the managing directorship of ACT(A) to go back to the Vestey family's Blue Star Line, and had been succeeded by Alexander Macintosh, whom he had recruited when ACT was first established.

These two were the first non-executive chairmanships I had ever held, and they provided a fascinating challenge in the exercise of leadership without executive authority. How one does that I find hard to explain. It seems to come by encouragement more than anything else – by making executives feel that you are there to help them to do their jobs, and that your advice is always available when they need it.

These continuing appointments maintained my regular visits to Australia, which pleased me greatly. And, being free of executive responsibility and the grindstone, I now had time to reflect on some aspects of my quarter-century's work.

These days a man can move around the world so easily that it is difficult to remember that man has crossed the oceans only since the fifteenth century. Until then, he was essentially landlocked. On the sea he was limited to edging his way along the coasts, or exceptionally, drifting on the currents.

The adventurous Phoenician traders in the age before Christ took their courage and galleys out of the Mediterranean, and crossed the sea to Cornwall's tin. In the ninth century AD the Vikings made their way to Dublin and the Norsemen established a settlement in Normandy. But navigation was at its most elementary. Not until the eleventh century did the Amalfitans discover navigation techniques which enabled their tiny republic to dominate others along the Italian west coast.

In spite of advances in the science of navigation, the boat's ability to move very far from shore was limited by its one mast and limited sail. No one knew how to build a hull to carry more. Then, in the fifteenth century, man discovered how to construct a ship capable of bearing the weight and strain of three or four masts with as many tiers of sail. This was achieved by building a strong structure of crossmembers first, setting the masts firmly in it, and then building a hull round the structure. Previously the hulls had been fashioned first and the crossmembers fitted in afterwards.

This was a technological advance of tremendous significance. It became possible for man to cross the oceans and to open up the world for the first time in history – all within the short space of fifty years. By 1492 Christopher Columbus had crossed the Atlantic and discovered the New World.

For the next four centuries people of enterprise made their way round our world by sail. The English first settled at Jamestown, Virginia, in 1607; and in 1620 the Mayflower Pilgrims founded Plymouth colony in Massachussetts. The Dutch established a settlement at Table Bay, Cape of Good Hope, in 1652. Around that time Dutch captains made landfalls on west Australia (Terra Australis), blown beyond the East Indies by the roaring forties. Abel Tasman, the greatest of Dutch navigators, discovered Tasmania and New Zealand in 1642, but it was not until 1770 that Captain James Cook in the *Endeavour* sighted south-east Australia and discovered Botany Bay.

The old world had found another new continent. In 1788 Captain Phillip settled in Sydney Cove with the New South Wales regiment and the first batch of convicts from Britain. Meanwhile, the settlers in New England were developing the fast-sailing clipper ships, which proved so valuable to trade on the long voyages to China and elsewhere.

But the new-style sailing ships did not only make possible far-away settlements and trading posts. Men also used them in pursuit of international rivalries across the oceans. Hence the long-drawn-out wars against the Spanish. Not until the first years of the 19th century did Britain complete her mastery of the seas and start ruling the waves, to keep the peace in the interests of free trade.

However skilfully handled, sailing ships were still dependent on fickle winds. Moreover, their accommodation for passengers and seamen was sparse and rugged.

In the nineteenth century the growth of worldwide trade and travel was given a tremendous boost when marine engines were invented and then further developed by engineers such as Alfred Holt of Liverpool. Sail gave way to the steam-driven paddle and propeller. Ship schedules became more regular, and ships could be designed with ample space for passengers as well as cargo. Cunard's *Britannia*, still with a wooden hull, started transatlantic crossings in 1840; and the company's first iron-sided ship, *British Queen*, went into service in 1851. For the best part of the next century steamships provided us with a worldwide system of transport for passengers and every kind of freight.

But the steamship, and the turbine-driven motor-vessel which evolved from it, were destined to lose their passenger-liner custom by the third quarter of the present century.

On 17 December, 1903, the Wright brothers had made the first powered and controlled flight in a heavier-than-air machine, at Kitty Hawk, North Carolina. Man was learning how to fly. And, all at once, the first world war of 1914–18 added tremendous growth to the infant science of aircraft and engine construction and operation. So much so that by 1924 Imperial Airways had been founded to take over the work of four small private British airlines started in 1919 and 1920 to operate services between Britain and Europe. As its name implied, the objective of Imperial Airways was to link Britain with the British Empire by fast mail and, in due course, passenger services.

By the time the second world war broke out in 1939 we had still not proved it possible to fly commercially and direct across the North Atlantic. But by routeing aircraft on a long dog-leg via Bermuda, the Azores and Lisbon to Southampton, Pan American Airways carried mail and 21 passengers in one of their flying boats across the Atlantic in March 1939. The conquest of the Atlantic by air is a fascinating story.[1] Once again, a world war gave a tremendous impetus to the science of aviation. When the war was over, it became possible to start regular commercial air services across the North Atlantic in 1946.

In the following years, the airlines gradually took passenger traffic away from the ships – more rapidly on the shorter-haul deepsea route across the Atlantic, but more slowly on the longer-haul routes from Europe to South Africa, the Far East and Australia.

By a curious quirk of fate, it was the containership that finally clinched the matter. The containerships syphoned out of the passenger liners all their general cargo – and without the cargo revenue, the passenger liner could not possibly continue to pay its way, except as a cruise ship. P&O abandoned their passenger liner operations to Australia within two years of introducing their OCL containership operations in 1969. British & Commonwealth's Union Castle Line withdrew their remaining passenger liners in 1977, at the same time as they introduced their containerships on the South African run.

This in turn has brought about a chain reaction in the character and style of air travel. With no passenger liners operating regularly between Britain and Australia since 1971, air traffic between the two countries became predominantly end-to-end and therefore '3rd and 4th Freedom' in character. Until then the Kangaroo route had been heavily dependent on sector traffic, which could be picked up and set down as aircraft worked their way along. So it was commercially necessary to have intermediate stops. It was also technically necessary, because aircraft did not then have the range to do

[1]See David Beaty's *The Water Jump* (Secker & Warburg, 1976).

otherwise. When the greater part of the traffic became end-to-end in 1971, stops were no longer so commercially necessary. At the same time the technical qualities of the aircraft had improved, giving them the range to cover the 9,300 miles from Perth, Western Australia, to London against the prevailing wind with only one landing at Bombay. So, too, has it become possible (and is now politically and commercially convenient) to fly non-stop the 5,600 miles from London to Johannesburg.

The demise of the passenger liner after a reign of only about a hundred years is sad in many ways. But the coming of regular air transport has opened up the world to people of all ages, in ways that were unimaginable less than fifty years ago.

$$\star \quad \star \quad \star \quad \star \quad \star$$

That is all past history. We now have history in the making.

When I raised the question in 1967 of Australia entering overseas shipping in partnership with Britain's Blue Star, Ellerman and Port Lines, there was marked reluctance to consider it. The attitude of successive Australian Governments generally has been to regard Australia as a shipper country, not a shipping country – one that uses shipping but does not provide it unless essential.

The roots of this attitude run deep in Australian history and politics. British ships took succeeding generations of settlers to Australia, supplied them from home, and carried their exports to distant markets. It seemed natural to rely on others. The struggle to win a life for themselves out of their rugged land and climate was so great that Australians were only too glad to let others provide their oversea transport.

In time Australia had to provide its own coastal shipping. This grew up in conditions of monopoly, not exposed to foreign competition. Thus it became very costly – wages, manning levels and conditions of service for Australian seamen are such that it costs Australia more than twice as much to crew a ship as it would a foreign shipping company.

In Australian politics, the Country Party represents the large numbers of homesteaders, graziers and others whose livelihoods spring from the soil. Its existence has depended on the votes of those who work in these primary industries, who in turn have relied on economic foreign shipping to carry their exports. In no way will they pay freight rates based on Australian coastal-shipping costs.

The Liberal Party (roughly the equivalent of Britain's Conservative Party) has depended on a coalition with the Country

Party. So the Liberals also believed that Australia should be a shipper, not a shipping country.

Fortunately for Australia, the Minister for Trade and Industry in 1967 was a man of great character and wisdom. Sir John McEwen was also Deputy Prime Minister and leader of the Country Party, and his Permanent Secretary at the Ministry was Sir Alan Westerman. Within a couple of years John McEwen had won over the Cabinet: a limited incursion into overseas shipping would be useful to Australia by giving it an insight into the operation and economics of overseas shipping and by gaining admission to the closed society of shipping conferences.

Today, in its partnership with the British lines, the Australian National Line (ANL) now operate deep-sea containership services to the UK, Europe and the USA. But this has not been allowed to erode the general policy that Australia should remain a shipper country. ANL has developed services to south-east Asia and further north, but basically in ways that do not conflict with Country Party interests; and the great majority of Australia's trade with Japan is carried in Japanese ships.

Nobody else in politics and Government seems to have paused to consider how much Australia is losing by not having its own shipping. A country could expect to carry about half its overseas trade. As an island continent in the south-west of the vast Pacific Ocean, Australia has to be a great overseas trading nation.

The price Australia's customers are willing to pay for her exports is their landed cost at destination, including freight. By not retaining a substantial part of that freight, Australia is throwing money away. The cost of her imports is their landed cost in Australia, including freight. Again, Australia is throwing currency away – not merely a few cents, but many millions of dollars each year – by not carrying part of those imports.

In Britain we have developed our overseas shipping and aviation to the greatest possible extent. In the 16th century we were responding to the challenges of conquering new worlds, and of developing the full potential of sailing ships. In Cromwell's time the 1651 Navigation Act was passed because the Dutch had cornered most of the world's seaborne trade. We wanted to carry our own. At first this was a question of rivalry between nations. But by the start of the 18th century it was seen that there were strong economic reasons. So, too, with flying. International services did not start until 1919. At first it was a race to do new things. But gradually the economic advantages came to be seen.

Even Britain far from realises how profitable it is to operate her own international air and sea transport services.

How does a nation measure such profitability? In just the same way as in business – by counting whether we are better off with the service than without it, and by how much.

But there the analogy ends. A company makes this count in terms of its resources and of the extent to which revenue from customers exceeds the cost of providing the service. But a country's profit and loss account is with other countries, not with people or firms.

A country needs to measure the worth of an international service which it provides by calculating the extent to which it improves the balance of payments with the rest of the world. This is very different from normal business accounting. In fact, the profit or loss made by an international airline or shipping company is no guide at all to the worth of that company to its home country.

Take the accounts published by British Airways for the year ended 31 March 1980. On airline traffic revenue of £1,650 million it made a profit after tax (on a current cost accounting basis) of only about £10 million. That was the measure of the airline's worth to its shareholder, the Government, in that particular year.

Its worth to the country in that year was vastly different, measured by the contribution it made to Britain's balance of payments. It is not possible to calculate this precisely, because the corporation provides no figures on this subject in its report – only charts. Approximations must therefore suffice. In any case, precise figures are not necessary to make the case in principle.

The first calculation is to count the movement of foreign currencies into and out of the airline's hands. In 1979-80 British Airways appears to have earned some £950 million of foreign currencies in passenger fares and other revenues. Against this, it had to pay out nearly £550 million[1] in foreign currencies to meet its costs overseas. So the airline made a profit for the country of £400 million by bringing that net amount of foreign currencies into our national balance of payments account.

But that is by no means all that the operations of British Airways were worth to Britain in 1979-80. The airline earned some £450 million in sterling by carrying British passengers and air freight overseas. If Britain had not operated its own international services, all this sterling revenue would have had to be paid out to foreign airlines and would have drained Britain's balance of payments to that extent.

[1] BA states (Annual Report for 1979-80 p. 39) that its fuel expenditure is paid 'principally in sterling'. To cover the non-sterling part, this figure includes an estimated £100 million, roughly one quarter of total fuel costs.

The currency profit that this country derived from British Airways' international operations in that one year is therefore about £850 million.

That is a rough measure of the airline's worth to Britain at the present time. Without its international operations, we should be that much worse off.

British Airways, of course, is not Britain's only airline that provides international services. The same reasoning can also be applied in assessing the national worth of British Caledonian, Laker Airways and others. When the profit they bring to the nation's balance of payments account is added to that of British Airways, the total benefit Britain gets through its international air services is very great.

For the past few years the General Council of British Shipping has reported with pride the foreign currency earned for Britain by our shipping. But as we have seen, that is only part of the story. If Britain did not have a great fleet of merchant ships, British exporters would have to use foreign ships. This would adversely affect our balance of payments in a big way. The total benefit our merchant fleet brings to Britain's economy is greater to that extent.

Because all this is never brought out and explained properly, the public at large and possibly even the Government remain unaware of the enormous economic benefit of international air and shipping services to Britain. These are not only matters for pride. They earn and save the country vast amounts of foreign currency.

The same kind of calculation can be made for Qantas as Australia's overseas airline. The foreign currency which Qantas earns and saves for Australia, at approximately 60 per cent of total revenue, benefits the country's economy by some $A400 million a year.

The development of Qantas by Sir Hudson Fysh and his successors has been something of which Australians can be justly proud. In contrast to shipping it had a great advantage; it did not threaten the interests of politically powerful groups, which have blocked the development of overseas shipping. Government gave its overseas airline clearance to take off, and it has never had to turn back.

In determining Australia's policy towards its own overseas shipping, it is the gain in foreign currency that matters. The profit or loss of individual lines is of relatively little national significance.

Company profit or loss is of course an important indicator of the effectiveness with which the resources entrusted to it are managed, and adjusted to meet circumstances. But it is only a domestic indicator, to be used for internal control. So too the level of crewing

Mary, Lady McEwen, launching *ACT 1* at Bremen-Vegesack, watched by
Sir John McEwen, September 1968. *(Derek Rowe)*

Arrival of *ACT 1* at Sydney, completing her maiden south-bound voyage,
April 1969. *(ACTA Pty Ltd)*

The ACT(A) containership terminal and depot at East Swanson Dock, Port of Melbourne. *(Port of Melbourne Authority)*

The ACT(A)/ANL co-ordinating board take lunch in Melbourne, 11 May 1970. Round the table from left foreground: Alastair Lloyd (Ellerman Lines), Reg Robin (ANL), Philip Shirley (Cunard), Bert Weymouth (ANL), BS, Capt Sir John Williams (ANL), Edmund Vestey (Blue Star Line), Sir Alan Westerman (DTI, Canberra), Jim Payne (ACTA), Lindsay Duthie (DTI, Canberra), Eric Sutton (Port Line), John Morgan (ANL). *(Australian National Line)*

costs is a domestic problem. Neither should be allowed to affect decisions of national policy on overseas shipping.

Moreover, Australia's primary producers need no longer be concerned that their exports might be adversely affected. In the past ten years they have seen that domestic cost levels do not govern freight rates, which are fixed in negotiation between international shipping conferences and Australian producer groups.

There is no longer any economic case for Australia remaining a shipper country. In its balance of payments with the rest of the world, the Australian economy would benefit greatly from developing overseas shipping.

Australia is a great country. But as she moves into the 21st century and her foreign trading becomes ever more important she cannot afford to sit back and relax, not bothering to win for herself and her people the substantial currency gains that operation of her own overseas shipping would yield.

★   ★   ★   ★   ★

We have had nationalised industries since 1946 and we are unlikely to be without them in the foreseeable future. Their constitution is far from perfect; indeed, it was not to be expected that we should get it right first time. Now, over a third of a century later, it is high time to review it in the light of experience.

With John Reith, BOAC's first chairman, I always felt that the current constitution of a nationalised industry did not fit the circumstances of a business operating substantially outside Britain in the fierce heat of worldwide international competition. Admittedly, BOAC and BEA would never have developed so well if it had not been for the exchequer grants provided by Government in the first ten years after World War II. But the provision of money to cover the change from wartime to peacetime operations was no reason to put the airlines into the ill-fitting harness of nationalisation.

The 1980 move to denationalise British Airways and offer shares to the public is therefore very welcome. But BOAC and BEA could be made to work well and efficiently even when nationalised. This was proved again and again by Miles Thomas, Sholto Douglas and by all of us who succeeded them as chairmen or chief executives. Otherwise, British Airways would not be today the world's largest international airline.

There are lessons to be learned from BOAC's experience. They may be relevant to the running of major British domestic industries – the logical sphere in which to apply the principle of nationalisation if

Parliament wishes it. The lessons will certainly be relevant should future Governments renationalise British Airways.

It is farcical to imagine that a Government, just because an industry is nationalised, can draw a fixed rate of dividend or interest on the capital it provides, whether there are profits or not. There is the risk of fluctuation in every business; and transport by air or sea is inherently cyclical.

This is not because of management inefficiency; no-one can forecast with certainty how much of the product or service the customers are going to buy. Add to this the difficulty of forecasting costs accurately in such changing circumstances as we have seen with the price of fuel.

The up-and-down fluctuation in profits has to fall somewhere. It can fall only on industry's owners. And the owners of a nationalised industry are the Government. The capital provided by Government must therefore be regarded as risk capital or equity.

The Australian overseas airline Qantas provides an interesting case study. Qantas is not nationalised in the British sense but is wholly Government-owned. The Australian Government receive no more as dividend on capital than Qantas can afford to pay out of the profit available after financing future development.

In Britain the Government changed BOAC's capital structure in 1965 to allow part of its capital to be in the form of equity. That was good as far as it went. The change was not carried far enough, but at least it marked the dawn of reason.

It is sound policy to set profit targets for nationalised industries, to keep them up to scratch in circumstances of monopoly or near-monopoly. But profit fluctuation is inevitable in industry and must be accepted.

It should also be recognised that a single accounting year is too short a period for judging the effectiveness of management in a basic industry. For these reasons one year must be taken with another over a period of five years, as Parliament wisely provided in the original nationalising Acts. Unfortunately, Ministers and MPs tend to be influenced so much by short-term tactical considerations that this sensible provision has never been accorded the recognition it deserves.

Then there is the whole question of the balance of power between the industry and its 'sponsoring' Ministry. The power given to Ministers under the nationalising Acts need reconsideration. The Minister nominates the entire board of a nationalised industry; he has the power to appoint or remove anyone he wishes, subject only to the salutary practice of having to refer proposed chairmen to the

Prime Minister – though the PM may well be pre-occupied at the time with matters of greater national importance. When board vacancies arise the continuing board has never been consulted, although it probably knew much better than the Minister or his civil servants what sort of experience was most needed.

Fortunately for British Airways, the 1980 Bill may give the board power to appoint its own members. But that is a one-off case. The Minister's power of appointment needs reviewing in the case of all other nationalised industries.

When Herbert Morrison took the first tentative steps towards public ownership in the 1930s and set up the London Passenger Transport Board, he provided that nominations for chairman and directors should be put forward by a committee of five eminent persons outside politics and the civil service. That procedure was perhaps too cumbersome, but nowadays the power of patronage left in the hands of an individual Minister, with all its influence for good or ill on the way an industry is run, cannot be right. It breeds unsettlement within the board, which is not allowed to grow cohesively from within.

During the first six months or so of his appointment a new chairman is in a strong position *vis-à-vis* his Minister, because the Minister cannot afford to quarrel with the new man he has just appointed. But once that short honeymoon is over, the Minister's power to impose his own policy on a chairman at critical times is very great. Partly this is because the chairman needs to win the Minister's approval for much of what he wants to do – as when BOAC was forced in 1962 to give Cunard a bigger share of our new joint company than was commercially justified.

But even more is the Minister's power of influence derived from the honours system. Thinking back to some of the Government and Ministerial interferences BOAC had to suffer, I am convinced that the compliance of one chairman was bought by the Honours List. Shortly after agreeing to a Ministerial wish contrary to our commercial judgment and ordering many more of a new British aircraft than we needed, he was knighted. Later on, when a similar situation recurred, it is possible to wonder whether he might not have been made a peer if he had not died soon afterwards.

In the nature of politics, Ministers hold their office for only a short time. In the fourteen years I was in BOAC, we had no fewer than eight Ministers. Apart from Frank Pakenham and Harold Watkinson, who were allowed to stay with us for three and four years respectively, the other six Ministers held office for no more than sixteen months each on average.

The practice of appointing short-term transient Ministers may suit the procedures of politics. But it gives the bureaucracy enormous power behind the scenes. It is the Ministry civil servants who continue in office all the time. It is to them that each new Minister turns for briefing and advice when he takes office. He may come with his preconceived ideas, but the civil servants are there to persuade him what is or is not desirable in their view.

The trouble is that this back-stage influence is based on distant observation from the isolation of ivory towers, and not on knowledge gained from working in the industry itself. And that influence is insidious and all-pervasive.

The need for Ministers to depend on their civil servants for advice is a good and well-tried system for the traditional political process of government. But for the growing involvement of government in industry since World War II the system is not well-suited and needs to be changed. Well meaning our civil servants may be but, with a few notable exceptions, they simply do not possess the practical experience to advise Ministers on industry management problems.

The purpose of appointing independent outside directors to be non-executive members of a board is, or should be, to put qualified people in a position to supervise the performance of executive management on behalf of the shareholders. Nowadays it is of course increasingly accepted that management performance needs to be monitored on behalf of other people than shareholders, such as employees and local amenity groups. If wisely chosen, these outside non-executive board members will come to know far more than the Ministry civil servants about the problems besetting management from time to time and about the qualities of the senior executives.

Yet not once in my fourteen years with BOAC did a Minister consult the independent directors he and his predecessors had put on our board. It was not that our outside directors had been appointed merely to give them fees and perks as a gesture of thanks for services in another field. Many were highly experienced men of business and included senior directors of Alfred Holt (of Liverpool). Standard Telephones, Morgan Grenfell, Taylor Woodrow, Unilever and ICI. Ministers who 'sponsor' nationalised industries need to learn how to use the boards they have appointed.

The most effective way to protect the management of a nationalised industry from bureaucratic interference is by the issue to the public of a substantial part of its equity capital. Any influence brought to bear that is contrary to the commercial interests of the shareholding public can then be rejected out of hand. But such a remedy is possible in only a few cases, of which British Airways is one.

I have come to feel that the structure of a nationalised industry would be much improved if there were at the top a two-tier board – or, rather, two boards; a non-executive supervisory board and an executive management board, with the managing director or chief executive as the only link between the two. The Minister would appoint only the supervisory board, and he should look to them for briefing and advice when needed.

In making his appointments to the supervisory board the Minister could appoint one or two current (i.e. not retired) top civil servants from his own department and/or the Treasury. This would have the great advantage that representatives of the Government as owners would be involved on the inside in the industry's policy-making. It would also provide senior civil servants with practical experience of industrial direction.

Once again, Qantas provides an interesting case study; for many years the head of the Australian Treasury was on the Qantas board, which was wholly non-executive except for the chairman. This seemed to me so beneficial to both Government and airline that, when the co-ordinating board of the partnership between ACT(A) and the Government-owned Australian National Line was set up in 1969, I was glad to have on it the permanent head of the Department of Trade and Industry in Canberra, Sir Alan Westerman, and later the permanent head of the Department of Transport, Charles Halton.

It would be for the supervisory board to appoint the management board on the recommendation of the chief executive. In this way management would be effectively shielded from non-commercial influence by the Ministry. But the boards of nationalised industries should continue to be accountable to their sponsoring Minister; and their chairman and chief executive should be required to appear from time to time before the House of Commons Select Committee on Nationalised Industries.

*   *   *   *   *

Whatever changes may or may not be made in the constitution of nationalised industries, their efficiency and effectiveness come down in the end to the way they are managed.

Management today is having to adjust itself to a dramatic change in the balance of power throughout industry, in the private as well as the public sector. In nationalised industries we had to adapt ourselves in the 1950s to the greater power granted to unions through the setting up of national joint councils in which they had equal power with management. In the private sector the change in the balance of power did not manifest itself until the 1970s and in many cases management still does not know what has hit it.

On the one hand, management has lost much of its power to impose its will. Ownership of itself no longer carries the authority to direct people to do this or that. Managers, too, no longer have an accepted authority just because they are the bosses. People may still do what the owners or the management want, but only if they feel it is right and in their own interests.

This situation was brought about partly by the employer's loss of much of his arbitrary power to sack people for indiscipline or bad work. He has the right to hire; but his right to fire is matched by union insistence on multiple advance warnings and circumscribed by legal rights of appeal. The fear of dismissal by an employer has little of its former disciplinary power.

On the other hand, organised labour now has much more muscle. For one thing, a union's power over its members is almost beyond reason; by taking away a man's union card they can not only remove him from his job but also prevent him from practising his trade elsewhere.

But, of greater significance, organised labour has discovered that by stopping work it can exercise tremendous power over the management of industry and even the Government of the country. To get what it wants, it can hold its employers and the community to ransom by stopping the supply of the necessities of life.

The widespread use of this power became possible after the Conservative Government arranged in the early 1970s for supplementary social benefits to be paid to the wives of men on strike. However much sympathy one felt for strikers' families, the absence of cash in the home did ensure that people thought very hard before going on strike. With that hand no longer on the brake, there was little check on the use or abuse of union power – official or unofficial.

Ever since nationalisation was introduced the public sector was at a disadvantage when it came to pay bargaining. The unions knew that the Government stood behind a state-owned industry, and they would not take no from its management. Instead, they took pay disputes to 10 Downing Street for Government intervention. When inflation became rampant in the later 1970s they resorted to unrestricted secondary picketing to force Government to provide the money for higher wages not justified by productivity.

In the private sector, the unions know that there is no fairy godmother in the background; there is a cash limit beyond which they cannot push management. But that limit may be very high because of the great loss a company suffers from having its operations halted by a dispute. For that reason, Government deceives itself if it imagines that it can rely on private industry to control inflation by holding down the level of pay settlements.

Government deceives itself, too, if it regards high wage settlements as a main cause of inflation. They are a consequence of it. In the absence of an incomes policy, union leaders must seek pay rises in line with inflation merely to maintain the standard of living of their members. Responsibility for controlling inflation rests with Government, and Government alone. The buck cannot be passed.

Pay bargaining is only one aspect of management's relations with its workforce and is not the most important, though it attracts the most publicity. Whether in the private or the public sector, management works with its employees all the year round. In its day-to-day working, management must strive all the time to improve the value that a business adds to the product it makes or the service it provides for its customers. Yet, in the new power situation that has emerged in industry, management has lost its power to enforce its will and organised labour has won the power to block.

★   ★   ★   ★   ★

How can management manage without power? Or with the balance of power so stacked against it? Only by developing the art of personal leadership to a far greater extent than is practised today. Managers have to lead, not just direct people from their offices.

Managers too often feel that they alone know best. If the shop stewards don't agree, they just sit back and fume – and blame labour for the stalemate. Managers are hardly ever free from blame for troubles in industrial relations. They have too often disowned their responsibility of leadership. Yet men need leadership and respond to it. Too often they find it only in their unions.

Human leadership is a fundamental requirement of professional management. Managers must accept that the most important part of their job is to convince all concerned – middle managers, supervisors, shop floor, shop stewards, union officials and others – that what they, the managers, want done is in the company's and everyone's interest.

To do this successfully, managers have to give a lot of time to it – talking to the chaps at all levels and being ready to learn from them if they produce ideas that management has not thought of. Many managers would regard this as a dreadful waste of their valuable time. It is not.

When I joined BOAC in 1950 I found myself in a power situation that was a forerunner of that which has developed in the 1970s. All disagreements between us and the unions had to be referred to the National Joint Council. Miles Thomas set the pattern by showing what could be achieved by personal leadership and secured the unions' full support in reducing the number of people employed in the over-staffed airline by one in three.

I had fourteen years' experience of working on this basis. We had no power to impose our will without persuasion. It wasn't easy: there were fourteen card-carrying members of the Communist Party on our seventeen-man shop stewards committee at London's Heathrow airport. Yet in the early 1960s, before I had to leave BOAC, we got as good industrial and human relations in the airline as in the best of British industry.

Two hundred years or more ago our governors had to accept that they could continue to govern only with the consent of the governed. Today managers have to come to terms with the fact that they can manage only with the consent of the managed.

It is in winning that consent that the art of personal leadership is so important. Responsibility for leadership in a business cannot be delegated by the man at the top to professional personnel directors or officers. It is the head man, the chief executive, who will attract or repel the loyalty of the workforce – who will break down (or build up) the barrier between 'them' and 'us'.

I used to talk often with Lord Montgomery about how to exercise leadership in an industrial environment, with no powers of military discipline in the background. After one of his visits to BOAC headquarters, he re-capped his views in a letter to me from his home at Isington Mill, near Alton, as follows:

> 'Man is not a machine. He is a mobile and living organism, with a spirit and a soul. Those who treat him as a pawn, to be moved about at will, always come to grief.
>
> 'The worker wants to see his chief; and the boss must be out and about with his workers and talk with them individually – and occasionally collectively. The men will then learn that their best interests are safe in the hands of their leader; a mutual confidence will in due course be generated, and when that happens you have a pearl of very great price.'

Because it was foreign to his own experience, Monty did not mention that the boss, the leader, must also set out to win the confidence of the officials of the unions of which his men are members. That included, I believe he has clearly set out the nature of the challenge facing British management – and the opportunity.

★   ★   ★   ★   ★

But management and unions can only achieve success within the economic framework of the country as a whole. It is also necessary for Government to show real human leadership, and not merely juggle with taxes, interest rates and the borrowing requirements of the public sector.

Britons have lived for some 35 years in a welfare state. When it was first introduced in the 1940s the benefits made available took only a small part of our gross national product. At that time the country's productivity was increasing each year in returning from a wartime to a peacetime economy, and we could well afford them.

Now, at the start of the 1980s, Britain's productivity is static, if not actually falling. Yet the benefits provided by the welfare state are far greater. Most people seem to take these benefits for granted and regard them as entitlements without having to work for them.

Unless they are matched by increased productivity all round, they contain the seeds of decay. So much money is being pumped into the economy through cash benefits and the provision of free social services that we find it difficult to avoid high inflation. And inflation is an evil that breeds great social injustice and strife.

The leadership task of Government is not only to provide a just economic environment within which management and unions can work constructively together to increase the nation's prosperity. It is also to lead everyone to realise that the benefits of the welfare state have to be worked for and earned; that in working for them we have to adapt to change and discard methods that are out-dated; that in adapting to change there will inevitably be hardships which must be overcome sympathetically; and that, unless we work productively enough to pay for them, we cannot continue to enjoy all the benefits and services of the welfare state that people want and politicians arrange.

If we can all be brought to accept this inescapable fact of life, and if management can rise to the challenge facing it and grasp its opportunity, then we shall have the chance to rebuild constructive human relationships and revive dynamic growth throughout British industry.

November 1980

Appendix

Royal Flights operated by BOAC for The Queen's Flight up to the end of 1963

Date	Passengers	Journey	Aircraft Commander	Aircraft Used
1951				
7–8 Oct	Princess Elizabeth Duke of Edinburgh	London–Montreal	O P Jones	Stratocruiser
1952				
31 Jan	Princess Elizabeth Duke of Edinburgh	London–Nairobi	R C Parker R G Ballantine	Argonaut
6–7 Feb	The Queen Duke of Edinburgh	Entebbe–London	R G Ballantine R C Parker	Argonaut
4–5 Aug	Duke of Edinburgh Duke of Kent	Helsinki–London	A M A Majendie	Comet 1
27 Sept–11 Nov	Duchess of Kent Duke of Kent	London–Colombo– Singapore–Hong Kong	E Rotteram W N C Griffiths	Argonaut
1953				
30 June–1 July 16–17 July	The Queen Mother Princess Margaret	London–Salisbury Salisbury–London	A P W Cane R R Rodley	Comet 1
23–25 Nov.	The Queen Duke of Edinburgh	London–Bermuda– Jamaica	A C Loraine	Stratocruiser

Date	Passengers	Journey	Aircraft Commander	Aircraft Used
1954				
28–30 April	The Queen Duke of Edinburgh	Aden–Entebbe–Tobruk	F A Taylor	Argonaut
1955				
31 Jan–1 Feb	Princess Margaret	London–Trinidad	P C Fair	Stratocruiser
2–3 March		Nassau–London		
1956				
27–28 Jan	The Queen Duke of Edinburgh	London–Lagos	R C Parker R G Ballantine	Argonaut
16–17 Feb		Lagos–London		
21–22 Sept	Princess Margaret	London–Mombasa	C B Houlder R E Hallam	Argonaut
25–26 Sept		Nairobi–London		
15 Oct	Duke of Edinburgh	London–Mombasa	Houlder/Hallam	Argonaut
1957				
1–2 March	Duchess of Kent	London–Accra	L V Messenger	Stratocruiser
7–8 March		Accra–London		
1–2 July	The Queen Mother	London–Salisbury	F Walton A S M Rendall	Britannia 102
16–17 July		Salisbury–London		
27–29 Aug	Duke and Duchess of Gloucester	Kinloss–Kuala Lumpur	J J Veasey R I B Winn	Britannia 102
5–6 Sept		Kuala Lumpur–Kinloss		
12 Oct	The Queen Duke of Edinburgh	London–Ottawa	G Store	DC–7C
21–22 Oct		New York–London		
12–13 Nov	Princess Royal	London–Lagos	J R Johnson	Argonaut
24–25 Nov		Kano–London		

Date	Passengers	Journey	Aircraft Commander	Aircraft Used
1958				
28 Jan–1 Feb	The Queen Mother	London-Montreal-Honolulu-Fiji-Fiji-Auckland	J Woodman/B C Frost/W J Craig F E Flower	DC-7C
13 March	The Queen Mother	Malta-London	D Smith	Britannia 102
19–20 April 6–7 May	Princess Margaret	London-Trinidad Nassau-London	D Anderson	Britannia 102
11–12 July 11–12 Aug	Princess Margaret	London-Vancouver Halifax-London	J T Percy	Britannia 312
28 Oct 1 Nov	Duke of Edinburgh	London-Ottawa Ottawa-Leuchars	T B Stoney	Comet 4
12–13 Nov 24–25 Nov	Duke and Duchess of Gloucester	London-Addis Ababa Aden-London	A Meagher	Britannia 312
1959				
20 Jan–18 Feb	Duke of Edinburgh	London-India-Pakistan-Burma	A P W Cane	Comet 4
28–30 April	Duke of Edinburgh	Nassau-Bermuda-London	G G Stead	Britannia 312
4–5 Feb 27 Feb	The Queen Mother	London-Nairobi Entebbe-London	J L Gregory N A Mervin-Smith	Britannia 312 Comet 4
11 Feb–19 Mch	Duchess of Kent Princess Alexandra	London-Mexico City-Panama-Lima-Santiago-Rio-Sao Paulo-London	D A Cracknell	Britannia 312

Date	Passengers	Journey	Aircraft Commander	Aircraft Used.
12-13 May	Duke and Duchess of Gloucester	London-Kano Lagos-London	R E Hallam B G Wallace	Britannia 312 Comet 4
18 June 2-3 Aug	The Queen Duke of Edinburgh	London-Newfoundland Halifax-London	R E Millichap	Comet 4
8 Aug 5-7 Oct	Princess Alexandra	London-Vancouver Bangkok-Delhi-Tehran-Istanbul-London	E J N Hengle	Comet 4
1960 10 May 30 May	The Queen Mother	London-Salisbury Salisbury-London	J T A Marsden B E P Bone	Britannia 102
7-11 June	Duke of Edinburgh	London-Ottawa-Toronto-New York-London	J A Kelly	Comet 4
25-26 Sept 15-16 Oct	Princess Alexandra	London-Lagos Lagos-London	R H Tapley	Britannia 312

Date	Passengers	Journey	Aircraft Commander	Aircraft Used
1961				
20 Jan–6 March	The Queen Duke of Edinburgh	London–Cyprus Delhi–Agra– Ahmedabad–Karachi– Quetta–Pershawar– Risalpur–Chaklala– Lahore–Dacca–Chittagong– Panagarh–Calcutta– Madras–Bangalore– Bombay–Benares– Gorakhpur–Tehran– Isfahan–Shiraz– Ankara–London	A Meagher	Britannia 312
29 Oct–11 Dec	Princess Alexandra	London–Vancouver– Tokyo–Hong Kong– Bangkok–Rangoon– Gan–Aden–Tripoli– London	J Nicholl F Hill	Britannia 312
9 Nov 6 Dec	The Queen Duke of Edinburgh	London–Accra Dakar–London	J Woodman	Boeing 707

Date	Passengers	Journey	Aircraft Commander	Aircraft Used
1962				
6-7 Feb 5-6 April	Duke of Edinburgh	London-Georgetown Kingston-London	B D Barrow	Britannia 312
13-15 Feb 6-7 March	Duke and Duchess of Gloucester	London-Malta-Nairobi Nairobi-London	R E Knights	Britannia 312
2-3 Aug 10-11 Aug	Princess Margaret Lord Snowdon	London-Kingston Montego Bay-London	R Hartley	Britannia 102
6-7 Oct 18-19 Oct	Duke and Duchess of Kent	London-Entebbe Entebbe-London	H J Rose	Britannia 312
1963				
31 Jan-1 Feb 27-28 March	The Queen Duke of Edinburgh	London-Vancouver- Honolulu-Fiji Perth-Sydney-Fiji Vancouver-London	T Nisbet J Percy A Andrew	Boeing 707
15-22 March	Duke and Duchess of Gloucester	London-Amman- Nicosia-Akrotiri- London	F C E Sarson	Comet 4
24 Nov	Duke of Edinburgh Sir A Douglas-Home Mr Harold Wilson	London-Washington *(for President Kennedy's funeral)*	D J Bellingham	Boeing 707
8-9 Dec 19 Dec	Duke of Edinburgh	London-Dar es Salaam Khartoum-London	R C Alabaster	Comet 4

Index